Land, Law and The Left

About the Author

Abhijit Guha (*b.* 1956) is Reader in Anthropology at Vidyasagar University. He earned his Master's and M.Phil degrees from Calcutta University and Ph.D. from Vidyasagar University. He is engaged in displacement, resettlement and rehabilitation research for the last 11 years and has worked with Walter Fernandes in a project on West Bengal. He is also associated with the post-graduate diploma course on Participatory Management of Resettlement and Rehabilitation at the School of Social Sciences, IGNOU, New Delhi. He was visiting fellow at the Department of Sociology, Delhi School of Economics, Delhi University during August-September 2006 and also taught at the West Bengal National University of Juridical Sciences, Kolkata. Dr Guha has published over 60 research papers, book reviews and comments in various national and international journals of repute which include *Current Anthropology, Population and Development Review* and *Economic and Political Weekly*. Also, he has presented papers at many conferences and seminars in India and abroad.

Land, Law and The Left

The Saga of Disempowerment of the Peasantry in the Era of Globalization

Abhijit Guha

Foreword by

Michael M. Cernea

CONCEPT PUBLISHING COMPANY, NEW DELHI-110059

Cataloging in Publication Data—DK
Courtesy: D.K. Agencies (P) Ltd. <docinfo@dkagencies.com>

Guha, Abhijit, 1956-
Land, law and the Left : the saga of disempowerment of the peasantry in the era of globalization / Abhijit Guha ; foreword by Michael M. Cernea.
p. cm.
Revision of the author's thesis (Ph. D.)—Vidyasagar University.
Study conducted at Kharagpur I Block of Paschim Medinipur District, West Bengal, India.
Includes bibliographical references (p.)
Includes index.
ISBN 8180693988

1. Eminent domain—India—West Bengal. 2. Peasantry—Government policy—India—West Bengal. 3. Forced migration—India—West Bengal. 4. Communism—India—West Bengal. I. Title.

DDC 343.541 402 52 22

ISBN-13: 978-81-8069-398-4
ISBN-10: 81-8069-398-8

First Published 2007

Published and Printed by
Ashok Kumar Mittal
Concept Publishing Company
A/15-16, Commercial Block, Mohan Garden
New Delhi-110059 (India)
Phones: 25351460, 25351794
Fax: 091-11-25357103
E-mail: publishing@conceptpub.com

DEDICATED

to the peasants of the villages of Kharagpur
who fought a heroic struggle against the
acquisition of agricultural land
in the mid-1990s.

Foreword

THE KNOWLEDGE BENEFITS OF DIGGING DEEPLY

Economic and Political Dimensions of Land Expropriation and Displacement

The book on involuntary population displacement written by Dr. Abhijit Guha covers only one out of India's many hundreds of administrative districts: Medinipur in the West Bengal state. This district is, however, a microcosm of the vast ocean of India's countrywide ubiquitous forced displacement processes. I would therefore like to use this Foreword as the opportunity to put Medinipur's displacements, and the book about them, within the broader national context of India's displacements, and within the international context of development–caused displacement in the developing world. I am doing so because, indeed, the analysis and findings reported in this book about land acquisition much surpass in significance the borders of the Medinipur district.

During the last 15-20 years, India's massive population displacements have caused extraordinary internal and international concerns. They have gained an unfortunate reputation, far worse than comparable processes in many other countries. Why is there such heightened public opinion concern?

At least three answers to this question, three factors explain this concern:

First : Impoverishment

Although involuntary population displacements are entailed by *development*-oriented projects—projects usually justified on grounds of reducing poverty, creating employment, and bringing economic growth—forced displacements themselves result in precisely the opposite effect for many people: displacement suddenly makes many poor people poorer, instead of lifting them from poverty. It destroys employment and eliminates income generating assets, it causes social disorganization, marginalization and downward mobility. This is contrary to sound social development, and obviously doesn't bring growth for the population involved. In short, these processes embody a paradoxical situation, in which the development discourse is falsified by the development practice.

Second : Legal and Policy Quasi-vacuum

Despite enormous domestic and international demand, India's government has declined, year after year and decade after decade, to institute a national resettlement policy, let alone a special law to govern resettlement and rehabilitation processes, as other developing countries have enacted. Such a law would compel more adequate resettlement practice, prevent abuse and require the earmarking of project financial resources to preempt impoverishment and improve, rather than worsen, the livelihood of those displaced and resettled. Yet deliberately maintaining an absence of specialized law and policy, and implicitly wiggle-room for arbitrariness, is a policy in itself. The policy vacuum has betrayed a lack of political will at the highest level for radically improving the practice of resettlement. It has led to growing dissatisfaction and intensifying pressures both against the lack of policy and adequate legislation, and against unacceptable practices on the ground.

Third : Resistance

In India, more than in any other developing country, local resistance to expropriation, insufficient and unfair compensation and forced displacement have gradually swelled into organized large-scale movements. The nature of the protests changed as well. What has at the outset emerged as a series of local, disparate protests and claims against the abuses and illegal dispossessions initiated by local authorities' or by various projects, appears over time to gradually turn, when considered at the aggregate national scale, into something of a different quality: these protests and discreet oppositions are coalescing into a broad and growing anti-state struggle, acquiring political and not just economic dimensions.

Seen against this triple-featured background, Guha's research takes on particular value, as it contributes to knowledge and debate along all the three factors mentioned: impoverishment, local abuses within the vacuum of national legislation and central policy, and people's responses to displacement.

The readers of this book will easily realize that Abhijit Guha's analysis of one district is a research-documented testimony of unmistakable macro-national relevance. This district embodies India's contemporary history.

Accelerated industrialization, urbanization processes, and the increased influx of foreign investments for the exploitation of India's natural resources have a common characteristic: *land seizures* on an broadening scale. These are not isolated instances of small and unconnected displacements, that would be effortlessly absorbed and converted into resettlement processes. These processes happen in a myriad places all over the vastness of India, amounting together to an aggregate, unrelenting land redistribution that changes age-old tenure systems and puts land into the hand of different owners. Land is pulled from under the feet of large numbers of land tillers, suddenly dis-embedded from their production systems. These dispossessions un-link and detach scores of people from their meager, yet daily source of income and livelihood. While facilitating rapid overall industrialization, these are the most economically-brutal and financially-brutal, impoverishing compulsory displacements. They leave in their wake enormous social debris. The sad name of these social debris is: *internally displaced populations*. The monumental social and economic problem caused by sudden and forced displacements is that these displaced populations are left floating *without access to an alternative production system.*

To undertake his research, the author decided to deconstruct step by step the process of displacement and to zero in on its key segment: the expropriation and acquisition of private lands by the state, or by the state at the behest of the private sector, and the mechanisms for what is called "compensation".

The Reader is Entitled to ask: What is new in this Research choice?

Certainly, every serious social science study of displacement and resettlement addresses land acquisition. Yet, because land expropriation is a common denominator in all displacements and is touched upon by almost every author, an inaccurate impression has taken hold among many resettlement researchers that there is nothing new to say about this process. Abhijit Guha has NOT embraced this common—but erroneous—view. On the contrary, his book digs deeply into this dimension and treats it as a strategic research site. He meticulously explores the politics and economics of acquisition, and the legal set of mechanisms and provisions put in place that make expropriation not just possible, but also hardly assailable by its victims.

The most interesting part of the research is the analysis of the *political* processes that underpin and accompany land acquisition and make room for introducing both the economic and legal regulations for compulsory expropriations.

In-depth analysis of these political aspects is rarely done, and represents a distinct contribution to the knowledge about involuntary resettlement. The author has not only carried out interviews with all categories of relevant people, done sample surveys and case histories, etc., he also reached deeply into a generally unstudied source of information: the detailed debates of West Bengal's State Legislative Assembly Proceedings, for and against the enactment in law of decisions regarding expropriations. The window thus opened up proves very illuminating.

The relevance of this information is enhanced by the fact that the State to which Medinipur District belongs, West Bengal, has been ruled for many years by a left-of-center government, and maintained in power through popular election after election. This State's governments have historically promoted a land reform generally favorable to small and landless farmers, one that was more radical than those of other States most elsewhere in India. Nonetheless, parts of those same lands are now being taken away through expropriations of the new owners, to give right of way to industrial projects.

Is this Process now an Agrarian Counter-Land-Reform ?

Taking away the land is not only an inflicted economic loss, but is also political dis-empowerment of the peasants. This, of course, raises major questions and gives the author room to analyze the political and economic premises of the new industrial projects, why they are undertaken, and the socio-economic effects of the displacements.

The politics of land acquisition in West Bengal, as in India at large, takes new twists when the State's power of "eminent domain" is used circuitously to expropriate land not just for public interest projects, but also for private-sector for-profit projects, such as the two pig-iron industrial enterprises researched in the study. The 1984 amendments to India's Land Acquisition Act made such use of the State's power legally possible, but socially very damaging, as it "liberates" the private sector projects from the obligation to negotiate directly, in a socially responsible way, until a reasonable land price freely acceptable to the land owners is agreed upon in a "*willing buyer-willing seller*" negotiation.

Thus, the meticulous empirical analysis reported by Guha in this book provides fresh "grist to the mill" for a major critique now gathering steam in the international resettlement literature: the critique of the fallacies of the current economics of displacement and resettlement. I've long articulated elsewhere[1] my own argument against the flawed economics of coerced displacement and resettlement and am pleased to find new evidence for it in the present volume. This evidence demonstrates, once again, that compensation for land expropriation is not in itself a remedy for the de-capitalization and asset-lessness inflicted on those forcibly displaced.

Sure enough, asset compensation at replacement cost level is mandatory and indispensable, and should of course be paid in full for the assets and opportunities taken away from those dispossessed. But compensation alone, even if ideally correct, is insufficient to reconstruct the productive system of the displaced "land-losers" and to restore and improve their livelihoods. And it is well known that the realities of compensation practices are far, far below from ideally correct compensation…

This is why, in my view, compensation proceeds must be supplemented with investment financing by the sponsors/owners of the projects that cause displacement. This investment financing should

---

[1]Michael M. Cernea (1999) "Why Economic Analysis Is Essential to Resettlement: A Sociologist's View." In M. Cernea (ed.) *The Economics of Involuntary Resettlement: Questions and Challenges*. World Bank: Washington, DC; see also Michael M. Cernea, "For a New Economics of Resettlement: A Sociological Critique of the Compensation Principle", in *International Social Science Journal,* Nr 175, 2003, Blackwell-UNESCO.

be placed into the reconstruction and improvement of resettlers' living standards and capacities. Financial resources may often be scarce, but that does not obviate the objective need for such financing. Scarcity can be overcome through specially tailored strategies: among others, for instance, by instituting legal arrangements to enable those displaced to share in the forthcoming revenues from the project they helped make possible.

The principal contribution of Guha's book is the increased understanding he produces to highlight the impoverishment risks embedded in land expropriation, when the State imposes land expropriation without adequate safeguards and without counter-risks measures to protect those affected against further pauperization.

Unfair compensation and absent development financing investments for welfare reconstruction transform the impoverishment risks of displacement into dire realities of aggravated impoverishment. The author's tool of choice for analyzing the unfolding of such impoverishment risks in West Bengal is the "*Impoverishment Risks and Reconstruction*" *(IRR)* model. Having developed this model, now widely used by researchers in numerous countries, I'm pleased to find that Guha employs this methodological and conceptual framework aptly, revealing pauperization risks inflicted on resettlers that project planners most often ignore or deliberately gloss over. With the empirical findings generated and organized along this conceptual framework, this book builds a forceful factual and intellectual argument. As a corollary, Guha also advances practical recommendations for changing the ways in which the economics and the politics of development-caused involuntary displacement are now handled. These recommendations appear valid not only for West-Bengal, but may help many other states in India.

While this book's manuscript has been awaiting publication, important developments have taken place in the policy realm of resettlement. The Government of India, after declining for decades to issue an all-India formal policy for development-caused resettlement, has finally acceded to civil society demands and published in February 2004 such a framework, issued by the Ministry of Rural Development. The long lasting and embarrassing absence of political will to end the morass of displacements that impoverish people seemed to come to an end. But at close examination, the content of that policy document deeply disappointed India's resettlement specialists who have been long waiting for it. The ensuing public debate severely indicted the February 2004 policy as an inadequate response to, and only a pseudo-remedy of, the complex negative effects of displacements. During 2005-2006, a joint policy-crafting effort initiated by a group of civil society organizations and researchers produced a new draft policy-statement, eventually approved by the National Advisory Council (NAC) and submitted to the Government for approval. It appears that this new framework is widely supported publicly. Yet in response, in mid-2006 the Ministry of Rural Development issued its own new draft National Rehabilitation Policy, a draft again critiqued publicly as being "on the whole a thoroughly unsatisfactory proposal". While MRD's 2004 policy is now replaced even by the Ministry that issued it, when the present Preface will reach print time the two substantially different drafts may still be on the public agenda, competing for Government adoption.

Whether the adoption of a new policy on resettlement in India will tackle better the complex land issues explored in the present book is still to be seen. But given the conundrum of deeply pathological effects resulting from coerced displacements, I think that Guha's challenging, solid monograph could not have been timelier. It offers research-derived findings which will further fuel the debate around induced landlessness, development and resettlement. And it offers knowledge to better guide the implementation, and measure the effectiveness, of India's forthcoming displacement and resettlement laws and policy, in terms of preventing new impoverishment risks rather than creating new poverty.

Michael M. Cernea
Washington DC
mcernea@worldbank.org

Preface

The book deals with the various dimensions of development caused displacement in West Bengal under the Left Front Government. The main theme centres round land acquisition by the government for industrial projects and its adverse impacts on the peasants. The whole issue has been appraised under the context of the pro-peasant policies of the Left Front Government in West Bengal. So it is basically a policy study. For achieving the target, a multidisciplinary methodological strategy has been adopted in which a variety of data sources have been tapped, that can be broadly divided into: (i) first hand empirical data collected through surveys and anthropological fieldwork, and (ii) archival data obtained from the District Collectorate, Block Development Office, Government reports, Census, Gazettes, Panchayat Offices, Newspapers and West Bengal Assembly Proceedings. Since the study adopted a specific problem, viz., a critical evaluation of the transformation of the development policy of the Left Front Government after the liberalization, the case studies of two big industrial projects launched during 1990-96 in an agricultural district (erstwhile Medinipur now Paschim Medinipur) have been undertaken. The timing of the empirical observations in the field again coincided with a brief period of peasant resistance against the land takeover, which gave the author an unique opportunity to collect quantitative and qualitative data through participatory methodology. The field observations revealed that although the peasants in this particular area have not been displaced from their homes, they were dispossessed from their major means of production that caused frustration and despondency to agriculture among this group of excellent farmers many of whom still survives on cultivation of crops. Our field observations revealed that the peasants did not remain passive recipients of the government policy and put up resistance by adopting legal and extra-legal means. It was found during the fieldwork that the peasant leaders became quite efficient in helping the project affected families to file objections regarding compensation and organizing mass movements against acquisition. Secondly, it was also found that a huge plot of land remained unutilized and many families also did not get any compensation. This constitutes the first part of the narrative of disempowerment of the peasantry in West Bengal. New research questions arose from within the field, viz. (i) how the administration tackles the objections under the existing legal framework? (ii) how land acquisition proceeds through its different stages? and (iii) what are the problems and built-in difficulties in the land acquisition law in providing relief to the various segments of the project affected families? In order to collect first hand information to these questions, which arose in the field, it became necessary to go straight to the Land Acquisition Department of the District Collectorate and conduct archival research in the style usually followed by an historian dealing with contemporary affairs. The archival investigation revealed many hitherto unexplored areas on the administrative and legal aspects of land acquisition. For example, it was learnt that land acquisition and land reforms operate in contrasting manner and their simultaneous operation have immense policy implications for the State of West Bengal. Besides this, archival search in the Land Acquisition Department yielded valuable information on the contemporary scenario of acquisition and also about how the administration looked at its own shortcomings and problems as regards land acquisition in the district. The overall dismal picture of land acquisition in terms of the huge volume of backlog and financial loss completes the second part of the gloomy narrative, which remains hidden from the public eye behind the rhetoric of development. People only come to know that such amount of land has been acquired for an industry but very rarely about the time taken to compensate a displaced family or the number of unfinished projects for which land has been acquired. The archival search in the Land Acquisition Department again raised some crucial research questions, which were: (i) how the policy makers in West Bengal viewed land acquisition? and (ii) what were the major issues on displacement that have been debated among the policy makers of the State? These questions led us to search the West Bengal Legislative Assembly Proceedings. Many interesting facts on land acquisition were revealed from debates and questions of the Assembly Proceedings for the period 1948-1994. For example, the policy makers of West Bengal continued land acquisition with a State Act which was more anti-people in nature than the colonial Act from 1948 to 1994 and irrespective of political affiliation the elected people's representatives never moved any bill to enact a legislation incorporating compulsory rehabilitative measures for project affected families. In the West Bengal Legislative Assembly the only adverse effect of land acquisition, which was emphasised, centred round the payment of compensation. The other adverse socio-economic and political impacts of land acquisition like loss of agricultural land and common property resource, the pushing back of land reforms, disempowerment of the small and marginal peasants, plight of the sharecroppers and overshadowing of the panchayat were never discussed on the floor of the Assembly, even during the regime of the LFG. This is the third part of our narrative of land acquisition in West Bengal. The analysis reveals that land acquisition for big industries without a rehabilitation policy and legislation in West Bengal is a self-defeating strategy since it causes dispossession and disempowerment of the small and marginal farmers and sharecroppers and more importantly, pushes back the land reform policy for which the State had drawn the attention of the researchers and policy makers of India and abroad. Finally, it can be stated that the study, is not limited to two cases of the installation of industrial projects in a particular district of West Bengal but addressed one of the current policy issues having national as well as international importance, viz., development caused displacement and rehabilitation.

Abhijit Guha
Department of Anthropology
Vidyasagar University
E-Mail : abhijitguhavu@rediffmail.com

Acknowledgements

In the first place, I would like to express my sincerest thanks to my students Tapan Barman, Laxman Jana and Raghunath Mondal who brought to my notice the problem of land acquisition in the Kalaikunda area and introduced me to the villagers of Paschim Amba and Gokulpur. They have also assisted me in collecting field data during the period of my research in the area. This work could not have been done without their help and cooperation. Four students of a latter batch, Jyotirmoy Tripathi, Dhruba Maity, Hiralal Manna and Jayanta Bari who did their M.Sc. dissertations under my guidance greatly helped me by sharing many valuable information on Gokulpur and Paschim Amba.

Secondly, I am greatly indebted to the villagers of the study area who despite their hardship and trouble helped me by giving valuable information on land acquisition, peasant resistance and displacement in the Gokulpur-Amba area. I would particularly like to thank Trilochan Rana (who led the peasant movement) for helping me throughout the fieldwork period. He also supplied me many important documents related to my research problem. I am also grateful to Mihir Maity and his father Gostha Maity of Baharapat village for their kind help and warm reception in the field whenever I went to the villages. I also express my deep gratitude to Nityananda Chakraborty, Nitai Karak and Durga Singh for their active help and cooperation in the field area.

For the collection of the archival materials in the District Collectorate of erstwhile Medinipur, I am greatly indebted to Arun Bal, IAS, then District Magistrate of Medinipur for giving me permission to handle many official data concerning land acquisition. I also express my gratitude to Sukumar Habar, the Land Acquisition Officer of the district and all the staff of his Department for providing me with the necessary information and advice required for my research. My special thanks go to Sripati Kumar who literally taught me about the administrative process of land acquisition. I am also indebted to Satya Sundar Acharya, Chittaranjan Ghosh and Sunil Pal of the Land Acquisition Department for making me aware about the land reforms process and its various administrative stages.

I am indebted to the employees of the Gram Panchayat Office of Kalaikunda and its Pradhan, Jugal Bhakta for providing me information about the role of panchayat in relation to land acquisition and also for providing me the Annual Reports of the Gram Panchayat.

My heartiest thanks to Aloke Mitra, Joint BDO and Biplab Saha, Block Welfare Officer of the Kharagpur block I for providing me with valuable official statistics about the block as well as on the BPL survey conducted by the staff of the block office.

I am indebted to Pranati Roy, Librarian, West Bengal Legislative Assembly for untiringly supplying me the volumes containing the Assmbly Proceedings. My special thanks to Aswini Giri of the Computer Section of the Assembly Library for helping me to identify the volumes which contained debates on West Bengal Land (Requisition and Acquisition) Act, 1948 within a very short period of time.

I am greatly indebted to Michael Cernea, who not only written The Foreword of my book but also kept on sending me articles and books written by him on displacement and rehabilitation. His articles not only provided theoretical guidance but also gave me constant inspiration to undertake this work.

My special thanks to Ajit Kumar Danda and Alan Reid for giving useful suggestions on my Ph.D. thesis which helped me a lot to strengthen my arguments in the book.

I am also grateful to Walter Fernandes with whom I worked in his research project on "Development-induced Displacement and Rehabilitation" in West Bengal for giving me a very good exposure on various methodological problems in the study of displacement. I owe a lot to Fernandes.

I must express my heartiest thanks to Debaprakash Pahari and Utpal Roy of the Department of Geography and Environment Management, Vidyasagar University for drawing the map of the study area. They have done their job in meticulous manner within a very short period of time.

I deeply acknowledge the contributions of Shyamsundar Roy, Correspondent of *The Statesman* who not only highlighted the problems of land acquisition in the Kalaikunda area but also brought into light many important information which helped me to use those materials in my research.

My sincere thanks to my esteemed colleagues Ambarish Mukherjee and Tarun Kumar Banerjee of the Political Science Department of Vidyasagar University who took all the troubles to go through some of the chapters of this book and gave many valuable suggestions. I am also indebted to my uncle Reghabendra Guha for reading the first draft of Chapter 3. He gave me many useful suggestions on the draft.

I also thankfully acknowledge the valuable suggestions given to me by Lokenath Roy, Anjan Ghosh and Gopal Chakraborty on some portions of the draft. I would specially like to thank Uttam Bhattacharya of the Centre for Studies in Social Sciences, Kolkata for providing me with many valuable data on land reforms in West Bengal as well as the unpublished paper of Partha Chatterjee on the rehabilitation strategies of the Government of West Bangal. Sachinandan Sau of the Economics Department of Vidyasagar University provided me with District Statistical Handbook of Medinipur for the year 1998 for which I am grateful to him. I also thank Uday Nandi for procuring WBIDC publications for me.

I am really thankful to S. Ramanathan of the Indira Gandhi Institute for Development Research, Mumbai for making me enlightened on the different dimensions of Socio-economic Impact Assessment of land acquisition for development projects.

My special thanks to my respected supervisor Prof. Rajat Kanti Das who despite his heavy pressure of work discussed and argued with me on almost all the aspects of my Ph.D. thesis before its submission and also on the book which is an updated and slightly revised version of my Ph.D. thesis.

I would like to thank my colleague and friend Falguni Chakraborty for helping me in all possible ways to complete my work by giving intellectual suggestions and practical help. I am also grateful to J.J. Roy Burman of the Tata Institute of Social Sciences, Mumbai who first suggested me to orient my research towards policy study. His occasional visits to Medinipur were very much stimulating for my research.

I also like to thank D.P. Mukherjee, Amitava Basu, Manis Raha, Vina Majumdar, G.P. Chattopadhya, Goutam Chando Roy and

R.K. Bhakat for constantly inspiring me to complete my Ph.D. thesis as early as possible.

I am greatly indebted to Jogendra Mohan Debnath, Former Registrar, Vidyasagar University for introducing me to the District Collectorate of Medinipur and the library of the West Bengal Legislative Assembly in Kolkata which helped me to collect data from those offices. My thanks to Biswajit Das who took the trouble to bring out my migration certificate from Kolkata University which was essential for getting registration at Vidyasagar University.

I am grateful to Professor Swapan Kumar Pramanick, the Vice-Chancellor, Benoy Kumar Chanda, Development Officer and Himansu Ghosh, the Registrar, Vidyasagar University for sanctioning me the subsidy towards the publication of the book from the UGC Unassigned Grants fund. I also owe a lot to the anonymous readers of my Ph.D. thesis who recommended it to be published in the form of a book.

I express my warmest thanks to my wife Pritilata Guha who continuously insisted me to undertake the work and complete the thesis at the earliest. I should also acknowledge the contributions of my sons Arani and Asi who continuously enquired about the progress of my work.

I would like to express my sincerest thanks to Biswajit Sarkar and Kaberi Khan for typing the successive drafts of the manuscript of my thesis with utmost care.

I would also like to thank Partha Chatterjee and Satanira Chakraborty for supplying me with some basic information on the industrial development of West Bengal from the website of the Government of West Bengal.

Last but not the least, I must thank Mr. Ashok Kumar Mittal and Mr. S.P. Sinha of the Concept Publishing Company, New Delhi for publishing this book under extreme care, precision and patience.

26 September 2006

Abhijit Guha
Department of Anthropology
Vidyasagar University
Medinipur-721 102
West Bengal

Contents

List of Tables

List of Figures

Abbreviations and Acronyms

APL	Above Poverty Level or Line
BDO	Block Development Officer
BPL	Below Poverty Level or Line
Comm.	Commerce
Comp.	Compensation
Const.	Construction
Cong.	Congress Party
CPI	Communist Party of India
CPI(M)	Communist Party of India (Marxist)
CPI(ML)	Communist Party of India (Marxist-Leninist)
CPR	Common Property Resources, Common Pool Resources
CTIL	Century Textiles and Industries Limited
DP	Displaced person; Dispossessed Person
DPC	District Planning Committee
DST	Department of Science and Technology
Est.	Establishment
GP	Gram Panchayat
Indu.	Industry; Industrial
ISI	Indian Social Institute
Kgp.	Kharagpur
KTPP	Kolaghat Thermal Power Plant
LA	Land Acquisition
LAO	Land Acquisition Officer
LFG	Left Front Government
MARG	Multiple Action Research Group
MLA	Member of the Legislative Assembly
NPRR	National Policy on Resettlement and Rehabilitation
NATMO	National Atlas and Thematic Mapping Organisation
NEP	New Economic Policy
NGO	Non-Governmental Organisation
NH	National Highway
PAP	Project Affected Person

PIR	Preliminary Enquiry Report
PRIA	Society for Participatory Research in Asia
PSP	Praja Socialist Party
Publ.	Publication
RB	Requiring Body
Reh.	Rehabilitation
Rly.	Railway
RSP	Revolutionary Socialist Party
SEIA	Socio-economic Impact Assessment
SP	Socialist Party
Stn.	Station
SUCI	Socialist Unity Centre of India
TML	Tata Metaliks Limited
Trans.	Transport
WBHDR	West Bengal Human Development Report
WBIDC	West Bengal Industrial Development Corporation

ONE

Introduction

"Today, social knowledge about displacement is shrinking the gaps, going deeper than ever before. To use a common concept in anthropology, it is "thick knowledge".

Michael Cernea (1999)

Statement of the Problem

This research deals with land acquisition and development induced displacement in West Bangal. Both these problems have varying connotations that depend on the specific geographical as well as socio-political contexts in which they occur. In recent period, development induced displacement of human populations and its various consequences have been receiving serious attention not only from the policy makers and the international funding agencies like World Bank and Asian Development Bank, but also from the experts of different social science disciplines. Development induced displacements are not similar in rural and urban areas in terms of the responses and treatments they receive from the media, political leaders, NGOs and policy makers. For example, the forcible eviction of hawkers from the pavements of Kolkata (this is the changed name of the city of Calcutta) through "Operation Sunshine" (the official name for the programme of eviction of hawkers, which, it was said would allow sunlight to reach the pavements usually covered by shops and stalls) by the Government of West Bengal raised more hue and cry in the media and the political circles than those caused by the displacement of small and marginal farmers in the rural areas of the state. In the same vein, the displacement of farmers and their rehabilitation in the Rajarhat area of the North 24-Parganas district of West Begnal for the establishment of a new township received considerable media attention as well as importance from the State Government owing to its spatial proximity with Kolkata. In fact, Rajarhat townhip is growing as an extension of Kolkata.

The issues of development and displacement are interwoven with the broader policy changes of the Government in a given period of time. The changes in the policy again are strongly influenced and shaped by the wider national and international politico-economic forces that have been changing their courses in a rapid manner in the era of globalisation. All these developments basically point to social transformations of various types at the local and global levels. Uprooting of the peasants from their traditional resource base by exogenous forces has become a global phenomenon which had received the attention of social scientists since long (Hobsbawm 1995 : 287-295). Within anthropology, the study of peasant society and culture *vis-a-vis* the researches on depeasantisation opened up new horizons for more policy oriented studies on the role of the state as well as market forces in bringing about rapid transformation of the peasant societies in the rural areas of Asia, Africa and Latin America. Suffice it to say, that a major part of this transformation takes place around land that still forms the backbone of the rural society. Quite a good number of anthropological studies on villages have dealt with the various dimensions of land based agrarian relationship in the Third World countries.

The studies undertaken by economists have shown how market forces played their role in the process of depeasantisation with the advent of colonialism in the non-western world. But it was not only market that displaced the peasants from their major means of production, the eminent domain of State also became the other all-pervasive institution which dispossessed the peasantry. Industrialisation and urbanisation were the two major processes that uprooted peasants in almost all the countries of Asia, Africa and Latin America during their colonial and post-colonial periods of history. So the making of the new nations in the post-colonial situation was also the period of displacement of the traditional peasant as well as artisan, communities from their natural resource bases, viz. land, water and forest.

This anthropological research is conducted under the broad framework wherein the peasant community of a particular region is studied at the *intersection of the local and the global politico-economic forces.* This is neither a typical social anthropological or sociological study of the Indian village nor a study of the impact of industrialisation on a traditional caste based village community. This is rather a policy oriented exploration which has its focus on the acquisition of agricultural land by the State Government for the establishment of two big industrial projects in the Kharagpur sub-division of Paschim Medinipur district in West Bengal. It needs to be emphasised here that a study on the beginning of the process of depeasantisation caused by industrialisation in the rural areas of West Bengal cannot afford to ignore the acquisition of land by the State. Moreover, the process of land acquisition has gained importance in the recent period, particularly since the wake of liberalisation through New Economic Policy in 1991. Economists, political scientists, environmentalists, social activists, politicians and some policy oriented NGOs in India have started to assess the short and long-term adverse impacts of land acquisition on the small and marginal farmers of the country. All these studies and/or policy statements have macro-level foci and a coordination of Indian NGOs have prepared a pro-people alternative draft legislation on land acquisition and placed it before the Central Government in the late 1990s. But despite these developments, studies on land acquisition in a specific locality are still very meagre in India. In West Bengal, no study has yet been carried out to describe and/or analyse the process of land acquisition for industrial projects and its first order consequences on the agriculturists in a locality. The present study makes a humble attempt to explore land acquisition from the both ends of the process. On the one hand, the research tries to reconstruct the process of land acquisition for two private industries in the Kharagpur I block of the Paschim Medinipur district by extracting relevant information from the departmental files and papers of the District Collectorate. It has also employed anthropological method of first-hand observations and interviews through fieldwork to describe and analyse the responses and/or consequences of this particular case of acquisition which has displaced the rural cultivators of Paschim Medinipur district to a significant extent. The present work has made an attempt to integrate the two ends of the data set in a descriptive account. The endeavour bears resemblance with methods of history as well as social anthropology, in which data sources range from official letters, and gazette notifications to structured interviews, repeated observations and group discussions with displaced persons in the study villages where the fieldwork was carried out.

Under this general background, the more specific issues of the present research may now be advanced. From the foregoing discussion, it is clear that the acquisition of land by the Government for any project has administrative, legal, economic, political and above all, policy dimensions. Furthermore, the land acquisition process varies in space and the range of this variation increases tremendously, when one takes into account the socio-economic and political aspects of the population affected by development projects. In this study, it would be observed that within the same locality having similar socio-economic and geographical backgrounds, the land acquisition process for the two industrial projects of same nature varied in terms of compensation, people's resistance and, above all, policy implications. But before going into the details of the specific case studies which would be described in Chapters 3 and 4, the general issues on land acquisition and the launching of development projects in India with special reference to West Bengal needs to be discussed first.

Objectives of the Study

This research has been carried out to achieve the specific objectives as mentioned below:

1. The study would make a modest attempt to generate a data base on the different aspects of land acquisition in West Bengal mainly by using two specific case studies from the rural areas of Kharagpur I block in Paschim Medinipur district. The different dimensions of land acquisition that will be studied are:

   (a) *The policy dimensions* of land acquisition.
   (b) The *administrative procedures* and their various facets.
   (c) The *problems and present status* of land acquisition in Paschim Medinipur district.
2. The second related objective of this study was to describe the *socio-economic* and *political consequences* of land acquisition among the cultivators of the study area on the basis of field based empirical data.
3. The third objective of this research was to document in details the *resistance* and *bargains* carried out by the people in the study area towards land acquisition in the form of administrative as well as extralegal means.
4. The fourth and the last objective of this work was to make an *overall evaluation of the emphasis of the development policy of the Left Front Government* in West Bengal in the recent period. In keeping with this objective, some policy recommendations regarding the acquisition of agricultural land in West Bengal are also made in the last section of Chapter 5.

Methodology and Sources of Data

The methodology of this study basically followed an anthropological approach in which the land acquisition for two specific industries involving the acquisition of about 700 acres of agricultural land has been studied in the form of a case study. The acquisition of land has been studied from two different angles. On the one hand, the acquisition process has been described from the administrative perspective, and, on the other, from the aspect of its various socio-economic consequences. For the collection of data on the land acquisition process different types of published and unpublished Government reports, letters, gazette notifications, compensation documents, petitions, memoranda etc. have been studied at the Land Acquisition Department of the Medinipur District Collectorate.

The fieldwork for this research, however, has not been made in the typical fashion of anthropological village study. As inhabitants of about 15 villages have been affected by land acquisition, for the two pig iron industries, data from 9 villages (in two phases) covering 194 households have been collected by following combination of non-random opportunity and snowball sampling. Besides fieldwork and consultation of Government records and reports the other sources of data were news items, published Government reports, published and unpublished research reports and also interviews with the officers, surveyors and other employees of the Land Acquisition Department of the Medinipur District Collectorate. The data from the field have been collected through observation, open-ended questions, interviews with unstructured and structured questionnaire schedules, and case history. In the following table the relationships between the objectives as well as methods and sources of data, of the research have been schematically represented.

Table 1.1 : Objectives, Methods and Sources of Data

Objectives	*Sources of Data*	*Methods and Techniques*
Policy dimensions of land acquisition.	Research papers, books, Government orders, newspaper reports, assembly proceedings	Recording.
Administrative procedures of land acquisition.	Government reports, note-sheets, official letters, project proposals, gazette notifications, compensation records.	Consultation with Land Acquisition Department officials and recording.
Socio-economic and Political consequences of land acquisition in the study area.	Fieldwork in the area.	Participant observation, interviews with questionnaire schedules, collection of case history, census etc.
Peasant resistance against land acquisition.	Fieldwork, Government files, petitions, memoranda, newspaper reports.	Interviews with the leaders of the movement, observation and recording.

Selection of the Problem and Schedule of Research

The problem for this study was selected with some specific purposes which have been stated in the section entitled *objectives of the present study* although certain factors were instrumental in the selection of the particular villages. During1994, three students in the Department of Anthropology at Vidyasagar University were assigned to collect socio-cultural as well as anthropometric data on the Kora tribals in the Paschim Amba village under the Kalaikunda gram panchayat (G.P.) in the Kharagpur I block of erstwhile Medinipur district by following typical anthropological field methods for their M.Sc. dissertation works. It was then found that many of the Kora informants had already lost agricultural land for the establishment of a pig-iron industry in the Kalaikunda G.P. and had spent their compensation money towards domestic consumption. Incidentally, the students also met a non-tribal landloser of the village who was organising a movement of the peasants displaced from their agricultural land. These casual observations and contacts which were not required for the routine anthropological dissertations induced the author of this study to visit the area for the first time in the middle of 1995. Thc period 1994-95 was also important in other respects. In 1994 the Left Front Government issued its industrial policy after the declaration of the New Economic Policy of 1991 by the Central Government. In this policy statement the leftist West Bengal Government for the first time emphasised the importance of large and medium industrial investments from domestic as well as foreign private entrepreneurs in certain growing sectors of the economy like leather and leather products, petro-chemicals, food processing, electronics and information technology, power and tourism. The macro-level policy changes of the State Government were also showing its first signs in the study area. Land for Tata Metaliks (the pig iron industry in the Kalaikunda G.P.) had already been acquired during the 1991-92 and the plant started its production by 1993. During 1995-96 the villagers came to know about the establishment of another pig-iron industry on the agricultural land under the Kalaikunda gram panchayat. The situation offered a unique opportunity to conduct micro-level anthropological study of a peasant community facing the impact of the changes in the context of policy of the Government.

At the initial stage, enquiries into the nature and objectives of the peasant movement that was being organised by some local leaders against land acquisition were taken up. It was the leader of the movement who first gave an idea about the nature and extent of land acquisition in the villages under the Kharagpur Police Station. Interviews with the participants of this movement during 1995 not only helped the researcher to understand the mood, aspiration, and anguish of a good number of project affected persons in connection with the establishment of industries but it also paved the way to conduct household level surveys on the landloser families in 1996. In addition, the organisers of the movement also gave us copies of a number of petitions and memoranda which they submitted to the district administration in connection with the various demands of the local people centring around land acquisition. At a later stage of fieldwork, detailed socio-economic information was collected on a village named Gokulpur (under Barkola gram panchayat of the Kharagpur I block) which not only enjoys a reputation in the locality for the production of a good variety of vegetables but was also affected by land acquisition in a considerable manner.

In the third phase of the work, field visits were carried out in the villages affected by land acquisition of another pig-iron plant in the same locality. Household schedules of landloser families were filled up during January to April 1999. Along with household surveys, observations were made on other aspects of the socio-economic life of the villagers. For example, data have been collected on the micro-level changes that have been taking place on the huge chunk of agricultural land acquired for the Century Company, which still remains unutilised for ten years. Data have also been collected from the local gram panchayat office about the role of the panchayat in connection with the dispossession of the peasants in the study area. General information regarding the socio-economic profile of the administrative block in which the land acquisition actually took place have also been collected from the Block Development Office in this phase of research.

The fourth phase of the research was carried out in the Land Acquisition Department of the erstwhile Medinipur District Collectorate from the middle of 1999 to the first quarter of 2000. Research work at the Land Acquisition Department enabled the author to collect information on the various administrative, legal and policy aspects of the land acquisition process in general and also on the specific cases of acquisition that took place in the area during the 1990s. The departmental files revealed many interesting interactions among the key actors in the process, viz. the government, the requiring body, i.e. the private company for which government has acquired the land, and the project affected people. Research in the Collectorate not only provided a good deal of documentary evidence on the different dimensions of land acquisition, but also placed the author in a situation where he could learn about the various problems of this intricate and lengthy administrative procedure, directly from the persons who are in charge of its implementation. In the last phase, data on land acquisition and displacement have been collected from the West Bengal Legislative Assembly Proceedings for a number of years from 1956 to 1996. The Assembly Proceedings have been consulted by working in the West Bengal State Legislative Assembly Library in Kolkata. Besides the phases of research work mentioned above, news items on land acquisition and related policy issues from English and Bengali national dailies have also been collected throughout the period of research, that is, from 1995 to the middle of 2001.

Table 1.2 : Schedule of Research

Time period	*Nature of work done*
First phase June 1995-Feb. 1996	First entry into the field and interaction with the peasant leaders of the movement against land acquisition.
Second phase March 1996-June 1996	Household level survey and general observation on five villages affected by land acquisition for Tata Metaliks.
Third phase Nov. 1997-Jan. 1998	General observation as well as collection of some case histories from the villages named Gokulpur and Amba.
Fourth phase (a) Jan. 1999-April 1999 (b) May 1999-Feb. 2000 (c) April 2001-May 2001 (d) Middle of May 2001-Aug. 2001	(a) Field visits to villages affected by the land acquisition for Century Company accompanied by data collection in panchayat and block offices. (b) Collection of data from the Land Acquisition Department of the Medinipur District Collectorate. (c) Collection of data from the Assembly Proceedings of the West Bengal Legislative Assembly for the years 1956, 1957, 1963, 1967, 1972-74, 1978, 1983, 1989, 1991-94 and 1996. (d) Writing of the thesis.

The different phases of data collection have been summarised in the form of a table (see Table 1.2).

An Overview of Literature

The problem of development induced displacement and resettlement has assumed considerable importance in recent years, particularly since early 1980s. For the general public as well as policy makers, the displaced people often remained an undifferentiated and residual category who have to suffer the trauma of losing their homes and land for the greater interest of various kinds of development projects. There are at least two major reasons behind the upsurge of interest and attention towards the problem of displacement all over the world. First and foremost among those is the resistance of the affected people to the development projects. Notable among those resistances came from people's movements against big dams in the 1970s and 80s in many regions of the world (McCully 1996).

The second reason lies in the direct involvement of the World Bank in the formulation of an operational policy on resettlement of persons displaced by development projects (World Bank 1980). In fact, although World Bank's resettlement policy had gone through an evolution over the years (World Bank 1990,1994 and 1998), its beginning coincided with the anti-dam movement against Sardar Sarovar Dam in India financed by World Bank (McCully 1996). The media, accordingly, has also played a very important role in popularising the problems of displacement and rehabilitation at the local and global levels. Along with the non-governmental organisations who are fighting against development induced displacement almost all over the globe, the media has become a key actor in this development *versus* displacement debate.

Historically, the current popularity of the various socio-economic and political issues, which centre around development induced displacement, has a more academic background. Michael Cernea, who has worked most extensively on displacement and rehabilitation traced the earliest roots of empirical research on the problem in the works of the anthropologists and sociologists. In one of his recent articles, Cernea has stated:

> Anthropologists and sociologists took the lead in this research from the outset, initiating resettlement research long before the issue became subject to public policy and analysis by other disciplines (Cernea 1999a :28).

From the overview of Cernea's article, it is found that empirical studies on displacement and resettlement have been carried out by scholars both in developed and developing countries. In the United States of America, one of the first seminal contributions in resettlement research was carried out by Herbert Gans in the urban relocation site in the Boston area as early as 1960s (Gans 1968). Another early study on resettlement was carried out by anthropologist Elizabeth Colson in the 1960s, in which along with Thayer Scudder she studied in detail the socio-cultural consequences of the impact of Kariba resettlement on the Gwembe Tonga in Africa (Colson 1971; Scudder 1962, 1973). Important studies on the impact of dams and human-made lakes on the local populations of various parts of Africa were carried out by David Brokensha (1968) and Thayer Scudder and also by David Butcher (1971). Political scientist Robert Chambers (1970) conducted a study on the resettlement of populations caused by a dam on the Volta river basin in Africa. B.K. Roy-Burman (1961) made a pioneering study in India on the social processes of displacement caused by industrialisation in Rourkela in the post-colonial period. This kind of early social empirical research on the adverse socio-cultural and, to some extent, environmental consequences created a rich bank of "thick knowledge" (to echo a popular phrase in anthropology coined by Clifford Geertz) having direct implications for planners and policy makers in both developed and developing countries. But ironically, this rich body of empirical data were neither used by the policy makers to formulate future development policies nor by the academicians for building up new theoretical models and paradigms (Cernea 1995). In the worlds of Cernea:

> .....the body of social science concepts and research findings about population displacement and resettlement, generated through decades of field study, was left 'on the shelf' for

long time, without being used in relevant policies and programmes (Cernea 1995:92).

But the scenario, however, started to change since around the end of the 1970s when the World Bank which, as a major international development funding agency, adopted for the first time an operational policy on resettlement caused by forced displacement of populations almost all over the world. In this 1995 article which was published in the UNESCO journal of social science, Cernea outlined five stages in the history of World Bank's policy on involuntary resettlement that started since February 1980 and after going through successive important phases culminated into 1993-94 policy declaration on resettlement.

This five-stage policy history has its necessary details, which was first described in volumes of literature published by the Bank from 1980 to 1994. The basic content of this policy guideline has been summarised in a recent book entitled *Development Projects and Impoverishment Risks* (1998) edited by H.M. Mathur and D. Marsden who have been working as development anthropologists in the World Bank. The summary of the policy guideline runs as follows :

1. Involuntary displacement should be avoided or minimized whenever feasible, because of its disruptive and impoverishing effects.
2. Where displacement is unavoidable, the objective of Bank policy is to assist displaced persons in their efforts to improve, or at least restore, former living standards and earning capacity.
3. Displaced person should be : (i) compensated for their losses at replacement cost, (ii) given opportunities to share in project benefits, and (iii) assisted in the transfer and in the transition period at the relocation site.
4. People should be moved in groups to minimise disruptions in the social cultural life.
5. Participation of resettlers and hosts in planning resettlement should be promoted.

6. New communities of resettlers should be equipped with infrastructure and services for their successful integration in the regional socio-economic context.
7. Host communities should be assisted to overcome possible adverse social and environmental effects from increased population density.
8. Indigenous people, ethnic minorities, pastoralists and other groups that may have customary rights to the land or other resources taken for the project, must be provided with adequate infrastructure, and other compensation. The absence of legal title to land should not be ground for denying such group compensation and rehabilitation.

An attempt may be made to evaluate the implications of this policy framework as developed by the World Bank. First of all, in this policy formulation the major emphasis is given to displacement of population who have not only lost their livelihood but also their homes and have been resettled in a new place. But there are numerous cases of displacement where the project affected people (PAP) have lost their agricultural land either wholly or partially but not their homes. This kind of situation does not demand resettlement but proper provisioning of alternative modes of subsistence for PAP. In a democratic system of governance, the local governments should be made accountable for the proper provisioning of this alternative modes of subsistence for the PAP. The World Bank guideline is virtually silent on this point.

Second, it is well known that one of the major hurdles for minimising the disruptive and impoverishing effects of development induced displacement is the land acquisition laws through which the state exercises its power of 'eminent domain'. Therefore, it almost goes without saying that the land acquisition laws (in case of India it is the colonial Land Acquisition Act that is still in vogue in the country) need basic structural changes and should be made more transparent and participatory. The World Bank policies on resettlement caused by development projects dealt more with the effects rather than the basic 'causes' behind those effects.

Third, acquisition of large amount of agricultural land for big development projects (e.g. industries, power plants, big dams etc.) adversely affects the pre-existing empowerment scenario of the rural areas of a country. And quite obviously, even within a small region that is affected by the same project there are differential impacts upon the various groups of people depending upon specific socio-economic conditions historically created through the combined effects of people's movements and concrerte policy measures adopted by the Government. Large scale acquisition of agricultural land reverses these empowering processes by disempowering people not only economically, but also from political and cultural points of view. So it is not sufficient to state that "involuntary displacement should be avoided or minimized whenever feasible". The far-reaching and long-term political and cultural effects of displacement and dispossession should be assessed through pre-acquisition social surveys. Social survey with this kind of objectives should also have been incorporated in the Bank's policy on resettlement and rehabilitation. To put it more precisely, the Bank policy on rehabilitation and resettlement has never stated in categorical terms that large scale acquisition of farmland should be avoided in regions where successful implementation of land reform policies coupled with various poverty alleviation schemes by a government have already empowered the farmers. One gathers the impression that World Bank's policy on resettlement is one which is directed more towards the "curative" aspect of this socio-political malaise rather than concentrating on its "preventive" part.

Description to Analysis

From the above general discussion on the brief history of anthropological and sociological research on displacement and resettlement, an attempt has been made to review some of the recent studies on displacement with special reference to India. In this connection, it should be pointed out that research on development induced displacement gradually moved from descriptive and empirical studies to more analytical and policy oriented works, particularly since the 1980s when the World Bank first issued its initial resettlement policy. Many of the anthropological and sociological researches on displacement have now started to criticise government policies on land acquisition and provision of cash compensation to the deprived families and they have also begun to suggest alternative paths for development (Cernea 1991; Cernea and Guggenheim 1993; Barth and Williams 1994; Mahapatra 1991; Mathur 1995). On the other hand, important action oriented researches have been initiated by a good number of NGOs almost all over the world since early eighties. The international organizations like International Rivers Network (IRN) have been formed by mid-nineties which in collaboration with European Rivers Network (ERN), Narmada Bachao Andolan (NBA) and Biobio Action Group (BAG) and Brazilian Movement of Dam-Affected people (MAB) organised the First International Meeting of People Affected by Dams in 1997 (proceeding of the meeting 1997). In India, NGOs like Indian Social Institute (ISI), Multiple Action Research Group (MARG), Society for Participatory Research in Asia (PRIYA) and Institute for Socio-economic Developoent (ISED) and many others have started to publish important case studies as well as macro-level research works in the form of books, papers, pamphlets and manuals on displacement and rehabilitation since mid-1980s. These research oriented activist groups through several rounds of national level meetings which started around early 1995 prepared a draft national policy on displacement and rehabilitation in 1996 (Fernandes 1998). In fact this alternative draft policy which was formulated by more than 1500 NGOs from all over India was a critical response to the draft rehabilitation policies formulated by the Ministries of Water Resource Development (MWRD 1994) and Rural Development (MRD 1994), National Thermal Power Corporation (NTPC 1993) and Coal India Limited (CIL 1994). All these draft policies have made their respective attempts to revise or reformulate the crucial issues of relocation, rehabilitation and compensation of project affected persons and, significantly, the NGO alternative criticised all those government level draft policies in categorical terms. The draft policy prepared by the NGOs was submitted to the Secretary of the Ministry of Rural Development in 1995. The main features of this draft policy are summarised below (NCPR 1995):

1. The most important dimension of the NGO draft is that it does not take displacement as an inevitable phenomena like a natural disaster (e.g. earthquake). It rather wanted to force the government to try for every possible non-displacing developmental measures before undertaking any project that may involve deprivation and displacement of people. In this respect the NGO draft is more committed to the displaced and project affected persons than the World Bank Policy guideline on resettlement.
2. The central thrust of the NGO draft rests on the concrete suggestions for overhauling the Land Acquisition Act, 1894 (Amended in 1984) in India. The makers of the draft felt through their experience of fieldwork and activism that mere formulation of a good policy on displacement and rehabilitation is not enough. Therefore, what is needed is a change in the Land Acquisition Act, which should be made pro-people and rehabilitation must be incorporated as a matter of constitutional right and not a subject of sympathy or concession offered to affected persons by the government. In this respect also the NGO draft goes much deeper into the problem than the policy drafts prepared by the World Bank and the various Ministries of the Government of India.
3. As regards the encompassing yet undefined phrase 'public purpose' in the colonial Land Acquisition Act, the draft strongly suggested to restrict its domain of application by defining the purpose in a participatory and democratic manner through the incorporation of informed consent of the persons affected by a particular project.
4. Another striking characteristic of the NGO draft is the very strong emphasis it gives to the loss of common property resources (grazing fields, water bodies, forests etc.) by land acquisition and the extreme dependence of tribal people on common property resources. The draft suggested the award of compensation to common property resource users who also suffer displacement through land acquisition. In this regard, the NGO draft bears similarity with the World Bank guideline on resettlement.

The foregoing discussion on the various academic as well as policy oriented developements that have been taking place around the issues of displacement and rehabilitation clearly reveals the inevitability of more empirical findings whether one wants to build up theories or formulate balanced and humane policies about one of the greatest problems of modern civilisation. The need for creating a strong database on displacement has been recognised not only by the academicians but also by the non-governmental organisations who are actively engaged in influencing the government in changing its policies on rehabilitation. The government on the other hand shows little urgency to accept and implement measures and policies favouring the affected people simply because development projects always get priority for various political and economic compulsions. For example, in the post-Independence period in India despite valuable studies conducted by individual scholars that generated a wide range of empirical information on the consequences of land acquisition both at the macro and micro-levels, virtually nothing has been done to change the Land Acquisition Act by incorporating the findings of those studies. But this, of course could not dampen the enthusiasm of independent scholars, research institutes and NGOs in conducting policy-oriented and prescriptive studies on the nature, extent and consequences of development induced displacement and rehabilitation. Most of these recent studies, however, owe a lot of intellectual debt to the theoretical model developed by anthropologist Michael Cernea who worked in the World Bank as a senior adviser in its Environment Department. Cernea has developed his model on "impoverishment risks" caused by "involuntary resettlement" by analysing a large body of empirical data on development induced displacement from almost all over the world. His ideas on "risk model" started to develop as early as 1986 when he wrote a number of technical papers on behalf of the World Bank. Cernea's views on displacement and the role of social scientists are rather unique. In one of his celebrated monographs "Putting People First" (1991) which he edited, Cernea wrote: "Social Scientists, by contrast, are all too aware of how development projects can make certain people worse off. But social scientists all too often speak to themselves:

historically they have been much better at recording development's tragedies than preventing them." This is his starting point. From there he began his search for the common social processes which are unleashed by the launching of development projects whether they are big dams, mines, industrial estates, power projects or defence installations. These social processes are basically disruptive in nature which tear apart the socio-economic fabric of the community life. Cernea calls this phenomenon "impoverishment" which typically reveals itself in the following seven main dimensions: (i) landlessness, (ii) homelessness, (iii) joblessness, (iv) marginalisation, (v) food insecurity, (vi) increased morbidity and mortality, and (vii) social disarticulation. In his more recent work Cernea used the phrase 'impoverishment risks' instead of the more academic word 'dimension' and added one more risk, viz. 'loss of access to common property' to the earlier seven point list of dimensions (Cernea 1996a; 1996b; 1997; 1998; 1999 and 2000). In a recent article, drawing heavily from the experiences of Orissa, anthropologist L.K. Mahapatra added 'loss of education' as 'another impoverish-ment risk' to Cernea's model which according to him bears a crucial importance in the Indian context (Mahapatra 1999). The theoretical model that has been termed by Cernea as the 'risks and reconstruction model' has several advantage for academic research as well as social planning. The advantages are enumerated below:

1. The model captures not only the economic risks (landlessness, joblessness and food insecurity) encountered by a community but it also draws one's attention to the socio-cultural (marginalization, and social disarticulation) as well as biological risks (increased morbidity and mortality) to which a displaced population becomes vulnerable whenever development projects are launched.
2. The advantage of adopting a risk model serves as a kind of warning to development planning because vulnerability of a population to certain risks also directs the planners to think about their avoidance. In fact the 'risk model' may

help the planners to formulate policies for achieving workable solutions towards livelihood reconstruction of displaced populations.

3. The simple and open ended nature of this model allow the future researchers to expand and elaborate upon the basic framework to suit the needs of new situations.
4. The risk model breaks down a multifaceted phenomenon like 'impoverishments caused by displacement' into several quantifiable (e.g. one can measure and count the extent of landlessness or food insecurity) yet interlinked dimensions (e.g. one can find out the relationship between homelessness with social disarticulation or joblessness with food insecurity etc.) for a holistic understanding of any impoverishment situation. Furthermore, the model allows a researcher to collect both quantitative and qualitative data on the eight dimensions and permits diachronic comparisons between two situations, for example, pre and post-displacement scenario of project affected populations.
5. At the synchronic level, the model makes room for observations about variation. The different dimensions of impoverishment helps one to assess the relative importance of those dimensions in particular displacement situations. For example, in one situation loss of land may become the dominant theme while in another marginalisation of women and tribals may assume greater importance. This type of relative importance of the different dimensions has policy value for livelihood reconstruction of the communities affected by various sorts of development projects.

The literature covered so far reveals a clear dominance of applied anthropological and sociological models in the study of development induced displacement and rehabilitation. But it should be noted that in the mainstream anthropology there is still very little recognition of this kind of studies either in the curriculum or in the research projects carried out by anthropologists and sociologists.

The Wenner-Gren Foundation for anthropological research, under its small grants programme for 1990 and 1991, awarded a total of 137 research grants to scholars in social-cultural anthropology all over the world for developing "innovative ideas" covering the full range of areas and subject matter of contemporary anthropology. Among these 137 research projects, there were only 2 (1.45%) which proposed to conduct field research on involuntary resettlement and forced migration in Peru and People's Republic of China respectively (Wenner-Gren Foundation for Anthropological Research 1990 and 1991).

Among the social scientists, the economists seem to have given less attention to this field. Economists are still carrying out researches on development projects by calculating the cost-benefit ratio in terms of monetary investment and profit without taking into account the socio-economic losses suffered by the communities who loss their social, economic and natural capitals in the process of so-called economic development. The recent exchange between Ravi Kanbur and Michael Cernea clearly revealed the differences in the approach of an economist and an anthropologist on resettlement. In the exchange, Kanbur presented an economic view on compensation principle for project affected families advocating the idea of 'safety nets' (Kanbur 2002), while Cernea argued in favour of "resettlement with development" rather than on compensation alone (Cernea 2002). Even the economists who work far away from the routine orbit of neo-classical school pay little attention to the loss of entitlement caused by displacement and relocation. The famous contemporary works of Amartya Sen and Jean Dreze which dealt not only with poverty and famines in particular but also entitlement failure in general have no reference to large scale food insecurity caused by displacement through the major development projects in Asia and Africa (Sen 1999 and Dreze and Sen 1998).

Most of the works in anthropological and sociological research on displacement and resettlement till today are greatly influenced by two theoretical models. The first was developed by Elizabeth Colson and Thayer Scudder (Scudder 1985; Scudder and Colson 1982), and the second by Michael Cernea. The theoretical model developed by Scudder and Colson basically attempted to find out some general behavioural patterns of the resettled communities. They suggested that resettlement everywhere is a stressful experience and the people who have some degree of success in getting resettled in a new place pass through two basic socio-psychological stages. In the first stage, the displaced people behave in a more routined manner and they avoid any kind of risk taking behaviour. But in the second stage, the individuals of resettled population show innovative behaviour and tries to get a control over the situation. Negotiations with the host population take place more frequently at this stage and finally, the resettled population develops a kind of integration in the wider regional setting through the attainment of economic and administrative ability (Asthana 1996).

By comparing the Scudder-Colson model with that of the risk and reconstruction model of Michael Cernea certain similarities as well as differences could be revealed. First the similarities. Both the models have made sincere attempts to bring out the common features in all kinds of displacement situations rather than on their differences. The models provide a fair degree of testability on empirical grounds, although it is more difficult to test the Scudder-Colson model than the model of Cernea. The major difference between these two models is that while Scudder and Colson gave more emphasis on the dynamics of socio-cultural adaptation among the displaced populations, Cernea wanted to develop a flexible repertoire of "risks" generated through involuntary resettlement. Secondly, the risk and reconstruction model of Cernea is more policy oriented than the Scudder-Colson model.

Gaps in Research: The West Bengal Scenario

Under this broad and general overview of literature on development-induced displacement and rehabilitation, a brief review of the works done so far in this field in West Bengal may be made. The first striking thing one observes in this regard is the virtual absence of any empirical and theoretical work on development induced displacement in West Bengal. This of course does not mean that displacement and rehabilitation are non-existent in West Bengal, which in the pre-Independece period, was the leading state in terms of industrialisation, and where, after Independence, large industries and thermal power plants have been built up displacing many families (including tribals) from their agricultural land and home. West Bengal has also experienced large scale mining on the western part of the state bordering Jharkhand. In an article published in 1989, Walter Fernandes and his co-workers, quoting from government sources, have shown that for the Durgapur Steel Plant in the Bardhaman district of West Bengal 6,633.44 hectares of land was acquired, which displaced 11,300 persons, 3.39 per cent of whom were tribals, (Fernandes *et al.* 1989). In the same article, Fernandes quoted another government source which showed that up to 1983 there were 114 mines (all are coal mines) in West Bengal although he did not give any concrete figure of the total number of displaced persons owing to the acquisition of land for the establishment of mines. Through extrapolation, Fernandes, however, arrived at an estimate of 1,380 displaced persons per mine in India which brings out a figure of 1,57,320 persons in case of West Bengal. In more recent period, particularly since the adoption of a liberalised economic policy by Central Government, quite a good number of development projects have been launched by the West Bengal Government and many more will be coming up in near future. The building up of a new township near Kolkata and the establishment of industries in the rural areas of West Bengal including a port centred industrial complex at Haldia in the Purba Medinipur district constitute the recent development package of the Government of West Bengal. For the successful implemention of this development policy large scale acquisition of land has already been taken place in West Bengal, which displaced quite a good number of small and marginal farmers. No published statistics on displaced (DP) and project affected presons (PAP), let alone their caste/tribe affiliation, are available from any official source of the Government of West Bengal. Displacement and rehabilitation have not yet entered into the official agenda of the Government of West Bengal just as the recording of *bargadars* (sharecroppers) and the number of landless labourers who have been given land by the government have become a routine procedure.

On the other hand, the West Bengal scenario is yet to figure in any substantial manner in the academic literature with respect to land acquisition, development induced displacement and rehabilitation. There exist at least four special volumes of important Indian journals devoted exclusively to displacement and rehabilitation but none of them contains any case study or policy-oriented paper on West Bengal. These journals are *Social Action* (Vol. 45, No.3, 1995, July-Sept.), *Lokayan Bulletin* (Vol. 11, No. 5, 1995), *Economic and Political Weekly* (Vol. XXXI, No. 24, June1996) and *Eastern Anthropologist* (Vol. 53, Nos.1-2, January-June 2000).

The same is true about monographs recently published from prestigious publishing houses, viz. *Development, Displacement and Rehabilitation* edited by Walter Fernandes and Enakshi Ganguly Thukral (1989); *The Uprooted* (1990) edited by V. Sudarsen and M.A. Kalam and *Development Projects and Impoverishment Risks* edited by Hari Mohan Mathur and David Marsden (2000). Very recently, Partha Chatterjee, a renowned political scientist, has undertaken a study on resettlement and rehabilitation in West Bengal. His paper, which is still unpublished was presented in a workshop on "Social Development Research" in West Bengal held during 6-7 July, 2000 at the Centre for Studies in Social Sciences, Kolkata. In this significant paper, Chatterjee has pointed out that participatory rehabilitation through NGOs has become a "mantra" which is being repeated by the governments, funding agencies, experts and activists but "little attention has been given to the specific forms of practice through which appropriate and adequate 'participation' can be ensured" (Chatterjee 2000). Chatterjee used three cases of displacement and consequent rehabilitation in West Bengal to assess the role of the political parties' *vis-à-vis* government bureaucracy in providing rehabilitation to PAP in West Bengal. His findings on the political processes that centred around the rehabilitation mechanisms of the recent industrialisation in Haldia (1988-91) and the establishment of new township in Rajarhat clearly demonstrated the dominance of the local political society over the government administration. Quite interestingly, in both the cases. the distribution of rehabilitation benefits was based on a ground-level agreement between the representatives of the ruling and the opposition political parties of West Bengal. The net result of this process was the distribution of a better and quicker rehabilitation package to the project affected families than it would have been made by the usual land acquisition procedure carried out by bureaucratic machinery alone. In West Bengal, it was the political society (represented by the political parties) rather than the civil society (represented by the NGOs), which took the role of mediator between the state and the PAP. The first published evidence of research on land acquisition and its various adverse impacts on the peasants in West Bengal comes from author's own work conducted in Paschim Medinipur district (Guha, *et al.* 1996; Guha *et al.* 1997; Guha 2004 a; Guha 2004 b). In contrast to the work of Partha Chatterjee the findings of the author show how the ruling party overlooked the issue of rehabilitation as well as the undermining of village based decentralised planning and land reforms by putting emphasis on industrialisation (Guha 2004 a and 2004 b).

Standpoint of the Research

At this stage, the reasons behind taking up the problem of land acquisition in the erstwhile Medinipur district of West Bengal should be mentioned.

Firstly, land acquisition in West Bengal has a special significance in the context of the pro-peasant land reform policies adopted and implemented by the Left Front Government in West Bengal since it came to power in 1977. Almost all the studies conducted by the researchers on displacement in other states of India did not take into consideration the dampening effects of land acquisition on small peasants and sharecroppers who are the real beneficiaries of land reforms.

The second reason lies in the spatial proximity of the Gokulpur-Amba region from the Vidyasagar University campus which provided the author a unique opportunity of conducting repeated field visits in the study area and establish long-standing contacts with the project affected people and the local panchayat members. This has enabled the author to collect information on the various aspects of land acquisition in the area over a long period of time.

In this study an attempt has been made to describe the process of land acquisition in the Gokulpur-Amba area of the Kharagpur I block from a holistic perspective. The research strategy adopted in this work has not followed the usual anthropological holism in which any socio-cultural formation is viewed as an integrated system. The traditional anthropological description concentrates more on the local society (a tribal community or a village community) and its various system maintenance functions are explained with the help of ecological, structure-functional, cognitive and psychological orientation (Johnson 1978). This study has made an attempt to develop a kind of descriptive holism in which a group of villages have been put under the wider context formed by the aquisition of cultivable land for the private industries.

Agricultural land is not only a socio-cultural and economic category for the peasants in a rural setting but the rights of the people over land depend on the functioning of a specific set of legal, administrative and policy apparatus with which a particular state power is endowed in a given period of time. The functioning of the legal, administrative and policy mechanism of the state power do not again operate in a cultural vacuum. The differing and sometimes quite opposing perspectives on issues around development form the cultural context within which the state apparatus functions.

The acquisition of privately owned agricultural land by the leftist state government in West Bengal under the wider context of the New Economic Policy and globalisation severely affected the rights of rural cultivators on their agricultural land in the Gokulpur-Amba region of the Paschim Medinipur district. The rural cultivators in the Gokulpur-Amba region on the other could not form a homogenous group of peasantry in terms of the losses they suffered as well as the resistances they have put up against the functioning of the legal and administrative apparatus of the state power.

In this research, an attempt has first been made to describe the geographical context of erstwhile Medinipur district in general and Kharagpur block I in particular mainly from a broad economic perspective drawing heavily from government sources as well as from our field level observations. These are described in Chapter 2 which revealed the predominating dependence of the people of the study area on traditional form of agriculture and the preponderance of the people below the poverty line.

Chapter 3 deals with the dimensions of land acquisition in India and West Bengal. It takes into consideration the legal, administrative and policy perspective that emerged out the amendments on Land Acquisition Act, government reports, evaluation of the land acquisition process by the NGOs and the debates and dialogues among the elected people's representatives in the West Bengal Legislative Assembly. In the last section of Chapter 3 an attempt has been made to explore the ground realities of land acquisition in the present field area in some details based on the District Collectorate sources and specific field observations.

The third level of analysis draws heavily on the findings about the various consequences of land acquisition in terms of socio-economic as well as political dimensions which constitute the major portion of Chapter 4. In this chapter, the empirical scheme of data collection developed by Michael Cernea in his seven point impoverishment model has mainly been followed. The findings however, differed from the empirical model generated by Cernea and his followers who have worked in India in one major respect. In the 'impoverishment model' there is no discussion on the political disempowerment or marginalisation of the peasants through land acquisition process. In West Bengal, the subject of political empowerment of the rural poor has tremendous policy relevance owing to the success of the state in land reform and decentralisation of power through the elected panchayats. This question of the loss of political empowerment of the rural poor who were empowered by the left government just a few years ago, has been taken up here. In this chapter, the peasant resistance against land acquisition in the study area has also been briefly analysed.

In the fifth and concluding chapter, an attempt has been made to summarise the findings of the study on land acquisition from a policy perspective. Basically, this chapter constitutes the fourth level of holistic perspective that dealt with the policy implications of land acquisition and its various consequences in West Bengal.

TWO

The Context of Land Acquisition

> *In the agricultural sector, West Bengal continues to register high growth in food grain production and yield. ..... Index of agricultural production grew by 18.2% in the period 1991-1996. This has increased the overall purchasing power in the rural areas.*
>
> ***Destination West Bengal (1999)***

Medinipur District—Pre-eminence of Agriculture

Midnapore or Medinipur is the southernmost district of the Burdwan division of West Bengal. It was the largest district (22°51′10″ N to 21°36′35″ N and 88°12′40″ E to 86°35′50″E) in West Bengal which covered an area of 14,081 sq. km. with a total population of 8,349,890 according to 1991 census. The density of population of this district was 593 persons per sq.km. which was much lesser than the West Bengal average of 767 per sq.km. The district had 7 subdivisions, 46 police stations and 54 development blocks and was divided into two parts, Medinipur East and Medinipur West (NATMO 1996).

Medinipur was not only the largest district of West Bengal before its bifurcation in 2002 into Purba and Paschim Medinipur but it was also the most varied in its the physical aspects. Topographically, the district could broadly be divided into three parts: (a) almost entirely flat plains on the eastern part which is bounded by the districts of Hughly and Haora, (b) the undulating extensions of Chhotanagpur plateau of Bihar on the north and west. Geologically, this region consists of a hard laterite formation, and (c) the coastal plain of the south and south-west which is geographically part of Orissa and is subject to tidal waves and to the inroads of the Bay of Bengal.

The major rivers of the erstwhile Medinipur district are the *Rupnarayan, Kangsabati, Subarnarekha, Haldi, Kaliaghai* and *Silabati*. The district is gradually sloping from the Chhotanagpur plateau (300 mts.) to the 'Kanthi' (a former sub-division of the district which is now a subdivision of Purba Medinipur) littoral plain of Bay of Bengal.

The climate of Medinipur is monsoonal type. The annual range of temperature varies between 9°C and 43°C. While the average annual rainfall is 1470 mm. The Kanthi littoral part receives high rainfall which gradually decreases towards the north-west. The climate of the north and west of the district is very different from that of the swamps in the east and south. In the north and north-west the climate is characterised by dry, hot summer with moderate rainfall and short winter season. The east and south of the district is like that of the 24-Parganas of West Bengal characterised by hot and humid climate.

The great variation of the district in terms of topography, climate and geology is also reflected in the varieties of soil, flora and fauna. The pre and post-Independence District Gazetteers and Census Handbooks have recorded this tremendous diversity of Medinipur district in vivid details *(Bengal District Gazetteer, Midnapore 1911; District Census Handbook, Midnapore 1951 and District Census Handbook, Midnapore 1961*).

The district is predominantly rural in terms of the distribution of its population and agriculture supports the majority of its people. According to 1991 census, about 89.9 per cent of the people in erstwhile Medinipur District lived in the rural areas whereas 19 urban centres supported only 10.1 per cent of the population. (NATMO 1996). This means that the population of Medinipur distinctively depends on agriculture and its related activities. Almost hundred years ago, the scenario was not very much different at least in terms of figures. L.S.S. O'Malley recorded:

> Agriculture supports 77.2 per cent of the population, industries 9.8 per cent, the professions 2.9 per cent, and commerce 0.5 per cent. The population is more distinctively agricultural than in any other part of West or Central

> Bengal...... There are seven towns in the district, but none are of any great size.......Altogethet 3 per cent of the population is contained in these seven towns....... (O'Malley 1911).

In the post-Independence period, the importance of agriculture did not at all decline in Medinipur and out of the total working population the percentage of people engaged in agriculture far exceeded the state average. The 1961 District Census Handbook under its separate section entitled "Agriculture" emphatically stated:

> The district of Midnapore is pre-eminently an agricultural district and agriculture forms the major industry of the district. Most of the workers of this district are engaged in agricultural pursuits.... In the state of West Bengal, as a whole, only 54 pet cent of the total working population are engaged in agriculture against the district's percentage of 76. (District Census Handbook Vol. 1, 1961).

A research paper on the land use pattern of Western Midnapore by an eminent economic geographer was included in the District Census Handbook of 1961 which succinctly summarised the economic activities of the district in the following manner:

(1) Agriculture is the principal economic activity, not only because it is the major occupation employing the largest number of population, but also for the fact that all other occupations are abjectly dependent on it; and
(2) On the prospects of a single-crop, i.e. *aman* paddy, the entire economy stands or falls (Chakraborty 1961).

Since 1872 when the Collector of Medinipur returned the district's area as 4,836 sq.miles (3,095,040 acres) till late 1990s, rice had remained the single most cultivated crop for which the highest amount of land was put under cultivation. Medinipur is mainly an *aman* rice producing area, which is sown in the months of June, July and August and reaped in November, December and

January. The other varieties of rice (the *aus, boro* and high-yielding variety), vegetables, pulses, oilseeds, and fibre crops are also grown in the district.

L.S.S. O'Malley recorded that the cultivable land of the district may be divided into three classes, viz., high land, low land and *diara* or river land. The high land is sandy and found around the village sites above flood level and *rabi* crops are grown in it. Locally, it is known as *kala*. This *kala* land is further sub-divided into *bastu* or homestead land, and *dhosa*, in which *aus* paddy as well as pulses or oilseeds are grown. The low lands, which are locally known as *jala*, lie in between the villages. This *jala* land is mostly clayey and remains under water during the rains; the only crop grown on it is rice, but in rare cases, when near homesteads a summer oilseed *(til)* is grown. *Diara* lands are formed by river silt and are most sought after by the farmers. These lands are most suitable for growing *rabi* crops, pulses, wheat, barley, oilseeds and various vegetables (O'Malley 1911).

The land tenure scenario of Medinipur district had undergone important changes after the end of the British rule. In the pre-Independence period the land tenurial system was characterised by a variety of estates which existed in the pre-British period and continued during the British rule. The colonial administration, however, quickly tried to bring all kinds of estates and rent free lands into the purview of a revenue earning state power. A number of peasant rebellions collaborated by local indigenous landlords took place in the early years of British colonial rule in Medinipur and adjoining districts which centred around land and forest (Roy 1996). After Independence, *zamindary* abolition and land reforms took place in Medinipur like the rest of the state and the district registered a preponderance of households having landholdings of smaller sizes as early as 1961. The data obtained on households of the district during the 1961 census enumeration revealed that a little less than three-fourth (73 per cent) of the total households in the district depend on agriculture. The 1961 survey also showed that about 56 per cent of the total cultivating households of Medinipur had land below 2.5 acres while another 24 per cent had lands of holding size varying between 2.5 to 4.9 acres. One tenth of the cultivating households have lands varying between 5 to 7.4 acres in size while there were about 190 households having land above 50 acres. The 1961 census survey also recorded at about 32 per cent sharecroppers (*bargadars*) of the total cultivating households of the district among whom more than a quarter held even below one acre in size *(District Census Handbook,* Midnapore 1961).

The Kharagpur Block—The Area and Population

The villages of the study area come under the administrative jurisdiction of Kharagpur-I block of the present Paschim Medinipur district. The Kharagpur-I block is situated in the western part of the district and is bounded in the north by the Kasai river. On the west and the south of the block lie the Jhargram sub-division while the Kharagpur township is located in the east. Although the two major townships of the district are situated almost in the vicinity of this block it is chiefly an agricultural area with few patches of *sal* forest. The area is characterised by vast open cultivable lands interspersed with village settlements connected by unmetalled roads.

The block has an area of 201 sq. km. or 27,979.21 hectares within which 18,500 hectares are under cultivation (66.12 per cent) according to a survey conducted by the Block Development Office in 1997-98. The same survey has also found that out of the total cultivated area at about 6,905 hectares are under more than one crop which turns out to be 37.32 per cent of the cultivated land of the block. The total population of the block is 1,21,685 of which the males outnumber the females (male 62,314 and female 59,364), and there are 22,666 scheduled castes (18.62 per cent) and 29,974 (24.63 per cent) belong to the scheduled tribes. Among the scheduled castes the females (11,683 souls) outnumber the males (10,983 individuals) while within the scheduled tribe population the sex ratio is in favour of the males (15,528 males and 14,448 females). The population density of the block turns out to be a little more than 605 persons per sq. km. while the average household size is slightly above 5 persons. The district statistical handbook, which is based on 1991 census data, however differs from the survey conducted by the Kharagpur I Block Development Office. According to 1991 census figures the total population of the block has been recorded as 1,21,659 while the area of the block is 281.94 sq. km. and this gives a population density of 432 persons per sq.km. with 268 mouzas of which 225 are inhabited (*District Statistical Handbook*, Medinipur 1998).

The Scenario of Poverty

The occupational profile of the block reveals not only the dependence of the population on agriculture but also the poor economic condition of the people. Out of 41,124 main workers 16,180, i.e., 39.34 per cent are landless agricultural labourers while 11,509 (27.98 per cent) are cultivators. Together, these two categories constitute 67.32 per cent of the total main workers of this administrative unit of the district.

The other adjoining blocks, viz. Kharagpur II, Medinipur (Sadar), Sankrail, Jhargram, Keshiary and Narayangarh bear similarities with Kharagpur I when we consider the percentage share of landless agricultural labourers. The highest position being taken by Kharagpur II (48.13 per cent) while the lowest by Narayangarh (38.67 per cent) [*Ibid.*]. In terms of other important development indicators Kharagpur I block presents a rather backward picture when compared with the adjoining blocks. For example, the literacy percentage of this block is only 58.38 (the district percentage being 81.27) whereas Narayangarh, Kharagpur II and Keshiary registered 70.06, 64.02 and 61.84 percentages respectively; only the percentage is lower in Jhargram and Midnapore (Sadar), than it is in Kharagpur I. The number of electrified villages also show a gloomy picture for the block—only 29.33 per cent of of the total number of inhabited villages have electric facilities while the same percentage is 70.35, 50.5, 39.74 and 30.30 for Midnapore Sadar, Keshiary, Narayangarh and Jhargram respectively [*Ibid.*]. When the small savings collection of the block is taken into consideration, Kharagpur I is found to occupy the fifth position among the six other adjoining blocks, the highest position being taken up by Kharagpur II. Since a substantial segment of the population in this region is dependent on the cultivation of *aman* paddy it may be worthwhile to look at the production data of this particular crop. The production data show that although the yield rate as well as the total production of *aman* rice has increased considerably over a period of one year, the land area under cultivation of this crop has declined from 191.5 thousand hectares in 1996-97 to 158.8 thousand hactares in 1997-98. This has also happened in case of the neighbouring block Kharagpur II. The area under *aus* paddy cultivation has also declined in case of these two blocks over the period 1996-97 to 1997-98. The area under *boro* paddy cultivation has, however, increased in these two blocks during the same period [*Ibid.*].

Here an attempt has been made to make a comparative assessment of Kharagpur I block in terms of some economic and developemental parameters with the six other adjoining blocks of Paschim Medinipur. This comparative assessment may throw some light on the relative position of our study area on the basis of some important criteria as recorded in the 1991 census. These economic and developmental criteria include: (i) number of villages having electricity, (ii) literacy percentage, (iii) small savings collection, (vi) *aman* rice yield, (v) total number of main workers, (vi) total number of cultivators, (vii) number of landless agricultural labourers, and (viii) number of non-workers (i.e., persons in the 15-64 age group) and their percentage out of the total population of the block. We have also made a ranking on each of these criteria and marked it in smaller bold face numbers in italics from one to seven. Except for columns VII, VIII and X in all the other columns a higher numeral represents a better position for the block while in case of column VII (i.e., number of cultivators) a higher ranking only represents that more people are dependant on cultivation of land. While in cases of columns, VIII (number of agricultural labourer) and X (the percentage of non-workers out of the total population) higher rank indicates an inferior economic condition of a particular block. In simple terms, the first four criteria (i.e., from columns II to V) can be called development indicators while the criteria included under columns VII,VIII and X can be designated as economic indicators. Now in terms of the development indicatiors, Kharagpur I block comes to the bottom level of the scale except for the

Table 2.1 : A Comparison of six Blocks with Kharagpur I on the Basis of Selected Developmental and Economic Indicators

Name of the block	*Inhabited villages*	*Villages electrified*	*Literacy in percentage*	*Small savings collection 1997-98 (in '000 Rs.)*	*Aman paddy yield Kg/Ha (1997-98)*	*Total main workers*	*Cultivators*	*Agri. Labourer*	*Non-workers 1991*	*Percentage of Non-workers to total population*
	I	II	III	IV	V	VI	VII	VIII	IX	X
Kharagpur I	225	66 *6* (29.33)	58.38 *5*	9970 *5*	2165 *3*	41,124	11,509 7 [27.98]	16,180 *4* [39.34]	77.395	63.61 *1*
Kharagpur II	323	127 *4* (39.31)	64.02 *2*	37,849 *1*	2362 *1*	47,524	15,431 *6* (32.46)	22,874 *1* [48.13]	84.708	61.89 *2*
Midnapore (Sadar)	226	159 *1* (70.35)	50.06 *7*	861 *7*	1628 *7*	43,603	14,828 *5* [41.40]	18,055 *3* [41.40]	76,569	61.59 *4*
Jhargram	485	147 *5* (30.30)	56.51 *6*	20,728 *3*	1979 *4*	50,501	22,681 *4* [44.91]	19.238 *6* [38.09]	75,664	56,66 *6*
Sankrail	246	41*7* 16.66	61.32 *4*	8,429 *6*	1963 *5*	35,885	18,242 *2* [50.83]	13,313 7 [37.09]	45,210	51.55 *7*
Keshiary	200	101 *2* (50.5)	61.84 *3*	13,968 *4*	1,706 *6*	43,876	19,118 *3* [46.38]	20,351 *2* [46.38]	64,814	57.92 *5*
Narayangarh	463	184 *3* (39.74)	70.06 *1*	26,260 *2*	22,13 *2*	64,702	35,491 *1* [54.85]	25,026 *5* [38.67]	1,40,557	61.73 *3*

( ) Represents the percentage of villages electrified out of the total number of inhabited villages.
[ ] Represents percentage out of total main workers.
Source: District Statistical Handbook, Midnapore 1998, Bureau of Applied Economics and Statistics, Government of West Bengal.

column V which shows the yield rate of *aman* paddy. For the three economic criteria the block shows very low number of cultivators but a higher figure of landless agricultural labourers as well as the highest percentage of non-workers against its total population (63.61 per cent). [see Table 2.1].

In order to understand the nature and extent of the poverty among the different categories of the rural population in the country, the Ministry of Rural Areas and Employment, Government of India, had undertaken a programme of household survey in 1997. The basic objective of this survey was to identify the rural families living below the poverty line for bringing them under various anti-poverty programmes implemented by the Ministry for the ninth year plan (1997-2002). Accordingly, the expert group of the Ministry recommended a multiple criteria classification of the poor families by using not only annual family income but also other qualitative parameters like housing condition, consumer durables used etc. (*Compendium on Socio-economic Survey of Rural Households* 1997). This household survey for Kharagpur block I was carried out in 1997-98. The unpublished results of this survey was procured for this research from the Block Development Office. The data from this survey have been arranged against the gram panchayats (the lowest rung of the three tier elected local government in West Bengal) of the block which are seven in number. Table 2.2 summarises the findings of the survey.

There are altogether seven gram panchayats within Kharagpur Block I, viz., (a) Arjuni (b) Barkola, (c) Bhetia, (d) Gopali, (e) Hariatara, (f) Kalaikunda, and (g) Khelar. The blocks have varying population strength and composition.

All the gram panchayats have scheduled caste and scheduled tribe population although the numbers again vary from one panchayat to another. The Kalaikunda gram panchayat which contains our study villages stands second in terms of the population strength while as regards the scheduled tribe component of the population this block occupies the fourth position (23.11per cent).

The most striking feature of this table is the number of families living below the poverty line as they have been brought out through the household survey conducted by the Block Development Office

Table 2.2 : Population Figures and Families Living Below and Above Poverty Levels in Seven Gram Panchayats of Kharagpur I Block

Gram Panchayat	*Population*					*Family*		*Total*
	M	*F*	*SC*	*ST*	*T*	*Above poverty line*	*Below poverty line*	
Arjuni	9,089	8,423	2,925 (16.70)	2,366 (13.51)	17,512 (14.39)	1,004 (28.16)	2,561 (71.83)	3,565
Barkola	12,285	11,474	4,551 (19.14)	4,551 (19.14)	23,769 (19.53)	1,155 (23.81)	3,694 (76.18)	4,849
Bhetia	8,036	7,586	2,829 (18.06)	4,493 (28.68)	15,622 (13.65)	440 (15.65)	2,370 (84.34)	2,810
Gopali	8,989	8,707	2,113 (11.94)	6,824 (38.56)	17.696 (14.54)	1,176 (37.33)	1,974 (62.66)	3,150
Hariatara	5,105	5,107	1,163 (11.38)	2,345 (22.96)	10,212 (8.39)	412 (17.63)	1,924 (82.36)	2,336
Kalaikunda	12.042	11,433	4,129 (17.58)	5,427 (23.11)	23,475 (19.29)	1,356 (29.08)	3,306 (70.91)	4.662
Khelar	6,768	6,634	4,956 (36.98)	3.968 (29.61)	13,399 11.01)	437 (14.42)	2,776 (86.39)	3,213
	62,314	59,364	22,666	29,974	1,21,685	5,980 (24.32)	18,605 (75.67)	24,585

Figures in parentheses represent perentages out of column total.
SC–Scheduled Caste
ST–Scheduled Tribe
Source : Block Development Office, Kharagpur-I. The figures on families below the poverty line were sent to the office of the District Rural Development Agency (DRDA) by the BDO, Kharagpur-I through a letter bearing Memo No. 2453 dated 19.11.1997 under the heading 'Final Status Report'.

in 1997-98. The figures reveal the predominating number of families living below the poverty level in all the gram panchayats, the highest percentage being shown by the Khelar gram panchayat (86.39 per cent), while the lowest is by Gopali (62.66 per cent), the latter containing the highest percentage of scheduled tribe population. In Kalaikunda gram panchayat 70 per cent of the families live below the poverty level. If we take the average household or family size of this block as 5 then at least 93,025 individuals of the Kharagpur Block, i.e., 76.45 per cent of the total population are living below the poverty level. If we use the same method of estimation, then in case of Kalaikunda gram panchayat there would be 3306 × 5, i.e., 16,530 individuals living below the poverty line which turns out to be 70.41per cent of the total population of the said gram panchayat.

The last point to be mentioned in this connection is that according to the directives issued by the Ministry of Rural Areas and Employment, an operationl list of poor families was to be prepared out of the total number of BPL (below poverty line) families living in all the gram panchayats of the block. The objective behind the preparation of the operational list was to generate various employment schemes in order to push them up from the poverty level. The Ministry had also developed six categories of poor families, which should constiute the total number of families under the operational list. These six categories are named below: (1) landless labourers, (2) rural artisans, (3) women headed families, (4) physically handicapped, (5) bargadars, and (6) pattaholders.

In Kharagpur I, this operational list was prepared and sent to the District Rural Development Agency by the Block Development Officer in November 1997. The operartional list contained 8,157 BPL families which is only 43.84 per cent of the total number of families who live below the poverty line. The following Table 2.3 summarises the operational list of BPL families under the six categories as recommended by the Ministry. It also shows the number of scheduled tribe, scheduled caste and other backward community (OBC) families who have been included in the six categories of the operational list. Incidentally, no funds from the Ministry had come to assist the families through various employment generation programmes, at the time of collection of these data during April 1999.

Table 2.3: Below Poverty Line Families in the Operational List of the Kharagpur I Block

Landless labourer	*Rural artisan*	*Women headed*	*Physically handicapped*	*Bargadar*	*Pattadar*	*Total*
5375 (65.89)	238 (2.91)	1571 (19.25)	61 (0.74)	111 (1.36)	801 (9.81)	8,157
Scheduled castes	Scheduled Tribes	OBC	Other	Total		
3043 (37.30)	2601 (31.88)	778 (9.53)	1735 (21.27)	8,157		

Gokulpur and Paschim Amba—Two Villages in the Field Area

After describing the geographical, demographic and economic profile of the Medinipur district and the Kharagpur I block in a nutshell, we would now enter into the specific villages where the fieldwork for this research was carried out. Fieldwork specially designed to find out the consequences of land acquisition for private industries was also conducted in other villages as well, but these two villages were selected for giving a fairly representative account of land acquisition in this area. The representative nature of these two villages derives mainly from the geographical location and the type of agriculture as practised by the villagers. The names of the two villages are Gokulpur and Paschim Amba under Barkola and Kalaikunda gram panchayats respectively. They are situated at about 7 kms. from the Medinipur town which is the District Headquarters of erstwhile Medinipur. These two villages are located very near to the river *Kasai* (also known as Kangsabati) [the largest river of the district] on the east and the west sides of the South-eastern railway track which runs from Medinipur to Kharagpur railway station (12 kms. from Medinipur). If you want to reach the villages Paschim Amba and Gokulpur from Medinipur then you have to cross the *Kasai* river and get down at Gokulpur railway station. Paschim Amba is on the western side of the railway track while Gokulpur is on the eastern side when one goes from Medinipur towards Kharagpur. The people of both the villages depend mainly on agriculture, although a good number of villagers work as temporary wage labourers in and around Medinipur and

Kharagpur townships. Cultivation of paddy in these villages depends primarily upon rainfall and no irrigation facilities, either river lift or canal irrigation, was found to be operative at the time of our fieldwork. The inhabitants of Gokulpur which is located almost on the south-eastern bank of the river *Kasai* cultivate a variety of vegetables on the lands adjoining their homesteads owing to the very good supply of groundwater from traditional dugwells. Almost every landowning household of this village has at least one dugwell and water is available in these wells throughout the season within 10-15 ft. from the ground level. Some families have small ponds and shallow tubewells. In general, the inhabitants of Gokulpur enjoy a good supply of water for carrying out agricultural activities throughout the year.

The village Paschim Amba is located on the western side of the S.E. Railway track. The inhabitants of Paschim Amba which is almost within a kilometre from Gokulpur, do not enjoy a good supply of groundwater for carrying out vegetable cultivation. The main agricultural activity on this side of the railway track centres round rainfed paddy cultivation which takes about four to six months of the year. But it is important to mention here that land for four private industries has been acquired during 1990-96, by the Government of West Bengal on the western side of the railway track and this has affected the peasants of Gokulpur and Paschim Amba in different manner. The peasants of Paschim Amba (a section of whom belongs to a scheduled tribe named Kora[1]) suffered the problems of landlessness more acutely than the inhabitants of Gokulpur since the former did not have any scope to cultivate vegetables and other kinds of crops (e.g. mustard) on lands near their homesteads owing to the poor groundwater condition. The villagers of Gokulpur, however, have been facing a different kind of problem due to the acquisition of their farmlands located on the western side. They are now facing a shortage of their food crop (paddy), which they used to grow on lands located on the western side.

The household survey conducted by the Kharagpur I Block Development Office for the identification of families living below the poverty line in the Kalaikunda and Barkola gram panchayats revealed almost the same kind of picture (seventy per cent of the people live below poverty level) as it was in case of the block as a whole. (see Table 2.4).

In this table, the number of BPL and APL families of gram samsads (the fourth tier of the panchayat which contain one or more mouza villages) in the two gram panchayats are arranged, which clearly shows the overwhelming majority of BPL families in our study area. The figures for Gokulpur and Amba (Purba and Paschim) show a higher percentage of BPL families in the latter. The field observations also corroborate with the spirit of this survey and the inhabitants of Gokulpur seem to be a little better off than that of the people of Amba. It may be noted here that both the BPL survey and our field observations were conducted almost at about the same time period when agricultural lands of the peasants of both the villages have been acquired for the industries.

Gokulpur—A Close Up

A brief outline of the location and economic condition of the village Gokulpur has been given and it was compared with Paschim Amba having some contrast in order to throw some light on the differential impact of land acquisition in the region. The socio-economic scenario of Gokulpur would now be described in some detail as revealed through anthropological fieldwork conducted in the early and middle part of the year 1998.

Gokulpur (J.L.No. 120) can be called a medium sized village having a population of 1746 individuals (930 males and 816 females) living in 329 households which gives an average household size of 5.30 (see Table 2.5)

The BPL survey, however, recorded a much higher figure of households (360 in number) for Gokulpur gram samsad, which was due to the fact that in the said survey other villages were also included under the Gokulpur gram samsad. The village is being inhabited by 18 castes and tribes of which the majority of the population belongs to the Sadgop[2] caste (43.87 per cent of the total population), who reside in 140 households (see Table 2.6).

Table 2.4 : Village-wise Break up of the Families Living Below and Above Poverty Line in Kalaikunda and Barkola Gram Panchayats in 1997

Name of Gram Samsads	*Kalaikunda*			*Name of Gram Samsad*	*Barkola*		
	APL	*BPL*	*T*		*APL*	*BPL*	*T*
Pratappur	74 (26.61)	204 (73.38)	278	Ajabpur	83 (28.42)	209 (71.57)	292
Panchrolya	64 (45.07)	78 (54.92)	278	Gokulpur	116 (32.22)	244 (67.77)	360
Rajpura	26 (31.70)	56 (68.29)	82	Shymraipur	127 (32.90)	259 (67.09)	386
Sadatpur	418 (72.69)	157 (27.30)	575	Khastaluk	86 (39.81)	130 (60.18)	216
Dhuliapata	48 (34.53)	91 (65.46)	139	Barkola (Purba)	56 (30.60)	127 (69.39)	183
Kasputia	48 (32.21)	101 (67.78)	149	Barkola (Paschim)	92 (39.65)	140 (60.34)	232
Kalaikunda	54 (23.07)	180 (76.92)	234	Bargai	43 (22.99)	144 (77.00)	187
Radhanagar	25 (14.20)	151 (85.79)	176	Nayekpara	73 (25.70)	211 (74.29)	284
Niranjanbar	35 (22.43)	121 (77.56)	156	Keshpal	30 (21.42)	110 (78.57)	140
Chandabila	40 (20.00)	160 (80.00)	200	Sofiabad	64 (25.6)	186 (74.4)	250
Jagganathpur	35 (16.20)	181 (83.79)	216	Mohanpur	24 (7.84)	282 (92.15)	306
Khalkona	35 (11.25)	276 (88.74)	311	Satkui	54	477	531
Gumraipal	45 (10.81)	371 (89.18)	416	Matkatpur	110 (34.16)	211 (65.52)	322
Kholapatna	53 (15.49)	289 (89.50)	342	Rupnarayanpur (Purba)	18 (9.27)	175 (90.20)	194
Mahespur	95 (20.65)	365 (79.34)	460	Rupnarayanpur (Paschim)	52 (15.43)	285 (84.56)	337
Kantapal	97 (27.95)	250 (72.04)	347	Jafala	82 (19.95)	329 (80.04)	411
Amba (Madhya)	100	105 (51.21)	205	Walipur	45 (20.45)	175 (79.54)	220
Amba (Purba Paschim)	63 (48.78)	171 (73.07)	234				
Grand Total	1356 (29.08)	3306 (70.91)	4662		1155 (23.81)	3694 (76.18)	4849

Figures in parentheses represent percentages out of each row total.

Source : Unpublished survey conducted by the Block Development Office.

Table 2.5 : Age Scx Composition of the Village Gokulpur

Age group	*Male*			*Female*			*Total*	
0-4	(8.817)	82	(4.696)	(9.436)	77	(4.410)	159	(9.106)
5-9	(15.053)	140	(8.018)	(13.480)	110	(6.300)	250	(14.318)
10-14	(13.655)	127	(7.273)	(10.416)	85	(4.868)	212	(12.142)
15-19	(9.354)	87	(4.982)	(8.946)	73	(4.180)	160	(9.163)
20-24	(8.709)	81	(4.639)	(10.049)	82	(4.696)	163	(9.335)
25-29	(10.430)	97	(5.555)	(11.274)	92	(5.269)	189	(10.824)
30-34	(6.236)	58	(3.321)	(8.578)	70	(4.009)	128	(7.331)
35-39	(9.247)	686	(4.925)	(6.617)	54	(3.092)	140	(8.018)
40-44	(4.193)	39	(2.233)	(4.289)	35	(2.004)	74	(4.238)
45-49	(4.086)	38	(2.176)	(3.431)	28	(1.603)	66	(3.780)
50-54	(2.365)	22	(1.260)	(3.431)	28	(1.603)	50	(2.863)
55-59	(1.827)	17	(0.973)	(2.205)	18	(1.030)	35	(2.004)
60-64	(1.935)	18	(1.030)	(3.676)	30	(1.718)	48	(2.749)
65-69	(1.397)	13	(0.744)	(1.838)	15	(0.859)	28	(1.603)
70+	(2.688)	25	(1.431)	(2.328)	19	(1.088)	44	(2.577)
		930			816		1746	

Figures in parentheses represent percentages. The left side figures represent the percentage out of each column while on the right side show percentage out of grand total.

The landholding pattern of the village shows preponderance of landless families (34 per cent), and through field survey it was learnt that this pre-dominance of landless families existed even before the acquisition of agricultural land of the inhabitants of Gokulpur. The landholding pattern of Gokulpur actually reveals the poor economic condition of the villagers wherein small landholding families constitute the majority of the population. Therefore, the acquisition of the farmland of the inhabitants of the village further worsened the economic condition of the villagers.

The Koras of Paschim Amba—A Case of Non-migrant Rural Poor

If the Sadgops of the Gokulpur village represent a peasant community who are undergoing the process of depeasantisation through impoverishments caused by land acquisition, then the Koras of Paschim Amba can be called a community of rural poor who survive by selling their labour in the urban and rural areas of Kharagpur and Medinipur. The Koras hardly own a piece of agricultural land (see Table 2.8) on which they can grow a crop for their subsistence but they own mud houses and small homesteads to which they return every night after working as daily labour either in the agricultural fields of others or as non-agricultural temporary wage-earners in and around Kharagpur.

Table 2.6 : Distribution of the Castes and Communities in Gokulpur

	Number of households	*Number of individuals*	*Mean household size*
Sadgop	140 (42.553)	766 (43.87)	5.47
Tanti	47 (14.28)	235 (13.45)	5
Mahishya	35 (10.63)	175 (10.20)	5
Santal	23 (6.99)	112 (6.41)	4.86
Bauri	20 (6.07)	97 (5.55)	4.85
Lodha	12 (3.64)	54 (3.09)	4.5
Kayastha	9 (2.73)	52 (2.97)	5.77
Dome	8 (2.43)	48 (2.74)	6
Brahmin	5 (1.51)	38 (2.17)	7.6
Napit	6 (1.82)	37 (2.11)	6.16
Kamar	3 (0.91)	24 (1.37)	8
Baisnab	5 (1.51)	22 (1.26)	4.4
Teli	2 (0.60)	18 (1.03)	9
Pod	3 (0.91)	18 (1.03)	6
Kora	4 (1.21)	15 (0.85)	3.75
Munchi	3 (0.91)	14 (0.80)	4.66
Kol	2 (0.60)	11 (0.63)	5.5
Rajput	2 (0.60)	10 (0.57)	5
Total	329	1746	5.30

Figures in parentheses represent percentages.

Table 2.7 : Landholding Pattern of Gokulpur

Size category (in acres)	*Number of households*	
Landless	112	(34.042)
≤0.5	65	(19.756)
0.5 - 1.5	98	(29.787)
1.5 - 2.5	33	(10.030)
2.5 - 3.5	14	(4.255)
3.5 - 4.5	2	(0.607)
4.5 - 5.5	1	(0.303)
5.5 - 6.5	1	(0.303)
6.5 - 7.5	NIL	
7.5+	3	(0.911)
Total	329	

Figures in parentheses represent percentages.

Table 2.8 : Land Holding Pattern of the Koras of Paschim Amba

Amount of land (in acres)	*Number of Households*		*Average Household Size*
Landless	43	(76.79)	4.95
≤0.5	4	(7.14)	5.75
0.5-1.5	6	(10.71)	6.6
1.5-2.5	7	(1.78)	3.0
2.5 & above	2	(3.57)	9.0
	56	(100)	

Figures in parentheses represent percentages.

So the Koras cannot be regarded as migrant rural poor and no land has yet been given to these landless Kora families of Paschim Amba by the Government of West Bengal through land reform measures.

The establishment of private industrial plants, of which one is situated within Amba (a coke oven plant) and the other (a pig-iron industry) in an adjoining mouza, has in fact increased the scope of daily wage based employment for the Kora men and women. The acquisition of agricultural land has not affected the Koras in the manner they affected the Sadgops, since many of the Koras were landless labourers before the acquisition. But the prospect of their employment as agricultural labourers in the lands of Sadgop cultivators has, however, declined due to the impovrishment of the latter through land acquisition. The majority of the Koras of Paschim Amba were found to earn their livelihood by working as agricultural labourer at the time of our fieldwork (see Table 2.9).

Table 2.9 : Types of Work Done by the Koras of Paschim Amba

(Number of Persons)

Season	*Cultivation in own land*	*Agricultural labour*	*Non-Agricultural labour*
Summer Season	44	15	155
Rainy Season	55	195	55
Winter Season	50	181	102
	149	381	312

The foregoing brief account of the Sadgops of Gokulpur and the Koras of Paschim Amba shows how the pre-existing geographical and socio-economic conditions of the two groups of rural poor form the contours of socio-economic transformation that have been unleashed through the acquisition of the fertile agricultural land in a rural area of Paschim Medinipur. The differential impact of land acquisition on the Sadgop and Kora communities has developed its unique character when a peasant movement against land acquisition started in 1995-96. The movement attained a level of militancy for a brief period, but its leadership mainly came from the Sadgop cultivators while the tribals like Kora and Lodha were never found to be the active participants of the movement.

NOTES

1. Koras are listed as a scheduled tribe by the Government of India and they are found in many rural areas of Medinipur district. According to the early British administrator ethnographers Koras are allied to the Mundas of the Singhbhum district in Jharkhand (presently bifurcated into East and West Singhbhum) and have migrated to West Bengal, from

their traditional homeland in Chhotanagpur, Bihar (Mitra,1951). The Koras still earn their livelihood as day labourers as well as small and marginal farmers.

2. Sadgops are one of the clean castes of the Hindu order who have taken to agriculture and claim themselves to be superior to milkmen or Goala caste (Mitra,1951). In Purba and Paschim Medinipur districts, the Sadgops earn thier livelihood as enterprising agriculturists who are most often found to occupy the fertile riverine plains of the district. They are also found in the urban areas in the service sector.

THREE

Legal, Administrative and Policy Dimensions of Land Acquisition

It is necessary to identify the laws of the land that are to displace, compensate and rehabilitate people and to examine their contents in detail. After such an appraisal it will be possible to pinpoint the glaring shortcomings of the law and of the underlying policies.

K. Vaswani, V. Dhagamwar and E.G. Thukral (1990)

The Backdrop

In India, the system of keeping records of cultivable land by the state for the purpose of revenue collection originated in pre-colonial period, while a systematic legal and administrative machinery for acquiring land from private owners developed during the colonial regime. The all-embracing nature of the colonial state power found one of its successful expressions through the enactment of the Land Acquisition Act in 1894. The succession of some landmark events, which led to the enactment of this enabling piece of legislation, showed a consolidation of British colonial power in the Indian subcontinent. This consolidation of the colonial power was not only a political phenomenon, but it also ushered in a chain of technological as well as economic events which needed a well organised legal and bureaucratic structure. In 1820, coal mining in Raniganj (West Bengal) and extensive irrigation network started in North India. The construction of the first Indian steamship, coffee and tea plantations in Mysore and Assam started by the late 1830s. Between 1850 to 1880, the first telegraph lines, railways, modern cotton and jute mills were established. This period also witnessed the first legislation, which curtailed the access of the local people to forests and mechanised mining as well as growth of manufacturing sector of the economy. In 1893 the first Indian Petroleum Refinery was established and in the next year, that is, in 1894, the Land Acquisition Act was enacted for acquiring privately owned land by the state for public purposes. The succession of events, which led to the enactment of this Act, clearly showed that it was the need of the time.Mining, plantation, establishment of railway lines, manufacturing industries, beginning of major irrigation works, and road building, all needed land which again was already under various forms of state controlled and customary tenurial systems that existed from the pre-colonial period. This enabling Act empowered the state to acquire any privately owned as well as common property land for public purposes. The Act provided the legitimacy behind the acquisition which otherwise would have to be done with the application of brute force. After Independence, the Government of India did not abolish this piece of colonial legislation and acquisition of private land continued with the help of the Land Acquisition Act, 1894. The first major change in the Act was introduced in 1894 through an amendment by the Central Government. The said amendment resulted in some beneficial changes for the project affected people (PAP) which are enumerated below :

(1) Payment of 12 per cent per annum interest on land value to the person whose land has been acquired commencing from the date of notification to the date of declaration of the compensation award.
(2) Payment of solatium (i.e. compensation for losses suffered or injured feelings) at the rate of 30 per cent. Earlier it was 15 per cent.
(3) A provision was made to those not satisfied with the collector's award to apply for a redetermination of the compensation.
(4) The amendment also tried to minimise the undue delay that characterises land acquisition proceedings.

But along with above beneficial changes the amendment had also conferred greater discretionary power on the government and introduced the acquisition of land for private companies. Before the amendment, private companies procured land from the market by paying the market price. The amendment enabled the private companies to get land from government, which meant that the latter had to acquire land beforehand on behalf of the company.

In India, every State Government has the right to amend the provisions of the Land Acquisition Act,1894 in its application to that particular state and since Independence, the different states have made several amendments. As a result, at present there exists a good deal of inter-state variation with regard to the various technical aspects of the land acquisition proceedings. Most of these inter-state variations centre round matters related with notification, survey, objections to notification, payment of compensation and the authority who is empowered to set in motion the acquisition proceedings. The LA Act, however, is basically a Central concern, since State Government can make amendments as long as the changes are not opposed to the Central Act and the Central Government has the power to modify an amendment or declare it invalid (Vaswani, Dhagamwar and Thukral 1990).

Basic Features of the Land Acquisition Act

According to the Land Acquisition Act, the state can exercise its right of *eminent domain* wherein it is the ultimate owner of all land, which it can acquire for public purposes after paying full compensations calculated on the basis of market value. Despite several amendments of the Act after Independence, the two basic principles of land acquisition, viz. (i) public purpose, and (ii) compensation on market value remain unchanged. The various criticisms of Land Acquisition Act in India have also centred round these two cardinal principles. One of the major criticisms of the Land Acquisition Act is that the expression "public purpose" is nowhere defined in the Act and in India the courts do not have the power to decide whether the purpose behind a particular acquisition was a public purpose. The court can only direct the Collector to hear the objections of a person whose land has been acquired, but the Collector may not always listen to the objections raised by the legal owner of the land.

The second criticism is anthropological in nature. It says that the calculation of compensation on the basis of market value not only deprives the landowner, but it also hides the various socio-cultural dimensions of land ownership in an agrarian society. Land does not only have a market price at the time of acquisition, but it also serves various social, political and psychological functions to its owner. The ownership of a small piece of land can empower a landless family and increase the status and prestige of that family in the local social milieu. A piece of land supports a family for a number of generations, not simply its present members at the time of acquisition. But these important dimensions of land and its ownership in an agricultural society are not considered for calculation of its value while giving compensation to a landloser.

Beside these two criticisms, there are others which grew out of the lengthy discourse and debate carried out by activists, scholars, legal experts and non-governmental organisations on the various shortcomings of this Act. The criticisms are as follows :

1. The Land Acquisition Act only deals with compensation and not rehabilitation of project affected persons (PAP) whose land have been acquired. The responsibility of the state towards the affected persons ends with the payment of compensation.
2. The Act considers the payment of compensation to individuals who have legal ownership right over land. This means that under this Act no compensation is payable to landless labourers, forest land users and forest produce collectors, artisans and shifting hill cultivators because they do not have any legal right over land, although these groups of people are also affected when agricultural and forest lands are acquired for development projects. In West Bengal, the State Government had to make an amendment in the Land Acquisition Act in order to provide compensation to sharecroppers (*bargadars*), who also suffered loss of livelihood because of acquisition of agricultural land.

3. The Land Acquisition Act only recognises individual property rights, but not community rights over land. As a consequence, the *usufructory rights* of the tribal and non-tribal communities over common land do not find any place in this law. So when village common lands are acquired, no compensation in any form is provided to the village communities who derive various types of benefits (e.g. cattle grazing, fuelwood collection etc.) from these lands. The Land Acquisition Act does not have any scope for this kind of compensation for loss of common pool resources (CPR). Interestingly, in the vast rural areas of India, privately owned agricultural lands are also used as common grazing lands by the villagers in the post-harvest season. The Land Acquisition Act has no provision to compensate the villagers who may not be the owners of a particular piece of agricultural land but enjoyed *usufructory rights* of cattle grazing on agricultural land after the harvest of the crops. Even the recent Environmental Impact Assessment (EIA) does not have any provision to calculate the economic costs for the loss of common property resource in agricultural land (Guha 2004).

The foregoing discussion on the basic features of Land Acquisition Act reveals that in a country like India with immense socio-cultural diversities and regional variation, there is ample scope for studying the land acquisition process from an anthropological perspective. Each case of land acquisition in a particular state or in a specific region has its own peculiarities and historical antecedents. Every case of acquisition also elicits specific type of responses from the PAP that depends on the nature of socio-economic and political composition of a particular area. Anthropological study of land acquisition may include, among others, a descriptive account of a specific case of land acquisition, which would give adequate importance to the view of each group of participants in the process. Usually, anthropologists study only the human groups who are affected by land acquisition by employing participant observation.

In this research the process of land acquisition for two private companies and its various consequences have been studied by anthropological fieldwork and through the collection of documentary evidences from the concerned administrative offices of the District Collectorate.

Stages of Land Acquisition and Rights of the Project Affected People

In India, land required for any developmental purpose has to be acquired by State Governments through the Central Acquisition Act or various State Acts. The acquisition of land is basically an administrative process, which proceeds through several interconnected stages (Land Acquisition Act, 1894). The different stages in the Central Act are described in the following paragraphs:

(a) *Stage 1.* Under section 4 of the Act a notification is made by the State Government wherein the purpose for which land is to be acquired is mentioned. The other details in the notification include, (i) the amount of land acquired, (ii) the date of notification, (iii) the mouza(s) in which the land to be acquired, and (iv) the sections of the Act by which the land would be acquired. This notification would have to be published in the Government Gazette as well as in two daily newspapers of which one would be in the regional language. The District Collector also issues a public notice at convenient places in the area.

(b) *Stage 2.* Under section 5 (a) of the Act, any person who has an interest in the land (e.g. landowner or sharecropper) may file an objection against acquisition in writing within 30 days from the date of publication of the notice. The Collector may give an opportunity to the objector of being heard and after making any further enquiry will submit the case to the government, although the decision of the Collector on the objections is final.

(c) *Stage 3.* Under section 6, a declaration notification is made by the government which is a conclusive evidence that the land is needed for a public purpose or for a company. This declaration is made within one year from the date of publication of notice.

(d) *Stage 4.* In the fourth stage of land acquisition, a notice is again issued by the Collector under section 9 of Land Acquisition Act to all those persons who have an interest in the land. Through this notice the Collector invites "interested persons" to claim compensation.

(e) *Stage 5.* In this stage, the Collector conducts an enquiry under section 11 against the claim of the interested person and also makes an assessment of the compensation to make an 'award'. The Land Acquisition Act stipulated that the 'award' would have to be made within two yeras from the date of publications of the declaration under section 6. This 'award' becomes final under section 12 of the Act. If any dispute arises, the Collector may refer the matter to the Court for its decision under section 30.

(f) *Stage 6.* At this stage, that is, after the declaration of the 'award' the Collector can take possession of land under section 16 of the Act. But in case of urgency, the Collector may immediately after the notification under section 9, can take possession of land under section 17 without making an 'award', although in this case the Collector will have to make 80 per cent of the estimated compensation to the landlosers.

(g) *Stage 7.* The 'award' made by the Collector under section 11 is not final. Any interested person not satisfied with the award may write to the Collector to refer the matter to the Court under section 18.

(h) *Stage 8.* The sections 23 and 24 of the Act deal with the parameters to be used by Court as well as the Collector for the assessment of compensation. The parameters include, (i) the market value of the land on the date of publication of notification under section 4, (ii) damage caused to crops etc. while taking possession of land or during measurement, (iii) damage to earnings or property while taking over a part of property, (iv) cost of change of residence or place of business as a result of acquisition, and (v) loss of profit between date of publication of declaration and the actual time of taking possession of land.

(i) *Stage 9.* This stage deals with the payments of compensation. In case of delay in the payment of compensation, an interest on the valuation of the land ranging from 9 per cent to 15 per cent per annum would have to be paid.

The different stages of the Land Acquisition Act show that after the first notification nearly one year may easily pass before the declaration and another 23 months may also be covered by the government before it can make any award since under the Act the declaration of the award can be made within two years after the publication of declaration notification. In case of agricultural land it is found that people are not allowed to cultivate as soon as the first notification is issued, although the actual possession may take a considerable period of time.

Secondly, it may also be very difficult for illiterate villagers to know about the first notification in the gazette and newspapers.

Thirdly, it is also very difficult for poor and illiterate villagers to submit objections in writing unless some political and social activists give support to them. No State Government in India has formed any department or special cell to help the poor villagers to file objections and demand proper justice when their major means of livelihood, that is, cultivable land, is acquired. Two Delhi based NGOs have published activists' manuals (in English) for guiding the project affected persons to demand proper compensation and social justice in connection with land acquisition. A booklet entitled *The Land Acquisition Act* (1989) published by The Society for Participatory Research in Asia (PRIA) has enumerated the different areas of intervention, where the project affected people can raise certain legitimate issues once land acquisition process is set in motion by the Government. For example, quite often, the public purpose in the first notification is not mentioned or the declaration is issued after one year from the date of first notice under section 4 and the like. In these cases, legitimate objections can be raised within the existing framework of the Land Acquisition Act, which may bring relief to the affected persons (Singh and Katyayan 1989).

The socio-legal manual entitled *The Land Acquisition Act And You* (1990) published by Multiple Action Research Group (MARG) is an exhaustive monograph that explains the operation of each and every section of the Land Acquisition Act with the help of concrete examples. In a Chapter entitled *What is Wrong With the Act* (pp. 110-113), the authors point out that the Land Acquisition Act does not give any power to the affected people by which the acquisition can be prevented. Project affected people by going to Courts and raising legitimate objections can only delay the process of acquisition and enhance the rate of compensation. The authors of the monograph have recommended that the demand for proper rehabilitation should be one of the crucial issues around which people affected by land acquisition can organise themselves and put pressure on the elected peoples' representatives and the Government (Vaswani, Dhagamwar and Thukral 1990).

Review of Land Acquisition by the Central Government

The recent activities and publications by the NGOs in India around land acquisition, displacement and rehabilitation have brought the issue before the general public in a popular way. It is true to a large extent that the consciousness of the educated layperson has increased about the various shortcomings of the Land Acquisition Act, although the political parties still seem to be not much interested in this vital issue like the NGOs. On the other hand, the Central Government of India, though not in a popular way has reviewed the various problems of land acquisition by different high-powered expert committees. Since Independence, the Law Commission has reviewed the various dimensions of Land Acquisition and the Commission in its 10th report made some recommendations on the subject. Besides, Law Commission, a landmark report was prepared on land acquisition and rehabilitation by the then Ministry of Food, Agriculture, Community Development and Cooperation in 1967.

The reference to this report, however, is not found in the recent literature published by the activists and the NGOs. The report was entitled as *Report of the Group of Experts on Land Acquisition* (1967) and was published by Department of Agriculture, Government of India. The expert group was constituted by 17 members (including bureaucrats, scientists and lawyers) which was chaired by Shri B. Sivaraman, then Secretary, Ministry of Food, Agriculture, Community Development and Cooperation. The group was empowered to deal with all questions related to land acquisition with particular reference to the following matters:

(i) procedure for acquisition,
(ii) principles for determining compensation, and
(iii) the delays that take place for the completion of the proceedings.

In the introductory part of the report it was stated:

> The Government of India has for some time past been considering remedial measure against delays and other difficulties in the acquisition of land for various development projects. It has also felt concerned about complaints with regard to the compensation. Although many of these problems have been examined in the past, first by the Law Commission and later by *ad hoc* committees, no workable arrangements have yet been evolved (Department of Agriculture, Government of India, 1967).

So it was in pursuance of the twin purpose of considering the *procedures* of land acquisition and the *principles* governing determination of compensation that the aforesaid expert group was formed. The group made the following observations on the Land Acquisition Act and its application in India:

(1) The problem of delay in the completion of the acquisition proceedings that used to end with the payment of compensation was the most important issue before the group which observed that a good deal of delay was due

chiefly to *administrative inaction* rather than any inherent defect in the law.

(2) The group endorsed the view that *acquisition of good agricultural land for non-agricultural purposes should be avoided as far as possible.* The committee recommended that the requisitioning department should consider this aspect in detail and whenever good agricultural land can be saved, alternative acquisition proposal should be submitted.

(3) The expert group also noted with concern that sometimes the requiring body (RB) asks for more land than what is required in the foreseeable future for the immediate purpose. The committee recommended that care should be taken by the Government in this regard so that the *requiring body applies for a minimum area of land which may be necessary in future.*

(4) One of the most important recommendations made by the expert group dealt with rehabilitation of displaced persons as a result of acquisition of land. The group observed that any person who is shifted from his land and habitation as a result of acquisition of his land should be deemed to be a displaced person (DP) and *the state has a moral responsibility for rehabilitation of the displaced people.* Under section 8.02 of the report the expert group stated unequivocally:

> In this connection, it was felt that the provision of section 23 (1) of the Land Acquisition Act implies the Government responsibility for rehabilitation. Projects where permanent labour is to be employed have been giving preference to dispossessed persons in matter of employment after necessary training ..... It may not be possible to lay down the law with regard to the exact nature of rehabilitative measures. But government must assume responsibility in principle (*Ibid.* 1967).

The foregoing description of the report of the expert group revealed the fact that the Government of India's deep concern with the various problems of Land Acquisition Act and observations as well as recommendations of the group, which were made as early as 1967, is quite congruent with the basic spirit of the recent World Bank Policy and the NGO draft on rehabilitation of persons displaced by development project. But there is, however, a significant difference between the NGO draft and the views of the expert group on the definition of the phrase 'public purpose' in the Land Acquisition Act. The expert group observed the fact that the LA Act neither defined "public purpose" nor did it lay down any criteria for determining it, and so concluded that "it would not be desirable to attempt a definition of the expression". The reason was also categorically stated by the group: "Any precise definition which may hold good in the present situation may not be applicable in a future context". Suffice it to note here that one of the persistent demands of the activists and NGOs engaged in raising the consciousness of the people with regard to land acquisition repeatedly stressed that the prospective PAP's should be given the legal right to take part in the determination of the public purpose of a given project. The NGO draft, which was submitted to the government in the mid-1990s, amended section 4.1 of the LA Act (i) to contain the reasons for the public purpose as well as (ii) the non-displacing and least displacing alternatives along with (iii) the details concerning the displaced and project affected persons (Fernandes 1998).

Land Acquisition in West Bengal

It has already been discussed in Chapter 1 that no systematic and comprehensive work on land acquisition in West Bengal exists till today. There is no baseline empirical survey on the nature and extent of land acquired in West Bengal for various development projects, nor is there any research on the specific problems of application of the Central and State Acts on land acquisition in West Bengal. Recently, Walter Fernandes and his team have undertaken a comprehensive macro-level empirical survey (sponsored by the Ministry of Rural Areas and Employment, Government of India and North-Eastern Social Research Council, a research oriented NGO) on the nature and extent of development induced displacement and rehabilitation in the 16 districts of West Bengal for the period 1951-1995. Being one of the research supervisors in the aforesaid research project for the South Bengal districts (Medinipur, Bankura, Puruliya and Hooghly), it is within the knowledge of the author that the results of this survey may be published in future (personal communication Walter Fernandes, 2000).

Since Independence, besides the colonial Land Acquisition Act of 1894, there existed another State Act entitled West Bengal Land (Requisition and Acquisition) Act, 1948. The latter Act is no more applicable in West Bengal since 31 March 1993 by a decision of the West Bengal Legislative Assembly. In fact, when this particular piece of legislation was first enacted in the State Assembly it was stipulated that the Act has to be renewed in the Assembly by a majority decision every five years since this is a very powerful and coercive law. The Government opinion was that the State of West Bengal, which had to receive millions of refugees from erstwhile East Pakistan just after Independence, needed huge amount of land for various developmental purposes. For this reason, the Government was in need of an Act, which was more powerful than the colonial Act in acquiring land from the private owners. By West Bengal Land (Requisition and Acquisition) Act the Government could first requisition a particular piece of land for which the payment of compensation may not be made while in the earlier LA Act of 1894 the government could not take possession of any land without payment of compensation. In the absence of any district by district published records on the amount of land acquired by West Bengal Government by the two Land Acquisition Acts it is not possible to make any assessment of the policy directions of the State Government in acquiring land by these two Acts which vary in their basic approach towards the payment of compensation to the project affected people. But the long period (1948-1993), that is nearly 45 years, during which the West Bengal Government has kept this powerful Act alive is itself an evidence of its frequent application. In terms of political composition, it should be noted that during this long period both Congress and Left ruled governments, who were in power, continuously renewed the Requisition and Acquisition Act of 1948 in the State Assembly.

In this research, a good deal of information have been collected on the attitudes of the different governments as well as the elected members of State Legislative Assembly from 1956 to 1994 belonging to various political parties of West Bengal by studying the published volumes of Assembly proceedings.

The debates and questions raised in the West Bengal Assembly in relation to land acquisition can be broadly classified into two sections, viz., (i) questions raised by the members on problems arising out of land acquisition in specific areas of West Bengal and the replies given by the concerned ministers, and (ii) the debates which took place at the time of placing the West Bengal Land (Requisition and Acquisition) Act, 1948 in the Assembly. The debates, as discussed below, reflect the stance of those involved in the decision-making process towards the problem at the highest political level of a state in a democratic system.

*Debates on West Bengal Land (Requisition and Acquisition Act) in the Legislative Assembly**

Since the promulgation of the 1948 Act on land acquisition (popularly known in administrative circles as Act-II while the colonial one as Act-I), debates and discussion on this legislation took place in the Assembly a number of times for amendments. In order to make amendments in the Act, it was placed in the form of a bill and after the debate the bill with the necessary changes and approval of the Assembly was sent to the President of India for his assent. From the records kept in the Assembly Library it has been found that the Act was placed 17 times in the house and got the assent of the President well within a period of 2 months. Another important fact

* All the names of the Ministers and MLA's mentioned in the sections on 'Debates' and 'Questions' are real which have been collected from the published Assembly Proceedings.

in this regard is that voting on the amendment of the Act had taken place only twice—once when the Congress Party was in power (on 20 February 1973) and at another time when the left parties were in government (on 28 March 1967). On both occasions, the parties which were in power won by a majority vote (Assembly proceedings Vol. 54; 1973 and Vol. XLIV; 1967).

With this general background, the salient points which were raised in the debates at the time of placing the bill in some of the sessions have been described below:

The Year 1956

The Minister Mr. Sankar Prasad Mitra (Congress Party), who was in charge of Land and Land Revenue as well as Judicial and Legislative Departments, placed the West Bengal (Requisition and Acquisition) Amendment Bill [hereafter W.B (Req. and Acq.)], 1956 in the 15th session of the Assembly on 12 July 1956.

The Minister reported that large scale acquisition of land was going on in Burdwan district for dam building by the Damodar Valley Corporation (DVC) and a total of 12,449.44 acres of land had been acquired by Act-II.

The Minister also stated that most of the areas in Burdwan district contained underground mines and minerals and the acquisition of these entailed heavy amount of compensation. Accordingly, in the bill it was proposed that the government might in appropriate cases exclude mines and minerals from acquisition.

The bill with necessary changes was then passed without any debate (Assembly Proceedings Vol. XV 1956).

The Year 1957

The Minister Mr. Bimal Chandra Sinha, who was in charge of the Land and Land Revenue Department, placed the W.B (Req. and Acq.) Act, 1948 for its continuance on 3 July 1957 in the 17th session of the Assembly. A debate followed wherein one member, Mr. Basant Kumar Panda of the Socialist Party (SP) said that this Act was no more required. Mr Subodh Banerjee of the Socialist

Unity Centre of India (SUCI) expressed his anxiety over the passing of this bill. He apprehended that poor slum dwellers of Calcutta might be evicted by this Act. Mr. Banerjee also stated that for development of the rural areas of the State there are other legislations which could be empolyed by the government. A member of the Communist Party of India (undivided CPI), Mr. Harekrishna Konar, who joined the Communist Party of India (Marxist) after the division of the CPI in 1964 and became the Land and Land Reforms Minister in 1967, when the left parties came to power in West Bengal for the first time, delivered a long speech. In his speech Mr. Konar opposed the bill by saying that the government should not pauperize lakhs of people in the name of development. He cited examples where the government had used bulldozers over the standing crops of the farmers and made big holes on the fields by the side of Khonnen railway station in Burdwan, as a result of which the farmers could not cultivate in those lands. Mr. Konar raised another point in which he said that the acquisition of the same amount of agricultural land from a rich and poor farmer had different implications; land acquisition always hit the poor farmer more severely than the rich (Assembly Proceedings Vol. XVII, 1957). The bill, however, was passed in the Assembly without any voting.

The Year 1963

The Minister Mr. Shymadas Bhattacharya of the Congress Party, who was in charge of the Land and Land Revenue Department, placed the W.B. Land Acquisition (Amendment) Bill, 1963 in the 36th session of the Assembly on 19 August 1963 for discussion among the members. This bill was placed to amend the Land Acquisition Act, 1894 for introducing a legal right for the sharecroppers (*bargadar*) to receive compensation for the acquisition of the land on which they had no ownership right. This bill can be called a landmark in the history of the amendments in Land Acquisition Act of India. In no state of India other than West Bengal an amendment like this has yet been introduced.

When the debate on this bill started one member, Mr. Sanat Kumar Raha of the CPI argued painstakingly for raising the rate of compensation for the *bargadars* from three times to five times so that the *bargadar* could purchase some land of his own and rehabilitate himself. He also pointed out that there must be an arrangement for spot enquiry whenever there would be a dispute with regard to the identification of a *bargadar*. The Minister, however, did not agree with Mr. Raha's proposal for a higher rate of compensation to the *bargadar* and succinctly replied by saying that he had listened to many speeches in the Assembly, but to his knowledge no member had yet tried to explain why there was no provision for paying compensation to the sharecroppers in the Land Acquisition Act of 1894. He further commented it would not be true to say that his Government had not done anything for the *bargadars;* earlier they did not get any compensation whatsoever (Assembly Proceedings Vol. XXXVI, 1963). The amendment was passed without any voting.

The Year 1967

The Minister in charge of the Land and Land Revenue Department, Mr. Harekrishna Konar of the CPI (M) placed the W.B. (Req. and Acq.) Amendment Bill for extending its tenure in the 44th session of the Assembly on 28 March 1967. During the debate, Mr. Siddhartha Sankar Roy of the Congress Party who became Chief Minister of West Bengal later, strongly opposed the bill on legal grounds by saying that in many cases regarding land acquisition in West Bengal the High Court had passed judgements against this Act. He used a Bengali word within a sentence in English to give an added emphasis. To quote Mr. Roy: "This Act is an oppressive and *Jabardast* (Bengali word meaning 'overbearing') piece of legislation." He also pointed out the arbitrary nature of the phrase "public purpose" in the Land Acquisition Act. After the speech of Mr. Roy noise and shouting among the members supporting and opposing the bill started and ultimately voting had to be organised by the Speaker. The bill was passed by a majority vote with 131 members voting in favour of the amendment and 72 members against it (Assembely Proceedings Vol. XLIV, 1967).

The Year 1970

The Minister Mr. Harekrishna Konar of the CPI (M) introduced the bill for the extension of Act-II and frankly admitted that he had nothing to say on it. He only stated that this Act is necessary for quicker work. No debate took place and the bill was passed in the 50th session of the State Assembly on 29 January 1970 when the United Front Government dominated by the left political parties was still in power for the second time in West Bengal (Assembly Proceedings Vol. 50; 1970).

The Year 1972

The Minister, Mr. Gurupada Khan (Cong. I) who was in charge of the Department of Land Utilisation and Reforms and Land & Land Revenue placed the W.B. (Req. and Acq.) (Amendment) Bill 1972 in the 52nd session of the Assembly on 10 April 1972. During the debate, the CPI member Mr. Saroj Roy stated that for the sake of development land should be quickly acquired but at the same time the process of the payment of compensation to the affected persons should also be expedited. It may be noted in this connection that CPI at that time was a partner of the government formed by the Congress Party, while CPI (M) was in the opposition. One member Mr. Abdul Bari Biswas, however, did not oppose the bill but also supported the view of the CPI member by stating that the rules for the payment of compensation for the rich and poor landowners should be different. The Congress members supported the bill by saying that for the development of the country land should be acquired, but they at the same time admitted that delay in providing compensation very often harassed the landlosers.

The Minister also stated that the government would give attention for quicker payment of compensation, but sharply reacted to the comments of CPI and CPI (M) members on their suggestions with regard to the payment of compensation to rich and poor farmers. He said that it was not possible to evolve different rules for different categories of landlosers since in the eyes of the law everyone was equal. The bill was passed without any voting (Assembly Proceedings Vol. 52; 1972).

The Year 1973

The Minister Mr. Gurupada Khan introduced the bill on the same subject in the 54th session of the State Assembly on 20 February 1973 for expanding its scope. The opposition member, Mr. Timirbaran Bhaduri of the Revolutionary Socialist Party (RSP) gave a long speech to oppose the bill. He was against this legislation on the ground that it was being employed against the poor people. The member then personally attacked the Minister by asking him where the poor farmer would go whose land had been acquired for erecting a building for the entertainment of the factory owner who happened to be a friend of the Minister? Another RSP member, Mr. Shis Muhammed stated from his "bitter experience" that the government was invariably acquiring the land of the small peasants, whereas the rich farmers were spared. One Congress member, Mr. Jogilal Mondal supported the bill by saying that land must be acquired for the establishment of schools and the construction of roads, but the Act should never be applied to the poor and the payment of compensation should be made within three months from the date of acquisition. Another Congress member, Mr. Rajanikanta Dolui pointed out that thousands of bighas of land were being simply kept unutilised after acquisition. So land should not be acquired unless it was very urgently required.

The Minister in his reply could not avoid answering the personal attack made by Mr. Timibaran Bhaduri and said that none of his friends had any factory. He further informed the House about the formation of an Expert Commttee consisting of Secretaries of the Land and Land Reforms Department, Commerce and Industries Department, Agriculture Department and three other nominated members.

The bill was then passed through voting wherein 59 members voted in favour of the amendment of the bill while only three members (all belong to RSP) voted against it and one member abstained from the process (Assembly proceedings, Vol. 54; 1973).

The Year 1978

The year 1978 was significant in the political history of West Bengal since the Left Front Government came to power in 1977, wining the election by massive popular support. And since that year the LFG is ruling the state till today by completing 29 years of continuous stay in power. The bill was placed by the Minister Mr. Benoy Krishna Choudhry, himself a peasant leader belonging to CPI(M) from the Burdwan district. The Minister justified the extension of Act-II for the completion of unfinished development programmes and also for combating the devastation caused by the flood that ravaged the state recently. One member stated that it was an oppressive Act and extreme delays were being made in payment of compensation. Another member criticised the government for not being transparent in informing the house about the methods employed for the calculation of compensation.

The Minister assured the house by saying that Act-II was not applied unless land was urgently needed and the value of the land was determined not by the old market price but at the current rate prevailing just before the time of acquisition. The bill was passed without voting (Assembly Proceedings Vol.69; 1978).

The Year 1983

The bill was placed by Mr. Benoy Krishna Choudhury for amending its 1(4) clause to continue the Act for another five years.No member of the opposition party was present in the house.The Minister justified the extension of the Act-II by citing a number of tasks for which land-required viz.,

(i) maintenance of essential supplies of commodities,
(ii) establishment of industrial townships for the creation of employment,
(iii) construction of irrigation and drainage network,
(iv) construction of houses in the urban and rural areas, and
(v) for various other developmental works.

All the members supported the bill but only one member pointed out about the delay in the payment of compensation but no member spoke about rehabilitation of the displaced persons. The bill was passed in the 80th session of the Assembly on 8 September 1983 (Assembly Proceedings Vol. 80; 1983).

The Year 1989

The Minister Benoy Choudhury placed the bill for extension of the Act for another five years. He justified the extension to expedite the programme related to public welfare. During the debate, the point on the delay towards the payment of compensation was raised as usual. A new issue was raised by one member belonging to the Left Front, who mentioned that the Congress Party was trying to create disturbances by making use of the harassment of small landholders caused by acquisition. The member further pointed out that even the supporters of the Left Front, who were affected by the delay in the payment of compensation, were getting disgruntled. The Minister only commented that he was also aware of difficulties in implementation of this Act.

The bill was passed without voting in the 92nd session of the Assembly on 14 March 1989 (Assembly Proceedings Vol. 92; 1989).

The Year 1994

The Minister Mr. Benoy Choudhury placed the W.B. (Req. and Acq.) (Amendment) Bill 1994 in the 103th session of the Assembly on 23 Ferbruary 1994 for its extension only for the completion of the huge number of pending cases under Act-II. In his speech, the Minister narrated the historical background of this particular legislation. Mr. Choudhury stated that since it was not possible for the government to acquire land quickly on the basis of the colonial Land Acquisition Act of 1894, the Act-II was needed and was introduced after Independence. The government originally decided to keep this Act in force upto 31 March 1951, but it had to be kept alive upto 31 March 1994 through successive amendments in the State Assembly. In 1993 the Government of India had communicated that it would not agree any more to extend Act-II, and the State Government too, in principle, was in agreement with this view of the Central Government, For this reason, the State Government, since April 1993, had almost stopped the application of this Act except in some special cases. Accordingly, orders have been sent to the districts to complete all the pending land acquisition cases started under the Act-II by 31 March 1993. The Minister then gave a huge figure of 15,000 unfinished land acquisition cases at different stages in the state. He admitted that the land requisitioned in these cases could neither be returned to the owner nor could those be transferred to the provisions of Act-I of 1894. During discussion three members supported the bill although they questioned about the delay in the payment of compensation. The bill was then passed without voting (Assembly Proceedings Vol. 103; 1994).

The debates and discussions that took place in the West Bengal Assembly around West Bengal Land (Requisition and Acquisition) Act, 1948 revealed certain interesting points which are enumerated below:

1. Without any exception, the political party in power (Congress or Left) invariably justified the extension of Act-II for quicker acquisition of land for various development works.
2. Both the Congress and the Left Parties criticised the oppressive character of the West Bengal Land (Requisition and Acquisition) Act, 1948 whenever they were in opposition although representatives of the parties in the Legislative Assembly went for vote on the bill twice only. It seems that whether the parties would go for vote depended on factors other than the immediate issue at hand.
3. The delay in the payment of compensation seemed to be the most commonly accepted issue which was raised in the Assembly and no substantial improvement seemed to have taken place with regard to the time taken for the payment of compensation.

4. No member ever raised the point that the government has a moral responsibility for rehabilitation of the displaced persons due to the acquisition of land. It may be noted in this connection that the Report of the Expert Group on Land Acquisition formed by the Ministry of Agriculture, Government of India, which was published in 1967 (discussed in the section 3.3.1), categorically mentioned rehabilitation of displaced persons as a "moral responsibility" of the government. Since 1967, no member of the West Bengal Legislative Assembly, irrespective of political affiliation, was found to have made use of the aforesaid report of the Expert Committee to demand rehabilitation of displaced persons during debate sessions on Act-II. Incidentally, the report is still available in the Library of the West Bengal Legislative Assembly.
5. It is only the Left Members who have suggested that the rates of compensation for the rich and the poor should also be different but they did not make any move towards the differential payment of compensation through amendments in either Act-I or Act-II since they are in power from 1977.
6. The speech delivered by the Land and Land Reforms Minister of the Left Front Government in the 103th session of the Assembly on 23 February 1994 revealed the pace at which the land acquisition process was in operation in West Bengal (15,000 pending cases under Act-II). One could easily infer from this the kind of harassment caused to the displaced persons in the districts of West Bengal although no member (belonging to Left or Congress Party) spoke on this issue in the Assembly. Every political party seemed to have taken the stand that this harassment of the people of West Bengal caused by land acquisition was an inevitable outcome which has to be shouldered by the poor farmers for the sake of development of the state.

Questions and Answers on Land Acquisition in the West Bengal Legislative Assembly

The questions which were admitted by the Speaker of the West Bengal Legislaltive Assembly on land acquisition revealed a definite pattern. The concerned Ministers were asked to reply on a variety of subjects on land acquisition viz. rate of compensation, employment for displaced persons, non-utilisation of land acquired for a specific project and the like. After consulting the questions and answers in the Assembly Proceedings for the years 1956-57, 1963, 1967, 1972-74, 1978, 1983, 1991-94 and 1996, same observations may be made relating to their relevance on the actual problem.

A lengthy question-answer session was found to take place in the Assembly on 21 August 1963 regarding the acquisition of cultivable land for the construction of Haldia port in the erstwhile Medinipur district (admitted question No. 1050). The questions and their replies revealed that about 955 acres of fertile agricultural land had been acquired by Land Acquisition Act, 1894, but it remained unutilised at the time when questions were raised in the Assembly. In course of the questioning by a number of members belonging to the ruling and opposition parties (e.g. Sushil Kumar Dhara of the Congress Party and Birendra Narayan Roy (Independent supported by CPI), it was revealed that some of the farmers had started to cultivate paddy on their acquired lands and the elected members were trying to elicit some statement from the Minister in favour of these farmers. The Minister, however, tried to evade from making any kind of commitment on this particular issue and passed on the responsibility to the port authority for whom the said land was acquired. He, however, admitted that the government would not have any objection if the farmers could make an unofficial arrangement with the port authority with regard to the cultivation of acquired land where no construction work had yet been started. The Minister finally assured the House by saying that priority would be given to provide jobs to the persons whose lands had been acquired for the port (Assembly Proceedings Vol. XXXVI; 1963).

Ten years later, two Congress MLAs (Shri Sukumar Das and Shri Sougata Roy) asked (admitted question No. 1440) the Minister of Land and Land Revenue Department about the total area of land acquired for the Haldia Petro-Chemical project in Medinipur and the rehabilitation measures taken for the displaced persons. The Minister replied that 906.035 acres had been acquired and Rs. 4,47,91,437.14 had already been paid as compensation while arrangements were being made to rehabilitate about 517 displaced persons on 130.25 acres of land (Assembly Proceedings Vol. 54; 1973).

During the tenure of the LFG, questions by the members in the Assembly showed almost the same pattern as followed twenty years ago. Questions of the non-payment of compensation to project affected persons, however, constituted the central point of consideration. For example, on 22 August 1991 Congress MLA Shri Atish Chandra Sinha cited specific cases of land acquisition in his constituency in Murshidabad district where the landowners had not yet received any compensation. He also gave examples of cases in which land acquisition had taken place in 1977-78 but no compensation payment had been made. On 28 August 1991 Shri Natabar Bagdi of the Congress Party wanted to know whether compensation payment had been made against land acquisition for irrigation schemes in Purulia district (admitted question No. 316). On the same date admitted under question number 1314, one member asked about the number of homeless persons who had been given jobs in the Kolaghat thermal power project in Medinipur district up to March 1991. The Minister reported that at about 599 displaced persons were recruited in the various departments of West Bengal State Electricity Board up to March 1991 (Assembly Proceedings Vol. 98; 1991).

In 1992, from an admitted question no. 247 made on 23 March 1992 one could know that about 17.19 acres of land had been acquired in Narendrapur in the South 24-Paraganas for a proposed wildlife sanctuary (Assembly Proceedings Vol. 99; 1992). From a question made by Shri Angad Bauri (question No. 1620) on June 1992, it was known that about 1156 persons had not been given compensation for land acquired in the two mouzas for a colliery in

Burdwan district (Assembly Proceedings Vol. 99; 1992). On 1 June 1992, under approver question number 2042, Shri Manas Bhuniya of the Congress Party wanted to know about land acquisition scenario in the Gokulpur area of Medinipur district for the establishment of the pig iron industry owned by the Tatas. The Minister in his reply stated that about 217.23 acres of land had been acquired for the Company and compensations had been given at the rates of Rs. 22,015.50 and Rs. 26,891.00 respectively (Assembly Proceedings Vol. 99; 1992).

In 1996, from a question made by Shri Suniti Chattaraj (Congress MLA) it was revealed that only one person had been given a job from among the landlosers for the establishment of Bakreswar thermal power project in the Birbhum district. In his reply, the Minister had also informed the House that in the same project 16 persons had been given casual employment (temporary) among whom there were *bargadars* and *pattaholders* (those landless persons who received land from the government in the land reform programme).

The questions and replies on various aspects of land acquisition in West Bengal Assembly followed a pattern, which did not change much over the years. The questions revolved around compensation and rehabilitation. The elected members seemed to be more concerned with the deprivation of the landlosers owing to non-payment of compensation. With only one notable exception, there was no occasion when the members asked questions on the justification of acquiring agricultural land for non-agricultural purposes. Only in 1963, Mr. Sushil Dhara made a general observation that the government should not misuse agricultural land by keeping it unutilised after acquisition in these days of acute food shortage. Another interesting aspect revealed through these questions was related with the possible impact of land acquisition on land reforms. There was no debate or question raised on this subject in the State Legislative Assembly in West Bengal. In a state, which has made notable achievements in providing land to the poor, it was really surprising not to find any member of any political party saying anything on the subject.

Land Acquisition in Medinipur District*

From the discussion on the Assembly Proceedings it may be noted that acquisition of agricultural land in erstwhile Medinipur district came up as an important subject in the State Legislative Assembly. Project specific questions (viz. Haldia port, Haldia Petro-chemicals project or Kolaghat thermal power project) were raised by the elected representatives of the people, which revealed some scattered quantitative information on the amount of land acquired for a particular type of development project in the district. No systematic and comprehensive database on land acquisition in the district for a particular year or period was available until 1993.

The first systematic attempt towards creating a database on the land acquisition for different categories of project had been made by the Land Acquisition Department of erstwhile Medinipur district in April 1993. The results of this maiden effort have not yet been published, but a typed copy in the form of a report is available in the Land Acquisition Department of the Medinipur District Collectorate. The report which was entitled *Land Acquisition Cases of Midnapore : Present Status, Problems, Future Strategy* (1993) was prepared to fulfil two important objectives, viz. (i) to create a database for all the pending cases of the LA Department at Medinipur, and (ii) to supervise and monitor the calculation of interests for all the pending cases under Act-II in order to reduce government liabilities. The finding of this government report presented an "alarming picture" in terms of pending LA cases as well as the government's financial burden with regard to the interest incurred due to the delay in the payment of compensation after the acquisition. Under the sub-section entitled "Present Status", the report mentioned quite emphatically "that 293 cases have not at all progressed after handing over of possession to the requiring body

* The Department file numbers, memo numbers of letters and all other official references including names which are mentioned in the sections on Land Acquisition in erstwhile Medinipur district are real and are mentioned with the kind permission of the then Land Acquisition officer. These official data are not also regarded as 'classified' or 'restricted' information.

(RB)". The LA Department had sent estimates for 80 per cent payment but the RBs did not show any interest over the land after taking possession of the same. No action has yet been taken by the LA office for many years. The report categorically stated:

> Action is being taken to send estimates to R.B. as the Government liability is mounting. In certain cases where estimates have been sent, there is no response from the R.B. and they express their inability to place fund as it is not included in their respective budget for that year. With the increase in the value of land the liability of the Government is increasing in a very alarming manner in addition to the deprivation suffered by landlosers due to non-payment (p.1).

It should be noted in this connection that the compensation money has to be deposited by the requiring body, i.e. the Department or Company which is in need of the land. It may be a government department (e.g. irrigation or electricity departments) or a private company (e.g. a private hotel or industry) which shall be responsible for placing the fund with the LA Department from which payment of compensation would be made. The various stages of the departmental procedure for running a land acquisition case have been discussed in the next section.

The case of acquisition of land for various governemt departments in Medinipur which were pending at the time of the preparation of the afore mentioned report showed a huge financial burden on the government itself. In the following table the Department-wise fund requirement of the pending LA cases are shown (see Table 3.1).

The grand total shows the financial burden on the State Government for carrying out the completion of the pending cases around Rs. 26 crores.

The report revealed that there were at least 418 LA cases for which gazette notification had been published but award has not yet been made. Assuming a 15 per cent interest every year the yearly interest to be paid by the government comes to around

Table 3.1 : Department-wise Fund Requirement of Pending Land Acquisition Cases in Erstwhile Medinipur District (up to 1993 April).

Name of the Government Department	*Approximate Amount (in Rupees)*
Agriculture	52,13,616.15
Agriculture Irrigation	6,13,581.00
Agriculture Marketing	1,00,30,881.00
Animal Husbandry	1,01,582.13
Co-operative	34,935.00
Development and Planning	4,77,885.73
Fishery	13,31,990.45
Forest	20,38,439.00
Irrigation	14,54,20,607.67
L.G.U.D.	34,62,536.00
P.W.D.	8,19,81,577.29
Power	10,87,362.79
Public Health Engineering	24,14,912.18
Refugee Relief	89,096.00
Relief	73,940.00
South-Eastern Railway	1,33,27,441.81
Transport	2,98,700.00
Grand Total	26,47,54,107.21

Source : Land Acquisition cases of Midnapore: Present Status, Problems, Future Strategy (1993) Unpublished Report, Land Acquisition Department, Medinipur District.

Rs. 151 lakhs and for the district alone the liability of the government is increased by a staggering amount of Rs. 41,000 everyday.

The report considered another grave aspect of the problem of land acquisition in Medinipur. Under a section entitled "Implication" (pp. 3-4) it noted that in case of the pending cases where the RBs did not seem to be interested in their finalisation, most of them had actually constructed a building, road or irrigation channels which made it impossible for the land to be returned to the PAPs. It is true that there was a provision for de-requisition of land requisitioned under Act-II, but for all practical purposes this rarely happened. To quote from the report:

> ...for most of the requisitioned lands the land character has been changed to suit the objective for which the acquisition was made. A completed irrigation project or an industrial estate or a hospital project on a requisitioned land cannot be de-requisitioned. (p.3)

The report further observed that even if it is assumed that all the RBs have placed their respective funds with the Collector for making compensation payment to the PAPs (in the report however this phrase was never used) by 31 March 1994, then also it would not be possible to make a payment of Rs. 26 crores since Medinipur Land Acquisition Department with its existing strength of skilled and specialised staff, working at the normal rate, could make an yearly payment of Rs. 4 crores only. At this rate, the district collectorate could complete the pending cases within 5-6 years in an ideal situation.

The version of the district administration on the present status of land acquisition in Medinipur district not only revealed its "alarming" and "severe" condition, but is also acted as an "eye-opener" (words used in the report itself) for those in the administration. The report, however, was lacking in certain important aspects of land acquisition which are mentioned below:

(1) It only calculated the burden of the government in monetary terms for making compensation payments under pending Act-II cases. There is no statistics on the total amount of land acquired so far in Medinipur district for any given period or year. There is also no figure on the amount of land acquired under different categories of projects in the district.

(2) The report never made any attempt to estimate the number of persons or families who have been affected by the land acquisition under the pending Act-II cases in different areas of the district. Except for mentioning the plight of the owners who turned into landloser in the pending cases, nowhere in the report was found any estimate or statistics about the number of PAPs in Medinipur.

(3) It did not also give any list of pending cases of land acquisition for private companies or joint sector business enterprises in Medinipur district. It only dealt with cases of land acquisition for various government departments.

The government report on land acquisition prepared by the Medinipur District Collectorate in 1993 meticulously recorded land acquisition in terms of its constraints and shortcomings. Despite its various lacunae, which have been described above, the report revealed how diffcult and complicated it was to acquire land for development projects. It also gave an indication about the fact that there was very little hope to arrange for all the compensation payment within five to six years. Under these circumstances, one can only imagine the kind of harassment caused to the project affected families who have neither received compensation for the acquisition of their cultivable land, nor have they been allowed to cultivate the land requisitioned by the government, but lying unutilised.

Facts and Figures on Land Acquisition in Medinipur District during 1991—97

The only authentic source of data on land acquisition is the published notification in a government gazette. In West Bengal, land acquisition notice under section 4 of the Land Acquisition Act is published in the *Calcutta Gazette.* In the gazette notifications for land acquisition the following information are available:

(i) *Departmental notice number and date:* This date is always an earlier one from that of the gazette publication date. From the notice number one can also understand the project category (e.g. C and I stand for commerce and industry, I and M for irrigation and water works, Tr. for transport and the like).

(ii) *Location:* This item gives information about the specific place where land for a particular project is acquired. Here name of the specific mouza with its jurisdiction list (J.L.) number and the police station as well as the name of the district are given.

(iii) *Amount:* The total amount of land in acres as well as hectares is provided in the gazette notification.

(iv) *Section(s) of the Act:* The specific Act (i.e. Act I or II or any other special Act) by which land is acquired for a particular project is always mentioned in the gazette notification. The specific sub-section by which a notification is made is also stated under this item.

(v) *Purpose:* This part of the gazette notification is very important, since the public purpose for which the given amount of land is acquired or requisitioned has to be mentioned under this item. This item provides information on the type of project undertaken.

(vi) *Gazette publication date :* This is the specific date on which the notification for land acquisition under section 4 is made. The declaration notifications under section 6 of the Land Acquisition Act are also published in the *Calcutta Gazette*.

In this study, all the gazette notifications have been collected from the *Calcutta Gazette* for erstwhile Medinipur district for the period 1991-97 (seven years). These notifications were available in the gazette section of the Land Acquisition Department of the district.

The period 1991-97 has been chosen for the following reasons. In 1991 the Central Government announced its New Economic Policy which brought about important changes in the business climate of the country. The government encouraged both foreign and domestic business investments. This created an increased

Table 3.2 : Land Acquisition Scenario in Erstwhile Medinipur During 1991-1997

Year	*Comm. and Industries*	*Transport (Roads, Rail)*	*Irrigation Drainage*	*Power stations*	*Health, Edu. Govt. Buld.*	*Tourism*	*Fishery*	*Rehab.*	*Urban Dev.*	*Total*
1991	165.24 (2.75) [1.15]	22.39 (3.56) [0.15]	5.31 (0.73) [0.03]							192.95 (1.34)
1992	41.86 (0.69) [0.29]	150.50 (23.95) [1.05]	37.65 (5.19) [0.26]	5.13 (1.86) [0.03]		5166.99 [36.08]				5402.14 (37.72)
1993	99.83 (1.66) [0.69]	36.50 (5.81) [0.25]	76.91 (10.60) [0.53]	26.74 (9.71) [0.18]	12.65 (3.65) [0.08]					252.64 (1.76)
1994	43.30 (0.72) [0.30]	194.30 (30.92) [1.35]	327.60 (45.16) [2.28]	10.65 (3.86) [0.07]	90.70 (26.18) [0.63]					666.57 (0.465)
1995	2975.49 (49.66) [20.77]	67.19 (10.69) [0.46]	151.91 (20.94) [1.06]	135.35 (49.15) [0.94]	209.14 (60.37) [1.46]		205.90 [1.43]			3744.98 (26.15)
1996	1309.54 (21.85) [9.14]	67.30 (10.71) [0.46]	70.9 (9.77) [0.49]	55.18 (20.03) [0.38]	33.91 (9.78) [0.23]					1536.83 (10.73)
1997	1356.35 (22.63) [9.47]	90.02 (14.32) [0.62]	55.1 (7.59) [0.38]	42.31 (15.36) [0.29]				670.73 [4.68]	308.80 [2.15]	2523.30 (17.62)
Total	5991.61 (99.96) [41.84]	628.20 (99.96) [4.38]	725.38 [5.06]	275.37 [1.92]	346.42 [2.41]	5166.99 [36.08]	205.90 [1.43]	670.73 [4.68]	308.80 [2.15]	14319.40 (99.97) [99.95]

( ) percentage out of column total.
[ ] percentage out of grand total.

demand for land to be provided within a shorter time-span in a competitive market economy. In West Bengal, the industrial and other business investments started to increase since early nineties so it was expected that the demand for land would also go up in this period. Secondly, gazette notifications up to 1997 could only be used, since notifications beyond that year were not ready for use when the research was carried out in the District Collectorate.

So, the notifications on land acquisition in Medinipur for the period 1991-97 were collected. All together, there were 624 notifications related to various purposes for which land was acquired in Medinipur district. Incidentally, in the land acquisition notices there is no information on the type of land (e.g. agricultural, homestead, wasteland etc.) that was acquired. The purposes for which land was acquired have been categorised as: (i) commerce and industry, (ii) transport (roads and railways), (iii) irrigation and drainage, (iv) power stations, (v) health, education and government infrastructure (e.g. health centres schools, government buildings), (vi) tourism, (vii) fishery, (viii) rehabilitation, and (ix) urban development. The gazette notifications from which these categories were formed have been enclosed in an appendix (see Appendix A) with all the details. The following table contains quantitative information regarding the different categories of land acquisition in Medinipur district for the period 1991-97.

The table shows that from 1991 to 1997 a total of 14,319.40 acres of land has been acquired for various development projects and land acquired for commercial and industrial purposes has the highest (41.84 per cent) share. Next to commerce and industries, come tourism for which 5,166.99 acres of land have been acquired only for once during this seven-year period. Land acquisition for commercial and industrial purposes shot up virtually from 1995, although land acquisition for industries took place in all the years since 1991. The construction of transport network, which has a relationship with the growth of industrial sector also, shows a rise after 1993. In terms of land acquisition, the share of the transport category rose up from 5.81 per cent to 30.92 per cent, which never fell below 10 upto 1997. Land acquisition for the installation of power stations (this also has a complementary relationship with industries and commerce) also increased after 1994 from 10.65 to 135.35 acres in 1995 and maintained a much higher level compared to years that preceded 1995. So it can be tentatively concluded that the advent of NEP and liberalisation have started to show up in terms of demand for land in Medinipur district from 1994-95. Interestingly, this was also the period in which the Government of West Bengal had decided to withdraw the acquisition of land by the West Bengal Land (Requisition and Acquisition) Act, 1948, and when the Medinipur District Collectorate was under heavy pressure from the burden of pending land acquisition cases under Act-II.

The table shows certain other interesting points in terms of social development. Land for the rehabilitation of project affected persons constitutes only 2.15 per cent of the total land acquired while health, education and government infrastructure comprise 2.41 per cent of the total.

From this brief and preliminary analysis of the land acquisition scenario in the wake of a liberalised economy, it can be stated that the Government of West Bengal paid more attention towards commercial and industrial investments in a district, which depended heavily on agriculture. The figures also reveal that the State Government has given least attention towards the rehabilitation of the project affected persons, although land acquisition for commercial and industrial projects which usually deprive a large number people who are depended on agricultural land. While tourism constituted about 78 per cent of the total amount of land acquired for various development projects after the adoption of NEP by the Central Government in 1991.

Land Acquisition for Two Private Companies in the Study Area

So far, the different steps of land acquisition right from the stage of first notification under section 4 in the government gazette and the newspapers have been discussed. Land acquisition comes to the knowledge of the general public from this stage, when notices to individual landowners in specific mouza villages (a revenue unit) are served. But there is a long administrative process before the

Fig. 1 : Stages of Land Acquisition for Private Industry by Act-I in West Bengal

Land Acquisition Process (LAP)

1. Proposal from the Requiring Body (RB) goes to the Ministry of Industry and Commerce.
2. Proposal goes to the Cabinet Committee (if the land to be acquired is more than 100 acres).
3. Proposal is sent to Land and Land Reforms Department, Calcutta.
4. Proposal sent to the District Collector of the concerned district.
5. District Collector sends it to the Land Acquisition Officer.
6. Land Acquisition Department conducts survey and prepares the Preliminary Enquiry Report (PIR).
7. Proposal and PIR are placed before a screening committee comprising the District Magistrate, Additional District Magistrate, Land Acquisition Officer, Member of the Legislative Assembly, Sabhapati (Chairperson) of the Panchayat Samity (the second tier of the elected local government) and a representative of the RB.
8. Notification u/s. 4 of the LA Act to landowners and publication of the notice in the gazette and two newspapers (one in regional language).
9. Hearing of objections from the landowners.
10. Publication of the agreement (between the government and RB) and declaration under section 6 of the LA Act.

Land Acquisition

11. Government empowers the Department u/s. 7 to start the Land Acquisition case.
12. Hearing of claims u/s. 11 of the LA Act for identification of actual owners entitled to get compensation.
13. Preparation of the rate report of estimate which is calculated on the basis of land value, solatium and requisition compensation.
14. Compensation is sanctioned by the District Collector.
15. Award note for compensation is prepared.
16. Requiring Body places fund with the Land Acquisition Department of the district.
17. Award is declared by the Collector.
18. Compensation payment is made to the landlosers.
19. Possession o the land is given to the RB.

stage of first notification, which involves the highest level of bureaucratic structure. These pre-notification stages always remain outside the domain of public knowledge and the decision (technically termed as 'proposal') for the acquisition of private land is taken by the cabinet of ministers, after which it goes down the administrative ladder ultimately reaching the district level. There are few important stages at the district level too. Before the notification, the district land acquisition department has to perform certain crucial tasks, viz. survey and land measurement, preparation of PIR, placement of the land acquisition proposal before the screening committee comprising District Collector, elected peoples' representatives and representatives of the requiring body for whom land has to be acquired. In this research, the process of land acquisition as followed in the case of two private companies in the Kalaikunda Gram Panchayat within Kharagpur Block I has been studied in detail and its consequencs examined. When a private company asks for land for the establishment of an industry, it sends a detailed proposal showing the specific location of such land in the settlement map. This proposal is sent to the Ministry of Commerce and Industry and can be called the first offical stage of land acquisition for a private industry. The following schematic diagram (Fig. 3.1) shows the different stages of land acquisition for private industry in West Bengal under the Land Acquisition Act, 1894 (amended in 1984). In this connection, it should be mentioned that a statutory body named West Bengal Industrial Development Corporation (WBIDC)[1] has recently been formed by the State Government for quicker processing of proposals for the establishment of industries.

In the departmental jargon, the first ten stages are put under "land acquisition process" (LAP) and the actual "land acquisition" (LA) starts from stage 11. Separate files are maintained for these two sets of processes. This is because of the fact that land acquisition actually signifies that the administration should now start the process of the payment of compensation.

Before stage 11, no such preparation is taken up, only objections about the rate of compensation from the interested persons are received by the Department and they are dealt with under the purview of the Act. The time taken to cover all these stages varies from case to case and depends upon a number of administrative and financial factors.

Land Acquisition for Tata Metaliks

Tata Metaliks is a heavy industry, which was established within the jurisdiction of the Kalaikunda Gram Panchayat during 1992. This is a pig-iron manufacturing plant which was found to produce about 290 tonnes of pig-iron per day in 1995-96. There are two other big industries owned by the Tata group that are located within a radius of five kilometres from Tata Metaliks. These two industries are : (i) Tata Bearings Ltd. and (ii) Tata Davy Ltd. (a heavy engineering unit) which are located in the Nimpura area of the Kharagpur sub-division. Tatas have set up most of their manufacturing units in Kharagpur because of its proximity to the steel city of Jamshedpur in Jharkhand. After the establishment of the Tata Metaliks, the company has built up a metal road on the western side connecting the plant with the National Highway 6 in a place named Sahachawk. The south-eastern railway line runs on the eastern side of the industry. The Kharagpur railway station is only about 5 kilometres and the Medinipur district headquarters is 7 kilometres from this place. Another small industry, named Wellman Incandescent Ltd. has also been established just by the side of the Tata Metaliks at Paschim Amba village in 1994-95 for supplying metallurgical coke to the latter. This coke is required as a fuel for the blast furnace of the pig-iron plant. The Wellman Company is also a private one and about 18 acres of agricultural land has been acquired through West Bengal Financial and Industrial Development Corporation in 1994 for this company.

From the District Land Acquisition Department files we found the first reference of land acquisition for Tata Metaliks in a letter dated 26 March 1991. [No. 135/1(1)-C1/Group-H]. The letter was addressed to the District Collector of Medinipur by one Assistant Secretary to the Government of West Bengal. In this letter, the Assistant Secretary stated that his Department has received a proposal from the Tata Metaliks which was forwarded by the WBIDC for the establishment of a pig-iron plant in Kharagpur police station.

Accordingly, the Assistant Secretary requested the District Collector of Medinipur to start the necessary administrative process for the acquisition of 233.05 acres of cultivable land in the Mahespur, Latibpur, Mathurakismat, Amba, Prithimpur and Ashapur mouzas under the Kharagpur police station by applying West Bengal Land (Requisition and Acquisition) Act of 1948. In his letter the Assistant Secretary also mentioned that this industry would be established for the purpose of increasing employment opportunities for the people of the region. In this connection we can recall that in his answer to a question on 1.6.1992 in the West Bengal Legislative Assembly the Land and Land Reforms Minister mentioned that 217.23 acres of land was acquired for the Tata Metaliks. We have found through our enquiries in the Land Acquisition Department of Medinipur district that a total of 53 gazette notifications were made for acquisition of 198.09 acres of land for Tata Metaliks. The reasons behind this kind of variation in the amount of land acquired in the different estimates may be due to bureaucratic processes. It may be better to accept the estimate placed on the West Bengal Legislative Assembly.

After one year since the Assistant Secretary had written to the District Collector, a detailed report was prepared by the Additional Land Acquisition Officer which was approved by the District Collector on 27 March 1992. This report was entitled as *Composite revised rate report for LA cases of Pig-iron Project, P.S. Kharagpur.* From this report certain important information about the land acquisition for Tata Metaliks were found which are mentioned below:

1. The land acquired for the pig-iron industry belonged to "Jal soem" class according to the age-old system of classification made by the Land and Land Reforms Department. The Department classified the land type into four classes in terms of their productivity which were ranked in the following order: (i) *Jal awal*, (ii) *Jal doem,* (iii) *Jal soem* and (iv) *Jal chaharam.*
2. The possessions on these lands were given to the company on different dates in the month of August 1991 and

declaration notifications were published from November 1991 to January 1992.

3. The value of these lands were fixed by the Collector at Rs. 16,935 per acre on 2.12.1991 and this rate was not accepted by most landlosers during payments in 14 land acquisition cases and submitted petitions for reference in the Court In this connection, we may again recall the answer given by the Minister on the floor of the Assembly where he mentioned the higher rates of Rs. 22,015.50 and Rs. 26,891.00 per acre respectively (Assembly Proceedings Vol. 99;1st June, 1992).
4. The district Land Acquisition Department conducted an inquiry and duly considered the sale data of land in this area from 1987 to 1990. The Department observed some features of these land which they mentioned in the report. It is better to quote from the report :

> ...the lands are basically monocrop agricultural lands having no irrigation facilities. There are no immediate prospect of being used as homestead land. ...Altogether 40 sales are available but the sales from the ranges Rs. 6,000 to Rs. 60,000 are considered for the preparation of the rate report.... Compared to the transaction in years prior to 1990 there have been abnormal hike in the price of lands in 1991 covered under this project. (*Report of the Land Acquisition Department Medinipur* dated 27.3.1992).

5. The Land Acquisition Department finally approved a rate of Rs. 20,686 per acre which according to the Additional Land Acquisition Officer "seemed to be more reasonable." The report however did not deal with the compensation for *bargadars* (sharecroppers) for whom a different kind of rate was fixed for awarding compensation. From the award forms (Form 13A) dealing with a particular case of land acquisition (Case No. 27 of 1991-92) in the Latibpur mouza we have found that *bargadars* were paid

compensation at the rate of Rs. 11,211.75 per acre and these payments were made in the month of May 1993.

The cases of land acquisition for Tata Metaliks have shown that the Government of West Bengal desired a quick acquisition of land for the company and that is why Act-II was employed for the said purpose.

Secondly, the report prepared by Additional LAO, Medinipur district revealed that the lack of irrigation facilities and monocrop nature of the acquired lands have been emphasised for the calculation of land value. In fact these two negative features (lack of irrigation and monocrop nature) of the acquired land strengthened the justification of their acquisition for non-agricultural purposes and also for having a lesser market price.

Last but not the least, the District Land Acquisition Department did not explore the possibilities of rehabilitation for the affected families in terms of providing jobs and/or land as compensation; the administration seemed to be concerned only with monetary compensation at the market price.

Land Acquisition for Century Textiles and Industries

The land acquisition for Century Textiles and Industries Ltd. is typical example of a pending case where a huge chunk of acquired agricultural land remained unutilised for more than five years. The first reference of land acquisition for this industry was found in a letter dated 3 December 1992 (No. 518-CI/b) from the Assistant Secretary to the Government of West Bengal addressed to the Collector of the Medinipur district. In his letter the Assistant Secretary informed the District Collector that he had received a proposal from the WBIDC for the acquisition of 1137.78 acres of land in 18 mouzas under Kharagpur police station for setting up of a sponge and pig-iron industry by M/s. Century Textiles and Industries Ltd. From this letter it was learnt that the decision for the acquisition of this huge chunk of land was approved in a meeting of the Cabinet Committee held on 2 July 1992. The Assistant Secretary directed the Collector to initiate land acquisition proceedings under West Bengal Land (Requisition and Acquisition) Act, 1948 immediately, because the project was "connected with an incidental increase in employment opportunities in the state." Since December 1992, there was no reference in the Land Acquisition Departmental files about the progress of the land acquisition procedures for the Century Company until April 1995. A letter addressed to the Managing Director WBIDC (No. CTI/PI/WBIDC/06 dated 06.04.1995) from the Century Textiles Company was found, according to which the Company agreed with WBIDC to procure 641.86 acres of land, of which 85 acres might be given from the land allocated to Tata Metaliks which remained unutilised. On 17.5.1995, the Century Textiles Company again wrote to the Executive Director of WBIDC to clear up certain confusions with the Collector of Medinipur district as the latter was not aware of acquiring 150 acres of land on the western side of a village road. The Company also urged upon the Executive Director to hand over the land since land acquisition might take 6 months which seemed to be "too long a period" for the Company to wait. After writing this letter the Company requested the Managing Director of WBIDC to release an amount of Rs. 50,000 towards the payment of contingency expenses for land acquisition as desired by the Additional District Magistrate of Medinipur. On 14 August, 1995 (memo No. 1477/L.A.) the Additional District Magistrate of Medinipur informed the Deputy Secretary, Land and Land Reforms Department that the Century Textiles Company "had tried private negotiations for obtaining the said land (818.5 acres) with the landowners and failed". A copy of this letter was also sent to the Executive Director of the WBIDC. In less than a month, the Deputy Secretary, Land and Land Reforms Department directed the Collector Medinipur to investigate the proposal of Century Company and send a report so that the case may be started under LA Act, 1894. This was owing to the fact that the Government of West Bengal had already decided not to pursue land acquisition case under Act-II. (Letter No. 5354 LA (II) 5C-47/95 dated 4 September 1995).

After this, notification under section 4 of the LA Act, 1894 for the acquisition of 526.71 acres of land was published first in

Ganasakti [a CPI (M) daily] on 28.10.1995 and then in *Amrita Bazar Patrika* on 30.10.95 and subsequently, in the *Calcutta Gazette* on 3.11.1995 for the establishment of sponge and pig-iron plant on 10 mouzas of Kharagpur police station under the Kalaikunda Gram Panchayat. The agreement and declaration notification was published again in *Ganasakti,* on 4.4.1996 and in the *Calcutta Gazette* on 8.4.1996. The District Land Acquisition Department then proceeded to prepare the rate report of the land acquired for the Company in order to make payment of compensation to the affected persons.

The land acquired for Century Company came under 10 mouzas of the Kharagpur police station, of which two fell within the Kharagpur municipality. The Land Acquisition Department considered the sale of lands for all those mouzas that took place during 1993-95 by taking figures from the Government Land Sub-Registration Office and arrived at varying market values for all kinds of land in those mouzas. The Additional District Magistrate prepared a rate report on 22.4.1996 for the 8 mouzas under acquisition which were as follows:

	Name of the Mouza	**Land value per acre**
Under Kharagpur	Malancha	Rs. 1,00,000/-
Municipality	Dhekia	Rs. 64,000/-
	Rajpura	
	Chaksonadhar	
	Niranjanbar	
Under Gram	Kalikapur	Rs. 50,000/-
Panchyat Area	Tarabamni	
	Sujatpur	

The reasons for this kind of variation in the valuation of land were stated in the report of the Additional District Magistrate dated 22.4.1996.The whole chunk of land distributed over the 8 mouzas had little variation in terms of its agricultural potential. The land in all the mouzas were classed under "*Jal*" by the villagers, which yielded only one crop in a year and did not have any access to irrigation facility. But the area towards the railway line and the national highway No. 6 which comprised the Malancha and Dhekia mouzas had a much greater number of land transactions owing to speculation in view of imminent urbanisation originating from the railway township of Kharagpur. For the affected peasants who have lost their land due to acquisition, this variation in their land value within a distance of less than a kilometre under almost similar type of agricultural conditions did not seem to have delivered justice to them. On 24.6.1996, forty-two landlosers of Rajpura mouza submitted a written petition to the District Collecter in which they stated that the reality was that agricultural production showed higher figures for Rajpura not Malancha. So the land value for the former mouza should be fixed at a higher rate for the calculation of compensation to the landlosers. Suffice it to say here that the District Land Acquisition Office had no other option but to reject the above-mentioned petition since the rates of land values were fixed on the basis of sale data collected from the concerned Government Office of the district.

From a note prepared by the Land Acquisition Department on the tentative cost of acquisition for Century Company, we came to know that a rate of Rs. 7,000 per acre was fixed for the payment of *bargadars* affected by the project.

The payment of compensation for the company started and it continued upto the end of March 1998 after which it came to a halt. The Century Textiles Company did not also start any construction work for its proposed sponge and pig-iron plant although buildings were constructed by the side of the land acquired for the security guards of the company. The company Managing Director Mr. B.K Birla in an interview with the correspondent of *The Statesman* (a leading English national daily) told that they would not proceed with the project as "the national market of pig-iron has become very much competitive because of the entry of China and Australia in the field". He also stated that this decision was conveyed to the State Government long back. The State Land and Land Reforms Minister, Mr. Surya Kanto Mishra, on the other hand, told the reporter of *The Statesman* : "We are not finding any taker for the land" (*The Statesman* 18 November 1999). In another detailed report published after 7 months by the same newspaper it

Table 3.3*: Succession of Important Events in the Case of Land Acquisition for Century Textiles and Industries

Date	*Event*
2 July, 1992	Cabinet of the Government of West Bengal approved the project for the acquisition of 1137.78 acres of land in 18 mouzas under Khagarpur Police Station by Act-II of 1948.
3 December, 1992	Asstt. Secretary writes to District Collecter to proceed
28 October, 1995	The first public notification published in the newspaper. Acquisition by Act-I was made. Land amount reduced to 526.71 acres in 10 mouzas.
29 December, 1995	The hearing of objections by the landloser completed.
10 January, 1996	Peasants prevented soil testing.
22 March, 1996	Mass deputation by the peasants at District Collectorate. Peasants demanded land for land or job and higher compensation.
2 April, 1996	Publication of agreement between the Company and the Govts. in the Calcutta Gazatte (see Appendix C).
10 April, 1996	Peasants submitted memorandum to boycott parliamentary election.
2 May, 1996	Poll boycott decision of the landlosers published in *The Statesman*.
22 May, 1996	CTIL got possession certificate over 238.86 acres of land.
21 June, 1996	The report of the objection hearing at Collector's Office completed and all objections overruled.
May-July, 1996	Farmers were not allowed to cultivate on the acquired land. By this time the payment of compensation started.
28 February, 1997	Land and Land Reforms Minister announces that state would reclaim unused land leased to industries.
11 April, 1997	CTIL got possession certificate over another 119.39 acres of land.
12 March, 1998	The Statesman reported about the adverse effects of acquisition in Kalaikunda.
21 June, 1998	Kalaikunda Gram Panchayat held meeting with the landlosers about the land which remained unused by the Company.
12 October, 1998-15 March, 1999	The order sheet of the Land Acquisition Deptt. reveals the non-payment of compensation to landlosers as the company has stopped placing funds since December 1996.
19 April, 1999	Land Acquisition Officer, Medinipur writes to the MD of WBIDC seeking advice over this hanging situation.
18 November, 1999	The Company MD tells the reporter of The Statesman that they are not interested to establish the plant, the Minister also expressed his helplessness over the matter.
7 December, 1999	Joint Secretary, Land and LR Department writes to District Collector to send report on the Acquisition.

* The facsimilies of some of the media reports on land acquisition are enclosed in Appendix B.

was stated that the State Government still seemed to be undecided over the fate of the land acquired for Century Textiles (*The Statesman* 5 July 2000). The individual landowners, who possessed plots of land in this area, also stopped cultivation since they received acquisition notices in 1996. It may be of interest in this context to mention that in one of its publications the WBIDC enlisted the sponge and pig-iron plant of the Century Textiles as an "upcoming" industrial unit in the Kharagpur area (*Destination West Bengal*, WBIDC, 1999; see Appendix D). From a letter dated 19.04.1999 (memo No. 592/LA) addressed to the Managing Director of WBIDC by the Land Acquisition Officer it was learnt that district administration sought advice regarding the fate of the land acquired for Century Company for which a payment of Rs. 3,48,884.84 was made, but the rest of compensation payment could not to be completed since the Company did not place any fund with the District Collector. The following table summarises the series of events that took place for the acquisition of agricultural land for Century Company which ultimately could not be established.

The whole land acquisition episode for Century Textiles revealed some of the maladies of the land acquisition process in India which are mentioned below :

1. The project affected people have not been given any role by the State Government in determining the fate of their major means of production even when it remain unutilised for more than five consecutive years.
2. The failure of the Company to purchase the required land through private negotiations show that the peasants were not ready to part with their agricultural land for the proposed pig-iron plant.
3. The reason behind the varying rates for the different plots under the same chunk of land showed the limitations of the prevalent procedure for the determination of market price of land under the purview of the LA Act, 1894.
4. It became almost impossible for the administration to return the land to its owners even when the same remain

unutilised beyond the stipulated period mentioned in the agreement.

5. The Government seemed to be a prisoner in the hands of the bureaucratic machinery in dealing with this kind of problem of land acquisition. The State Government virtually suppressed the latest information on Century Textiles when the former enlisted Century Company as one of the upcoming industries in the state even in January 1999.

One important point about the acquisition of land for Tata Metaliks and Century Textiles Companies deserves mention. Huge chunks of fertile agricultural land were selected by the Companies and the Cabinet Committee of the West Bengal Government gave approval to this selection. Even a casual travel through this area from Medinipur towards Kharagpur would reveal the presence of a huge tract of undulating lateritic non-agricultural land on the western side of the south-eastern railway track lying on the north bank of the *Kasai river.* The landlosers of this area, during our fieldwork repeatedly pointed out that the government should have acquired the non-agricultural land for the industries instead of taking their agricultural land. When this point was raised before the officers and employees of the Land Acquisition Department of the District Collectorate they simply stated that it was the decision of the Government which the concerned Department at the district level had to execute. One very experienced and veteran Assistant Land Acquisition Officer once commented to the author: "Well, the screening committee at the district level may turn down a proposal coming from the Writers' Building in Kolkata. But I have seen through my experience that whenever Kolkata wants acquisition Medinipur simply obeys the order. There is hardly any exception" (Free translation from Bengali). This comment epitomised the power of the *eminent domain* of the state in case of land acquisition for development projects in India.

NOTE

1. The West Bengal Industrial Development Corporation is the leading state level agency which primarily facilitates growth and promotion of medium and large scale industries. The agency has obtained the required mandate to implement changes, so that now life becomes simple for the investors in getting all clearances (*Destination West Bengal 1999*).

FOUR

Looking at Land Acquisition from the Field

Rare is the development project, policy or process that only creates winners. The displacement theme brings to centre stage the losers. One form or another of displacement is often part of the development footprint,

Ravi Kanbur (2002)

Prologue

In the previous chapter, an attempt has been made to describe the process of land acquisition from a holistic perspective by taking into account its legal, administrative, historical, and policy dimensions. The approach was anthropological because after covering all the dimensions mentioned above, an attempt was made to retrieve the functioning of certain institutions (e.g. Land Acquisition Department) and human actors (e.g. elected peoples' representatives in the assembly) that centre round the major means of production of a group of rural cultivators in erstwhile Medinipur district.

In this chapter, the other end of the process of land acquisition would be described. From the perspective of the people who were dispossessed and displaced by acquisition, this may be termed as the 'receiving end' of the process. Under the existing legal, administrative and policy framework, the people, whose livelihood was drastically altered by the takeover of agricultural land, were not allowed to play any role once the process of acquisition was initiated by the private companies and the concerned Departments of the Government of West Bengal, which, for no ostensible reason, took years to be completed. The people who were put first in the policy drafts of the international funding agencies and the NGOs, had actually been placed in the receiving end of the elaborate process through which the state power tried to usher a new era of industrial development in West Bengal.

Dispossession and Displacement

The new era of industrial development in West Bengal or for that matter, in any other state in India is bound to be accompanied by dispossession of the peasantry from their major means of production, that is land. Dispossession from one's own means of production is one kind of displacement in which the dispossessed family not only loses its economic security but also social status and empowerment achieved through political movements and land reforms. The international funding agencies like World Bank and the various national governments have also started to pay serious attention to the problem of development induced displacement. Most of the studies on displacement so far have quite justifiably given more emphasis on "forced migration" and involuntary resettlement of human groups (Cernea 1999b; Fernandes and Thukral 1989). But there are situations when people are forced to give up their rights over one of the most valued capitals possessed by them. In an agricultural society this precious capital is land which embodies not only an economic value but also manifests various social and cultural dimensions. Michael Cernea's pioneering study on displacement has shown that impoverishment has several 'dimensions' and the primary among them is *landlessness*. According to Cernea, landlessness is one of the most vital components of displacement which should be given a major importance in devising rehabilitation schemes. To quote Cernea: "Expropriation of land removes the main foundation upon which people's productive systems, commercial activities and livelihoods are constructed. This is the principal form of decapitalization and pauperization for most rural and many urban displacees, who lose this way both natural and manmade capital" (Cernea 1999b:17). So, dispossession of the rural cultivators from their agricultural land is intimately interwoven with displacement even when they are not forced to leave their homes.

This can also be viewed as a kind of displacement from one's own existing mode of survival.

The second aspect of dispossession of the farmers from their major means of production, that is agricultural land, is the differential impact of land acquisition on the heterogeneous group of agriculturists in a region. This is precisely because of the fact that when any government acquires agricultural land it does not take into consideration the pre-acquisition land holding pattern of a region.

Thirdly, dispossession also entails a political dimension. In a rural society where peasant movements had taken place in successive waves and the rights of sharecroppers as well as landless labourers have been ensured by a government just a few years ago, the acquisition of fertile agricultural land for capital intensive heavy industries by the same government not only dispossessed the farmers economically but it also created political disempowerment.

In this study on the consequences of land acquisition for the sake of two private industries all the three afore mentioned phenomena had been observed, viz. (i) landlessness, (ii) differential impact of land acquisition on the peasantry, and (iii) their political disempowerment. Although all the three phenomena took place within a very short period of time, neither large scale forced migration nor any long standing peasent movement had taken place owing to this dispossession, and the plight of the farmers of Kharagpur remained a little known event in the development and displacement discourse in the academic as well as activist circles of West Bengal and India. In the following sections an attempt would be made to depict some of the consequences of land acquisition with the help of quantitative as well as qualitative data.

Consequences of Land Acquisition for TML

Before describing the socio-economic consequences of land acquisition for Tata Metaliks (TML), a brief outline of the area from where sample households have been selected from the affected villages are provided alongwith the methodology adopted for this particular fieldwork.

The Area

The area lies on the bank of the river *Kasai* which is the largest river of the Medinipur district. Cultivation of paddy (staple of the district) in the villages under study depends primarily upon rainfall and no systematic irrigation facilities have yet been developed by the government. The villagers residing on the south-eastern bank of the river cultivate a variety of vegetables on the land adjoining their homesteads owing to a very good supply of groundwater tappped through traditional dugwells. But just west of the South Eastern Railway track the groundwater level is not very congenial for cultivation of vegetables. The main agricultural activity on this side of the railway track is rainfed paddy cultivation for about four to six months of the year. Land for the two big private industries has been acquired by the government on this side during 1991-96.

Selection of Households

The selection procedure of the households for the study followed a combination of purposive and opportunity sampling. At the outset, the main aim of the author was to locate the households whose farmlands have been acquired for the establishment of the Tata Metaliks. Instead of searching through the records of land ownership kept in the Land and Land Records department of the district, the present investigation depended directly upon fieldwork by following the traditional anthropological method of intensive interviews of the project affected people. Apart from knowing the current status of land ownership, (which are not promptly made up-to-date in the Land Records Office) micro-ecological variations and local level political movement centring round land acquisition within the first few weeks of fieldwork, it became also possible to know from the active members of the political movement the names of the villages whose inhabitants have been affected by the acquisition of agricultural land for the industries. Later, at the time of conducting the household survey, snowball sampling was taken recourse to, wherein the affected households gave the names of other such household heads whose land have also been acquired. Household

Fig. 2 : Map of the Study Area Showing the Location of the Villages Affected by Land Acquisition.

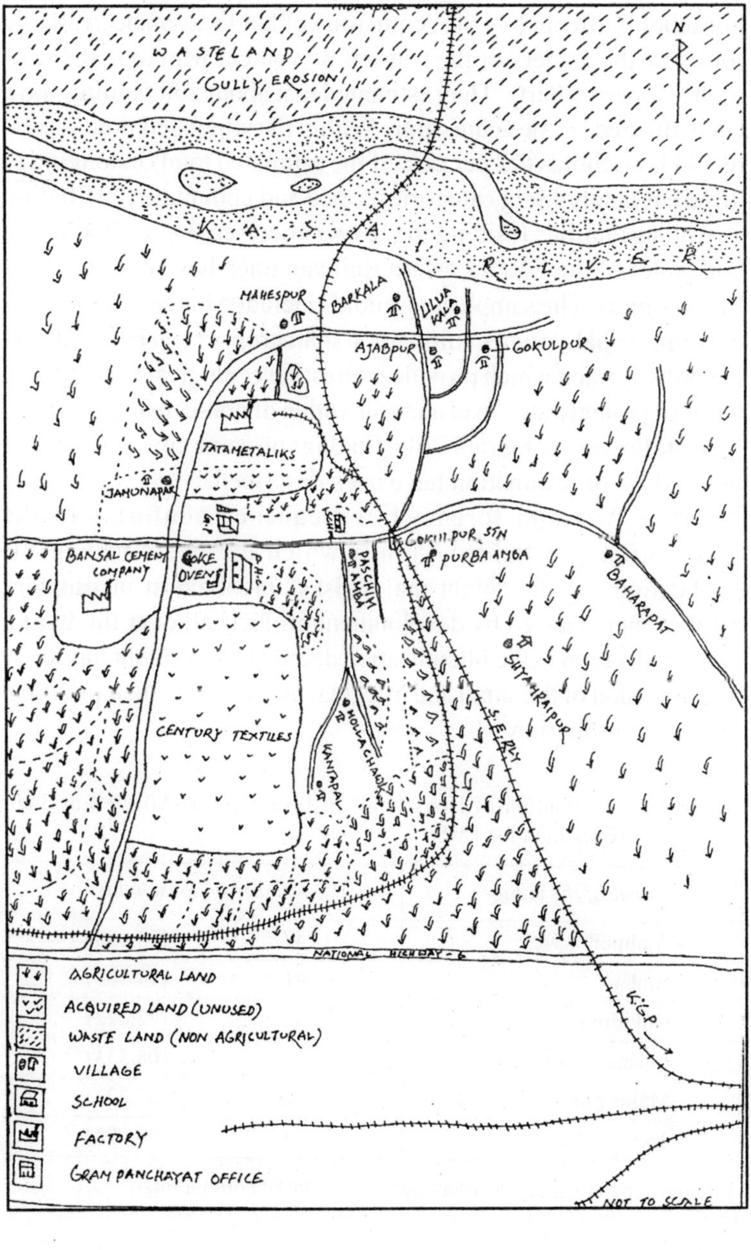

survey had to be completed within a period of three months owing to time constraints and as a result not all the affected households could be covered. A rough estimate about the total number of households affected by the acquisition of land was made available for us by the leaders of the peasant movement who took the help of the Congress Party. They estimated that about 200 families have been affected by the acquisition. Within the stipulated time, a total of 144 households (72 per cent of the estimated total) belonging to different landholding categories, caste and community affiliation as well as families residing in the two micro-ecological niches on both sides of the South Eastern Railway track have been covered by the survey. The sample households included hindu caste groups muslims, tribals, owner cultivators, sharecroppers on both sides of the railway track which provide interesting ecological variations in terms of groundwater level and cultivation of non-cereal food crops. In the following paragraphs, the findings on some consequences of the said act of acquisition have been described.

The first and foremost consequence conforms to the observation of Michael Cernea which he mentioned in his publications on the "eight major risks" involved in involuntary displacement caused by development projects all over the world. Industrialisation in the liberalisation decade in Medinipur has led to dispossession of the small and marginal farmers from their principal means of production.

Table 4.1: Distribution of Households in Five Villages Affected by Land Acquisition for TML

Name of the village	*Number of households*	
Ajabpur	47	(33.638)
Amba	21	(14.583)
Gokulpur	32	(22.222)
Liluakala	12	(08.333)
Mahespur	32	(22.222)
Total	144	(99.998)

Figures in parentheses represent percentage out of column total

From Table 4.1 it is found that the villages situated on the eastern side of the railway track (Ajabpur, Gokulpur and Liluakala) have been affected more in terms of the number of families who have lost their farmlands. The people of these villages are excellent farmers who keep themselves engaged throughout the year in agriculture. Besides paddy, they also grow almost all kinds of summer and winter vegetables like green chilli, lady's finger, mustard, water gourd, pumpkin, bitter gourd, brinzal, potato, cabbage, cauliflower, raddish and others.

These vegetables are grown in lands adjoining their homesteads which have not been acquired by the government. The villagers mainly sell these vegetables in the local market which fetch them some ready cash. On the other hand, some of the families who live in the village Paschim Amba, lying on the western side of railway track, belong to the *Kora* tribe. Many of the *Kora* women and men now work as temporary unskilled labourers in the coke oven industry.

Table 4.2 : Distribution of Households of Different Castes and Communities Affected by Land Acquisition for TML

Name of the caste/community	*Number of households*	
Baisnab	4	(2.777)
Brahmin	6	(4.166)
Kayastha	13	(9.027)
Kshatriya	15	(10.416)
Muslim	8	(5.555)
Napit	2	(1.388)
Sadgope	56	(38.888)
Scheduled Castes	12	(8.333)
Kora (Tribe)	24	(16.666)
Tantubay	3	(2.083)
Teli	1	(0.694)
Total	144	(99.368)

Figures in parentheses represent percentage out of column total

Table 4.2 shows that the households belonging to Sadgops, who are one of the most enterprising peasant castes of Western Bengal, have been affected most, while scheduled tribe and scheduled caste families comprise almost a quarter of the total number of affected households. Despite the presence of various constitutional safeguards and job reservation for the scheduled communities, there is no special provision for rehabilitation of these marginalised group in India. In this region too, these communities have become further marginalised due to the establishment of industries on their farmland and no step has yet been taken either by the State or the Central Government to rehabilitate these groups properly. It may be relevant here to cite a publication, *Tribal Problems in India* written by A.B. Bardhan, the General Secretary of the Communist Party of India. In a section under the rubric "How public-sector projects displace tribals", Bardhan gives statistics about the number of displaced tribal families and the amount of land taken away from them between 1968 and 1973. These figures include data from West Bengal, although, no separate estimate for the state is provided in the book. After presenting the statistics, the author categorically stated:

> This first impact of these projects has been the large scale displacement of tens of thousands of tribal families from their traditional homes. *While this is inevitable in the overall interests of the country,* (emphasis added) scant attention was paid to the rehabilitation of the uprooted tribals. To quote an instance, the Assistant Commissioners for scheduled castes and scheduled tribes for Bihar, Orissa and West Bengal found out after investigation that out of 14,501 tribal families who had been evicted from 62,494 acres, only 3,476 families had been allotted some sort of alternative land" (Bardhan 1973).

In the pre-acquisition stage, there was no landless families within the sample households and 75 per cent of these families belonged to the size category of 0.5-4.5 acres. According to the latest standards set by the Government of West Bengal, these families should be regarded as a marginal and small farmers. The pattern of landholding among the same families after land acquisition show that 15 per cent of the families have become landless and the number of households belonging to the lowest landholding category (≤0.5 acres) have increased from 19 to 35. On the other hand, the number of households within the size category 3.5-7.5 acres, have declined from 22 to 9 only (Tables 4.3 and 4.4).

Table 4.3 : Pre-acquisition Agricultural Landholding Pattern of Sample Households Affected by the Acquisition for TML

Size category of holdings (in acres)	*Number of households*	*Mean household size*
Landless	Nil	-
≤0.5	19 (13.194)	4.73
0.5 - 1.5	58 (40.277)	6.43
1.5 - 2.5	32 (22.222)	8.84
2.5 - 3.5	13 (9.027)	8.60
3.5 - 4.5	8 (5.555)	8.86
4.5 - 5.5	6 (4.166)	12.6
5.5 - 6.5	Nil	-
6.5 - 7.5	8 (5.555)	13.3
Total	144(99.996)	5.76

Figures in parentheses represent percentage out of column total

In Table 4.5, the distribution of sharecroppers according to the size category of their landholding has been shown. It is true that the number of sharecropper families constituted only 7.63 per cent of the total number of affected families but the overall importance of this phenomenon has to be assessed in the light of the land reforms policy of the LFG in West Bengal. Not only the political leaders of this government, but also the academic researchers have praised the communist government for increasing the bargaining capacity of the sharecroppers through the recording of their right over agricultural land (Lieten 1996). But here also the case of industrialisation in Paschim Medinipur under the wider context of the structural adjustment programme and economic

Table 4.4 : Post-acquisition Agricultural Landholding Pattern of Sample Households Affected by the Acquisition for TML

Size category of holdings (in acres)	*Number of households*		*Mean household size*
Landless	22	(15.277)	6.36
≤0.5	35	(24.305)	5.48
0.5 - 1.5	51	(35.416)	8.25
1.5 - 2.5	14	(9.722)	7.57
2.5 - 3.5	13	(9.027)	12.07
3.5 - 4.5	5	(3.472)	9.20
4.5 - 5.5	3	(2.083)	10.33
5.5 - 6.5	1	(0.694)	15.00
6.5 - 7.5	Nil	-	
Total	144	(99.996)	5.76

Figures in parentheses represent percentage out of column total

liberalisation policy shows that even a communist government, which was committed to uphold the interests of sharecroppers, could be a party to dispossess small and marginal farmers along with sharecroppers from their means of production.

Table 4.5 : Land Acquisition Scenario Among the Sharecropper Households Affected by Acquisition for TML

Amount of land in acres	*Number of households*
≤0.5	2
0.5 - 1.5	8
1.5 -2.5	NIL
2.5 - 3.5	1
Total	11

In Table 4.6, an attempt has been made to quantify the pattern of utilisation of the compensation money received by the landlosers in the study area. It needs to be mentioned at first that all the 144 households have received monetary compensation, although many landlosers during the field investigation reported that they were yet to get the full compensation money. Secondly, all the families have

Table 4.6 : Profile of Utilisation of Compensation Money by the Landloser Households Affected by the Acquisition for TML

Compensation category in rupees	*Purchase of agricultural land*	*Purchase of shallow tubewell*	*House-building and/ or repair*	*Domestic consumption*	*Marriage*	*Repayment of loan*	*Bank deposit*	*Business investment*
1,000-10,000	6	–	9	31	9	2	18	6
10,000-20,000	5	5	5	12	9	1	16	3
20,000-30,000	–	1	5	5	4	2	6	1
30,000-40,000	–	1	5	5	5	1	6	2
40,000-50,000	1	–	1	4	1	–	4	–
50,000-60,000	–	–	1	1	1	–	2	–
60,000-70,000	–	–	–	2	1	–	1	–
70,000-80,000	–	–	–	–	–	–	–	–
80,000-90,000	1	–	–	1	1	–	1	–
90,000-1,00,000	–	–	2	1	–	–	4	1
Total	13 (9.027)	7 (4.861)	28 (19.444)	62 (43.055)	31 (21.527)	6 (4.166)	58 (40.277)	13 (9.027)

Figures in parentheses represent percentage out of the total number of surveyed households

utilised the compensation money in more ways than one. Eight categories of utilisation of compensation money by the villagers could be identified, which were then arranged into ten compensation categories. But as the household members have spent the money under more than one utilisation category so any row total achieved is the result of addition of the same household more than once under different categories. Understandably, the sum of all the row totals will not be equal to the total number of households in the sample. However, each column total represents the actual number of households out of 144 under any particular utilisation category. This gives a fair idea as to how the villagers have tried to compensate their loss of land. The maximum number of affected households have spent some portion of the compensation money in domestic consumption, while the second highest number of households have deposited a part of the money in the bank. But if spending on marriage of the family members and house-building and repair are also considered to be domestic consumption then clearly the latter item predominates in the compensation utilisation process. The lower frequency of households who have tried to spend the money for agricultural purpose (for example, purchase of arable land or shallow tubewells) marks the beginning of the process of displacement of these small and marginal farmers from their traditional occupation and peasant way of life. In the next sub-section the consequences of land acquisition for Century Textile and Industries would be analysed.

Table 4.7 : Distribution of Households in Four Villages Affected by the Land Acquisition for CTIL

Name of the villages	*Number of households*
Shyamraipur	22 (44)
Baharapat	20 (40)
Kantapal	6 (12)
Molla chak	2 (4)
Total	50 (100)

Figures in parentheses represent percentage out of column total

Consequences of Land Acquisition for CTIL

About 50 households in four villages have been surveyed to study the consequences of land acquisition for Century Textiles and Industries Ltd. (CTIL). The same methodology was adopted in selecting the households and the results also show a similar pattern as found in case of acquisition for Tata Metaliks. The results are presented in the following tables.

From this table it is found that among the villages surveyed Shyamraipur and Baharapat occupied first and second positions in terms of affected households. Both the villages are located on the eastern side of the South Eastern Railway track and most of the inhabitants are engaged in cultivation of their lands for at least four to five months of the year. Although there are service-holders and petty businessmen in these villages, the life of the villagers still revolves around agriculture.

Table 4.8 : Distribution of Households of Different Castes and Communities Affected by Land Acquisition for CTIL

Name of Caste/community	*Number of households*
Lodha	16 (32.00)
Sadgope	27 (54.00)
Brahamin	01 (02.00)
Tantubay	01 (02.00)
Jelia Kaibarta (SC)	05 (10.00)
Total	50 (100.00)

Figures in parentheses represent percentage out of column total

In this table, the caste and community-wise distribution of affected households show that the Sadgopes (a numerically dominant cultivator caste in this area) occupy the highest position in terms of the total number of affected households and the Lodhas (a scheduled tribe) come second in the series. It is worth mentioning here that in some areas of Western Medinipur the Lodhas still practise hunting and gathering and the Government of West Bengal gives special attention for the development of this marginalised tribal community.

The pre and post-acquisition landholding patterns clearly reveal how landlessness has started to spread among the small farmers as a direct result of the West Bengal Government's decision to acquire farmland in this area. In the pre-acquisition stage there was no landless family in the sample taken, but after the acquisition eight families were found to be landless. The number of families in the size category 0.5 - 1.5 acres have increased considerably, while the same number has decreased substantially in the next higher category of landholding, viz. 1.5 -2.5 acres. The mean household size of the families in the different size categories of landholding shows that in the post-acquisition stage the affected households were supporting a higher family size than they were doing in the pre-acquisition stage with a lesser amount of landholding. This is a clear indication of the declining economic condition of the villagers caused by land acquisition.

Table 4.9 : Pre-acquisition Agricultural Landholding Pattern of Households Affected by Acquisition for CTIL

Size Category of land-holding (in acre)	*Number of households*	*Mean household size*
Landless	NIL	NIL
≤0.5	7(14.00)	5.42
0.5 - 1.5	15 (30.00)	4.73
1.5 - 2.5	10 (20.00)	6.60
2.5 - 3.5	8 (16.00)	7.50
3.5 - 4.5	4 (8.00)	11.75
4.5 - 5.5	2 (4.00)	11.00
5.5 - 6.5	1 (2.00)	9.00
6.5 - 7.5	–	
7.5 - 8.5	–	
8.5 - 9.5	–	
9.5 - Above	3(6.00)	8.33
Total	50 (100.00)	6.76

Figures in parentheses represent percentage out of column total.

In the following table we have made an attempt to quantify the pattern of utilisation of the compensation money by the households in the study area. Here it should be mentioned that all the families have utilised money in more ways than one. So here also, all the row totals are not equal to the total number of households in our sample. But each column total represents the actual number of households under any particular utilisation category. This table gives an idea as to how the villagers have tried to compensate their loss of major means of production. The data show that maximum number of landlosers have deposited some portion of their compensation money in the bank to meet future crises and domestic needs. While the second and third highest numbers fall under the categories of house building/repair and domestic consumption. The most conspicuous fact in this table is the lesser number of households who have spent some portion of the compensation money towards

Table 4.10 : Post-acquisition Agricultural Landholding Pattern of Households Affected by Acquisition for CTIL

Size category of land holding (in acre)	*Number of households*	*Mean household size*
Landless	8 (16.00)	4.37
≤0.5	9 (18.00)	5.55
0.5 - 1.5	21 (42.00)	6.85
1.5 - 2.5	4 (8.00)	9.25
2.5 - 3.5	3 (6.00)	9.66
3.5 - 4.5	2 (4.00)	9.00
4.5 - 5.5	–	
5.5 -6.5	–	
6.5 - 7.5	–	11.00
7.5 -8.5	1 (2.00)	–
8.5 - 9.5	–	–
9.5 - Above	2 (4.00)	7.00
Total	50 (100.00)	6.76

Figures in parentheses represent percentage out of column total

Table 4.11: Profile of Utilisation of Compensation Money by the Landloser Households Affected by Acquisition for CTIL

Compensation category in rupees	*Purchase of agricultural land*	*House building and/or repairing*	*Domestic Consumption*	*Marriage*	*Repayment of Loan*	*Bank deposit*	*Business investment*	*Health & clinic*	*Others*
1,000-10,000	2	1	–	1	1	–	1	1	1
10,000-20,000	5	4	2	1	1	2	–	–	3
20,000-30,000	–	1	–	–	4	3	1	3	–
30,000-40,000	–	1	–	–	–	–	–	–	–
40,000-50,000	–	2	2	1	–	2	–	–	–
50,000-60,000	–	–	–	1	–	1	–	–	–
60,000-70,000	1	–	2	1	1	2	2	2	–
70,000-80,000	–	–	1	1	1	3	–	–	–
80,000-90,000	–	–	1	2	1	1	–	1	1
90,000-1,00,000	–	–	–	–	–	–	–	–	–
1,00,000 above	2	9	4	4	4	10	2	3	1
	10 (20)	18 (36)	12 (24)	12 (24)	13 (26)	24 (48)	6 (12)	10 (20)	6 (12)

Figures in parentheses represent percentage out of the total number of surveyed households.

the purchase of agricultural land. This is another dimension of landlessness which also shows that the feeling of uncertainty over the possession of agricultural land has prevented the farmers from purchasing the same with the compensation money.

Peasant Protest: Not Always at the Receiving End

The protests launched by the landowning peasants of the Gokulpur-Amba area against land acquisition took many forms, even though these did not last long maintaining the same intensity. A good number of peasants took the statutory means to advance their objections against land acquisition under section 5A of the Land Acquisition Act during December 1995. A government report dated 21.6.96 vividly recorded the objections and described in detail how the latter were overruled. The objections submitted by 342 landlosers contained the following points: (i) The acquisition of agricultural land would affect the farmers seriously by throwing them out of employment, (ii) the landlosers will not get compensation at the rate they expect, and (iii) the proposed acquisition is against public interest and is beyond the purview of the Act. It is interesting to observe how the concerned officials of the Land Acquisition Department overruled all the objections raised by the farmers. Before rejecting the objections, the officials, however, recognised the severity and magnitude of the acquisition. To quote from the report :

> It is a fact that since large quantum of land is being acquired and the people chiefly subsists on agriculture many people will be seriously affected in earning their livelihood and avocation" (Departmental Report 1996).

But this was the only sentence in the whole report which upheld the interests of the peasants. The rest of the 3-page report was devoted to justify the acquisition through the elaboration of some arguments. The arguments of the officials centered round the low agricultural yield of the lands which are monocrop in nature. Moerover, the report also mentioned about the merits of the location of the land, which provided important infrastructural facilities for the industry like nearby railway line and the national highway. It is learnt from the report that during the hearing of the objections the petitioners could not "specify their individual difficulty in parting with the land" although the same report said that "most of the objectors submitted that they have no objection if employment is assured to them, in the company in favour of whom acquisition is being done." It is not clear from the report why the authors of the same could not understand the nature of "individual difficulty" in parting with the land which is their main source of livelihood. Three points raised in the report are quite significant and shows the bureaucratic way of dealing with such an action on the part of the government which was going to have a severe impact on the subsistence pattern of a group of rural cultivators in a monocrop region. Firstly, at one place the report mentioned : "It is worthwhile to point out that objections have been received only from 342 landowners for the acquisition of 526.71 acre which will affect at least 3000 landowners, if not more." It seems the official position rested on the logic that as the overwhelming majority of the farmers would not face any difficulty so there was no need to record any objection against this acquisition. Secondly, after citing the locational advantages of the land, the officals overruled objections regarding the question of earning a livelihood by saying that the proposal had been approved both by the screening committee and by the state after considering all the aspects. Incidentally, the screening committee for the approval of any project comprises the *Sabhadhipati* of the panchayat samity and the Member of the Legislative Assembly of the locality. It is obvious that these people's representatives who are members of political parties of the LFG would not object a proposal which has already been approved by the cabinet and the concerned ministries of their own government. Thirdly , the report dealt with the point 'job for land' simply by saying that the Land Acquisition Act does not provide any relief except compensation. But the government may take up the matter with the company particularly for those farmers who would become landless and would be devoid of any source of earning a livelihood. After having overruled all the objections, the procedure for land acquisition made headway.

Beside recording objections within the legal framework of the Land Acquisition Act, the farmers of this area also took recourse to extra-legal means to fight against the acquisition of their agricultural land. The information on this part of the peasant protest have been collected from interviews of the leaders and participants of this movement as well as from press reports and the various written memoranda submitted by the villagers to the district and state administration. In the following sub-section the succession of the important events of the peasant resistance has been described.

Protest to Resistance: Brief but Significant

The vast rural area which lies between Medinipur and Kharagpur townships is dominated by the two left political parties of the state, namely, CPI and CPI(M), which are also the major partners of the Left Front Government. The Congress, which is the opposition party in the state has some followers in the area. This party being the major supporter of economic liberalisation did not raise any objection when the news of industrialisation in this area came to be known. In fact, Congress welcomed this decision of the left government. They only raised doubts about whether the industrialists would at all choose West Bengal as a suitable site for industrialisation. In the study area Tata Metaliks has already been established on about 200 acres of agricultural land during 1991-92. Before the establishment of Tata Metaliks the leaders and cadres of CPI (M) and CPI organised meetings and continued individual level campaigns on the "bright possibility" of getting jobs by the landlosers in the industry. But when the Tata Metaliks started production, the promise for providing jobs was proved to be a false one and the peasants also experienced the lenghty as well as tedious process of getting compensation from the district administration. All of these caused sufficient disillusionment among the peasants a large section of whom were once hopeful about the positive effects of the establishment of industrial estates in this region.

The decision of the State Government to acquire agricultural land in the same area for CTIL was taken under this background. The pessimism created among the peasants owing to the establishment of Tata Metaliks inspired some of the inhabitants of this locality to agitate against the acquisition of land for another pig-iron industry. The movement gained much popularity under the leadership of Trilochan Rana [a former CPI(ML) activist] during 1995-96 who joined the trade union wing of Congress Party and put considerable pressure on the district administration.

Two interesting incidents may be mentioned in this regard which would throw some light about the reasons behind the popularity of this movement among the farmers. The first incident took place in the month of May 1995 when Trilochan Rana organised a good number of peasants to put a deputation to the Tata Metaliks Company authorities demanding some compensation for the damage caused by the movement of trucks carrying goods for the company over the unacquired agricultural fields (there was no crop in the fields at that time) of those farmers. The trucks damaged the dykes of the fields (*ails*) and the soil. Under the pressure of the peasants the company authority had to pay compensation in kind to 75 peasant families in presence of the pradhan (eleted head) of the Kalaikunda GP (Gram Panchayat). Some amount of fertiliser was given to those peasants whose lands were damaged.

In the second incident Trilochan Rana led a deputation to the district administration regarding the damage caused to the unacquired agricultural fields of some peasants for planting pillars to demarcate the acquired land for Century Textiles Company in Kantapal, Mollachak and other adjoining villages. Those cement pillars were fixed by digging at about 4 sq.ft. of land to a depth of 3-4 ft. and became permanent structures right on the agricultural fields of the peasants whose lands were not acquired. These pillars served as the boundary of the acquired land for CTIL. About 24 such pillars were constructed in early 1996. The peasants argued that cultivation of fields over a much wider area around those pillars was not possible owing to physical obstruction.

The district administration had to agree with this demand of the peasants and arranged for payment of Rs. 420 per annum as monetary compensation to those families affected by the construction of those pillars. This compensation payment continued for 2 years but with the decline of the movement the administration discontinued this compensation.

Both these incidents reveal that under the pressure of an intelligent and organised peasant movement the company authority as well as the Land Acquisition Department had arranged compensation for peasant families having no provision under the existing legal and administrative framework.

The movement reached its peak from the later part of 1995 upto April 1996 during which the farmers even went to the extent of violent means. In the first week of January 1996 hundreds of farmers in the Kalaikunda area stormed into the tent of the engineer who was conducting soil testing and land survey on behalf of Century Textiles Ltd. A leading national daily reported on 10 January 1996:

> Land survey and soil testing work in Mathurakismat Mouza in the Kaliakunda gram panchayat area of Kharagpur rural police station undertaken by Centuary Textiles—a Birla group of Industries—had to be abandoned following stiff resistance from villagers last week.... The farmers also blocked Sahachak for nine hours yesterday .... They also lodged a complaint with the police against the firm" (*The Statesman* 10 January 1996).

On 22 March 1996, the same national daily reported on a mass deputation by a group of peasants of the Kharagpur region before the district administration (*The Statesman* 22 March 1996). In this deputation , the peasants demanded land for land or a job for the members of the landloser families. They also demanded a compensation of 3 lakh rupees per acre of agricultural land. After this deputation, about 100 farmers came to Medinipur Collectorate on 10 April 1996 and submitted a mamorandum to the District Magistrate saying that they would boycott the ensuing parliamentary election to protest against the acquisition of fertile agricultural land for industrial projects.The farmers stated in their letter that this acquisition would disturb the local economy and distabilise the environmental balance of the region and this event was also reported in *The Statesman* on 2 May 1996. It is important to note in this connection that neither the state or district level Congress leadership, nor any MLA of this party showed any interest in supporting this movement of peasants in Kharagpur region. The local CPI(M) leadership and the elected panchayat members of this area not only remained silent about this spontaneous movement of the peasants but they also made every attempt to dampen this agitation by labelling it as a disturbance created by Congress to stall the progress of industrialisation under LFG. Without getting support from any opposition party and facing stiff resistance from the ruling left parties and lacking a coherent organisation, this localised peasant movement against land acquisition gradually lost its intensity.

The landlosers also tried to organise themselves by refusing to accept compensation money for a very brief period under the leadership of a few local leaders but this effort too did not last long and the movement finally came to a halt in the Kalaikunda region.

Dispossession of *Bargadars* by Land Acquisition

The *bargadars* occupy a special position in the land tenure system in West Bengal. Traditionally, they were the *bhagchasis* (sharecroppers) who did not enjoy any record of right on the land which they cultivated. *Bargadars* used to get a share (usually 50 per cent) of the crop and straw produced in a given plot of land. Before the introduction of the Land Reforms Act in the post-Independence period, there was no legal security for the *bargadars* if they were evicted from the land by the landowners. Even after the promulgation of Land Reforms Act in 1955, the landowners continued to exploit the *bargadars* in various ways by using their advantageous social position as well as superior political and economic power. The left political parties in West Bengal played a crucial role in upholding the interests of the *bargadars* by organising peasant movements and through the implementation of the legislation under a specific governmental programme named "Operation Barga". This programme recorded spectacular success in terms of the number of registered *bargadars* since the coming of the Left Front Government in 1977, although the initial enthusiasm has gradually declined over the years (Mukarji and Bandopadhyay 1993:41). The recently published *West Bengal Human*

Development Report (May 2004) by the Development and Planning Department of the Government of West Bengal in its second chapter entited "Land Reforms" noted a 'disturbing feature' regarding *bargadars*. To quote from the Report : "There have been recent reports of increasing land alienation by pattadars, and of eviction of bargadars, thus suggesting that the benefits of the land reform have been relatively short-lived at least for some rural households" (WBHDR 2004 : 40). Under the present legislation in West Bengal which has made the rights of *bargadar* hereditary, two kinds of crop sharing arrangements are recognised. In one, if the *bargadar* provides the inputs for agriculture (plough, bullocks, seeds, manure etc.), then he gets 75 per cent of the total crop produced while the landowner gets the rest 25 per cent. In another system, wherein the agricultural inputs are given by the landowner, the crop-sharing is done on a 50:50 basis. The major objective behind the registration of *bargadars* through operation barga is to prevent the eviction of *bargadars* who are the actual tillers of the land. The legislation, however, has no provision to protect the *bargadar* from eviction when the land is acquired for some public purpose, although West Bengal is the only state in India which had started to give monetary compensation to *bargadars* since 1963. It is interesting to note here that in the first National Policy on Resettlement and Rehabilitation (NPRR) published by the Ministry of Rural Development, Government of India in February 2004 does not contain any rehabilitation package for the sharecroppers (Guha 2005). The method of providing compensation to a registered *bargadar* is different from that of the landowner. Interestingly, when plots of land involving *bargadars* are acquired the Land Acquisition Department has to make calculation for payment of compensation both for the owner of the land and the *bargadar*. From the point of view of the requiring body for which the land is being acquired, the presence of recorded *bargadars* is not a very comfortable situation since for the same plot of land compensation has to be paid to two kinds of affected persons. From the perspective of the Land Acquisition Department too, the calculation of compensation for *bargadars* requires the culling of various kind of information from different departments of the government through a lengthy bureaucratic process, which is usually a time consuming affair. The different steps for the calculation of compensation of *bargadars* are described below.

In the first step, i.e. after the date of publication of notice under section 4 (1.a) of the Land Acquisition Act, the total quantum of land under *barga* cultivation is determined by taking help from the record of right (ROR) kept in the Land and Land Reforms Department at the block level. The Land Acquisition Officer (LAO) has to ask for the specific names of *bagadars* and the terms of crop sharing with their respective owners as well as the amount of land cultivated by each *bargadar* who would be affected by acquisition.

In the second step, the LAO writes to the Principal Agricultural Officer of the district to know about the yield of crops in the area under acquisition for the preceding three years. At this stage, the LAO also writes to the Agricultural Marketing Officer to get the market prices of the crop in the previous three years from the material data i.e. the date of publication of the acquisition notice under section 4 (1.a) of the LA Act.

In the last stage, with the help of the above data the rate of compensation for the *bargadars*, is calculated at the price of the net average of the crop produced in the *barga* land. The rate so determined shall again be fixed not more than six times of the net average of the produce. The compensation for a particular *bargadar* is calculated by taking into consideration the crop sharing arrangement (whether it is 50 per cent or 75 per cent) with the landowner.

There are two important points regarding the payment of compensation to the *bargadars* which must be mentioned. The first is that no *solatium* (which is 30 per cent of the land value) is given to the *bargadars* and the second is *requisition compensation* (i.e. the time taken to declare compensation award from the date of first notification) is not also provided to the *bargadar*. As a result of the facts mentioned in the foregiong paragraphs, the *bargadar*, being the actual tiller of the soil, is really at a disadvantageous position in the existing framework of land acquisition and award of compensation in West Bengal despite the special attention given by the government towards their empowerment through 'Operation Barga'. The *bargadars* almost invariably gets lesser amount of compensation at a much later date for same plot of acquired land than the owner of the land who often does not cultivate the land.

In case of land acquisition for the CTIL, it was found from the files of the Land Acquisition Department that in the Rajpura mouza the land value for the payment of compensation was fixed at Rs. 50,000 per acre in the year 1996. While in the same mouza the rate of compensation for the *bargadars* was fixed at the rate of Rs. 4,210 per acre. Even six times of this rate i.e. Rs. 4,210 × 6 turned out to be only Rs. 25,260 which is almost half the rate of the award value estimated for the landowners of the area.

In Malancha mouza (having highest rate of land value which was Rs. 1 lakh per acre under acquisition for Century Company) the *bargadars* received the compensation money more than two years after the landowners. The difference in the total amount of compensation received was also substantial. The rate of compensation for *bargadars* in Malancha mouza was fixed at the rate of Rs. 12,630 per acre. For almost the same amount of land acquired, the *bargadars* received remarkably lesser amount of compensation money (Deptt. Files LA case No. 8 and 12 of 1996 to 1997. In Table 4.12 four individual cases are shown in a comparative manner.

The reason for the delay towards the payment of compensation to *bargadars* stems mainly from the method of calculation of compensation, which requires information to be channelised through three government Departments, viz. Block Land and Land Reforms Office, Principal Agricultural Office and Agricultural Marketing Office. The lesser amount of compensation for *bargadars* arises from the basic tenet of the land ownership rules of India which does not recognise the recorded *bargadar* as one of the titleholders of the land. Through registration, the *bargadar* only achieves hereditary right to get a share of the crop produced in a given plot of land and a protection against eviction by the owner of the land. It may be noted in this connection that till today there has been no discussion or suggestion on the part of Government, political parties

Table 4.12 : A Comparison of the Landowners and Bargadars in Malancha Mouza Affected by Acquisition for CTIL

Sl. No.	*Name of the landowner*	*Amount of land acquired (in acres)*	*Total comp. received (in rupees)*	*Date of receipt of comp.*	*Name of the bargadar*	*Amount of land acquired (in acres)*	*Total comp. received (in rupees)*	*Date of receipt of comp.*
1.	Mangla Hansda	0.32	43,357.80	16.5.96	Dasu Behara	0.33	4,167.90	10.7.98
2.	Sandhyarani Das	0.75	1,01,619.85	16.5.96	Badal De	0.79	9,977.70	23.3.98
3.	Kalpana Bera	0.10	14,200.00	29.1.97	Bikram Behara and Rakhal Behara	0.10	1,263.00	23.3.98
4.	Arati Saha	1.16	1,57,172.05	16.5.96	Sanatan Hansda	2.43	30,282.00	7.10.96

Note : In the three cases where the amount of land acquired is not same for the owners and their respective bargadars, there were other owners whose names could not be collected since those files were not made available to the author during the period when archival research was being conducted in the district collectorate.

and NGOs to make compensation payment to the *bargadars* at par with that of their landowners of even at the rate of seventy-five per cent of the total compensation received by the landowner.

In the context of land acquisition, the recording of the rights of the *bargadars* is very much important since unrecorded *bargadars* are not entitled to get compensation from the LA Department. In the study area, an interesting case of a group of unrecorded *bargadars* and *pattaholders* (landless persons who are given land by the government) has been found whose claim for getting compensation against acquisition was summarily rejected by the LA Department of erstwhile Medinipur district. In Table 4.13 the particulars of some unrocorded *bargadars* are shown.

In a departmental file, a petition bearing memo No. 737/Ban-O-Bhumi dated 23 May 1996 from the Savapati, Kharagpur I, panchayat samity addressed to the Special Land Acquisition Officer Medinipur has been found which requested the special LAO to issue compensation notice to twenty unrecorded *bargadars* and sixty five *pattaholders* who have been affected by land acquisition for Century Textiles and Industries. The petition enclosed the individual applications of the said *bargadars* and *pattaholders* along with the details forwarded by one Ms. Mallicka Mudi, an elected member of Kharagpur I panchayat samity. All the individual applicants (most of whom were illiterate persons and gave their thumb impressions) stated in their petitions that as poor cultivators they could not record their names in the register, so the panchayat samity may enter their names after proper enquiry and make arrangements for getting proper compensation. In Table 4.13 the details of the *bargadars* are furnished.

Within seven days of the submission of the said petition, the special Land Acquisition Officer of the district wrote a letter (memo No. 730/LA dated 3.6.96) to the Savapati of the Kharagpur I panchayat samity. In that letter the LAO categorically stated that compensation to unrecorded *bargadars* could not be awarded and they have obtained a report from the concerned Block Land and Land Reforms Office containing an exhaustive list of *bargadars*. So no further claim of compensation in respect of *bargadars* could

Table 4.13 : The Particulars of Unrecorded Bargadars Affected by Acquisition for CTIL

Sl. No.	*Name of the bargadar*	*Name of the landowner*	*Name of the mouza with J.L. No.*	*Amount of land (in acres)*	*Remarks*
1.	Mahendra Nayek	Gouri Sarkar	Niranjanbar (154)	.0055	
2.	Sushen Nayek	do	Chaksonadhar (136)	.0122	
3.	Srimat Hebram	Sambhu Ganguly	Sujatpur (139)	.02	From the title it is evident that the bargadar belongs to Santal community who are listed as a scheduled tribe
4.	Bangu Mandi	Badal Chandra Pramanik	Niranjanbar (154)	.0062	Santal, ST
5.	Sukumar Patra	Name not given	Malancha (131)	.0105	
6.	Gostha Paloi	Gouri Sarkar	Sujatpur (139)	.0071	
7.	Dukha Nayek	Aloka Sen and 3 others	Malancha (131)	.01	
8.	Mohan Nayek	Rekha Ghosh and 2 others	Rajpura (130)	.015	
9.	Parameswar Nayek	Rekha Ghosh and 2 others	do	.025	
10.	Ghontu Nayek	do	do	.0085	
11.	Bangu Mandi	Raghu Kairi	Kantageria	.0176	Santal, ST
12.	Bangu Mandi	Raghu Kairi	Niranjanbar (154)	.0084	
13.	Sukhendu Bishal	Asoke Sen and others	Chaksonadhar (136)	0.61,0061	
14.	Mrigen Rana	Asoke Sen and 2 others	Malancha (131)	.005	
15.	Krishna Nayek	Santi Mitra and 2 others	Rajpura(130)	.017	
16.	Kalipada Chalak	Santi Mitra and 2 others	Rajpura (138)	.0103	
17.	Indra Kotal	Rabindra Chakraborty and Soumen Chakraborty	Malancha (131)	.0084	
18.	Mahendra Nayek	Biswanath Bhattacharya	Malancha (131)	.0315	
19.	Bhonda Nayek	Not mentioned	Rajpura (130)	.023	
20.	Srinath Mudi Laxman Mudi Chunaram Mudi	Anadi Pal and 5 others	Niranjanbar (154)	.025	Kora, ST

be legally entertained. Similarly, the claim for compensation of 65 *pattaholders* were also turned down by the district Land Acquisition Department. Interestingly, during the collection of information about *bargadar* compensation from the Land Acquisition Department this episode of the non-payment of compensation to unrecored *bargadars* was raised before a group of officials in the same office. Seeing the letter written by the *Savapati* of the panchayat samity one officer instantly commented: "I agree that the Block Land and Land Reforms Office failed to record those *bargadars* as alleged by the *Savapati.* But could the elected panchayat members evade their own responsibility in motivating the *bargadars* to record their names? What the panchayat members were doing in that area?" In the next section, the role of the gram panchayat in matters of land acquisition in the study area would be narrated.

Panchayats and Land Acquisition in the Kalaikunda Area

A lengthy literature exists on the positive role of panchayats (the elected local self-government) in the empowerment of the deprived classes in rural West Bengal, particularly since the coming of the LFG in power (Lieten 1996). Panchayat in West Bengal has become a unique statutory institution which cannot be avoided by the villagers in any matter related to the earning of their livelihood. No development programme in the rural areas of West Bengal can be executed without the involvement of the gram panchayats at the mouza level and panchayat samity at the block level. The panchayats are constitutional bodies which are responsable for, (i) the preparation of plans for economic development and social justice as well as (ii) the implementation of schemes for these two afore-mentioned objectives. The panchayats, however, have no legal power to acquire land for any developmental purpose. The legal manual published by the Department of Panchayats of the Government of West Bengal has a section on land acquisition which mentioned :

> If the gram panchayat needs any land for its own work within the purview of the Panchayat Act, then the panchayat can initiate a negotiation with the owner of the land for its takeover. If such negotiation fails, then the panchayat can apply to the District Magistrate for the acquisition of the said land and the District Magistrate would acquire the land for the panchayat (Clause 44).The panchayat, however has to take prior written permission from the State Government before taking possession of any land or corporate property.
>
> *(Translated from Bengali)*
>
> [*Bidhi Nirdeshika (Gram Panchayat)* 1994, Department of Panchayat, Government of West Bengal.]

The above paragraph from the manual for gram panchayats in West Bengal clearly reveals the legal and administrative superiority of the State Government over the panchayats in matters related with the acquisition of land within the jurisdiction of the latter. And if land is acquired by the State Government, which is not needed by a specific panchayat but falls within its area, then too the panchayat has not been given any statutory power to give objection to such acquisition under the framework of the land acquisition laws which are in vogue in West Bengal. The administrative procedure for land acquisition in West Bengal, however, has developed a system of keeping the *Savapati* (Chairperson) of the elected panchayat samity (the second tier of the panchayat) in the screening committee which considers the proposals submitted by the private companies that involve acquisition of land.

For the consideration of proposals for private industries in the Kharagpur I block screening committee meetings were held in which the concerned *Savapati* of the panchayat samity gave his suggestions before giving consent to the proposals. From the files of the Land Acquisition Department minutes of one such screening committee meetings were recovered, which revealed the role played by an elected member of the panchayat samity present in the meeting. The said screening committee meeting was held on 19.12.1994 in the chamber of the Additional District Magistrate in connection with the acquisition of land for three industrial projects involving about 40 acres of agricultural land. After the placement of the proposals along with their respective site plans by the LAO, the *Savapati* of the Kharagpur I panchayat samity pointed out that the members of the screening committee should be informed about the (i) provision of employment for the landlosers and (ii) the rehabilitation of poor landlosers for the establishment of those industries. The local Member of the State Legislative Assembly (MLA) also demanded that the said compaines should "spell out their employment policy". At this stage the Additional District Magistrate assured the members that he would take up the matter with the WBIDC and a convene a meeting with the companies on this issue. The representative of a particular company, who was present in the meeting informed that their employment potential is 150 but did not mention whether those persons would be selected from the landlosers or not. The members finally approved all the three proposals which was accordingly sent to the Asstt. Secretary to the Department of Commerce and Industries, Government of West Bengal.

The above description reveals the specific role played by the elected panchayat samity member in case of land acquisition within its jurisdiction for private industries. It is true that the *Savapati* of the panchayat samity raised the question of employment of landlosers in the industries for which land was being acquired, but the proposals were finally approved almost unconditionally. During the course of the fieldwork, many landlosers affected by the acquisition for Tata Metaliks and Century Textiles were repeatedly asked whether the local gram panchayats played any role to voice their demands for the employment of at least one person from every landloser family. The answer to this query, always without any exception, was given in the negative. When the gram panchayat *pradhans* were interviewed on this issue, they admitted that they could not do anything for the landlosers and one panchayat *pradhan* even stated:

> We were strongly against the acquisition of agricultural land since a lot of non-agricultural land existed in the vicinity. But we were helpless; it was a decision from the top.

The case of acquisition for Century Textiles, wherein a huge chunk of agricultural land (about 500 acres) had been simply kept vacant after the dispossession of the cultivators, the local gram panchayat was forced by a group of farmers to convene a meeting on 21 July 1998.The then Kalaikunda gram panchayat *pardhan* circulated a cyclostyled notice to all the affected farmers (including *bargadars* and *pattaholders*) in a meeting to discuss on the non-utilisation of this huge piece of land. The meeting was held in the office of the gram panchayat where more than a hundred farmers attended and discussed over the matter. The meeting finally entrusted the *Savapati* of the Kharagpur I panchayat samity to take the matter to the higher authorities of the government. Suffice it to say that nothing positive yielded even two years after that meeting and the farmers only expressed their total lack of faith and trust on this matter upon their elected panchayat at the time of conducting the last round of field visits in the Kalaikunda region in the winter of 1999.

Land Acquisition as Narrated by Some Affected Persons*

In this sub-section, some selected case studies in the form of personal narratives would be described in order to highlight the problems and crises encountered by the villagers affected by land acquisition for private industries. The case studies were collected in course of fieldwork from the persons who inhabited the village Gokulpur.

Case 1

Nirod Choudhury is a middle-aged man who belongs to the Sadgope caste and has been living in Gokulpur village for many generations. He has read upto class IV and his main occupation is agriculture. He inherited 2.5 acres of cultivable land from his father and the government has now acquired all of his land for Tata Metaliks

* The names of the persons in this section are not fictitious and are mentioned with the kind consent of them who were always eager to narrate their plight to the researcher in the field.

Company. He used to get food for his family of 6 from this land. Nirodbabu first heard about the news of acquisition from the villagers and he also came to know from them that every landloser faimly would be given monetary compensation as well as a job in Tata Company. He could still recollect that The would-be landlosers organised a number of meetings to press their demand for jobs to the administration. In the summer of 1989, when they were spreading manure in the fields, they received the notice of land acquisition through the local gram panchayat office. After receiving the notice they tried to organise an agitation in front of the office of the Tata Company at Nimpura, but nothing came out of it. During those days of turmoil, the Chief Minister of West Bengal, Mr. Jyoti Basu addressed a public meeting in the locality. Nirodbabu could recollect that in his speech the Minister assured that a job would be provided to a member of every landloser family.

After six or seven months he got the compensation money by cheque from the Bank of Baroda at Kharagpur at the rate of Rs. 22,000 per acre. He spent all the money in marrying off his daughter who was then 17 years old. Nirodbabu, however, did not sell out his two bullocks and the plough. He used to give them on hire at the rate of Rs. 60 per day to his neighbours who are in need of them for cultivation. He himself now works as a helper of a mason. His younger daughter has stopped going to school after studying upto Class VI level. His two sons have also stopped studying at schools and the older one (who read upto Class VI) has also started working as a day labourer in the locality. Although Nirodbabu's wife has not yet started to work outside home, but he did not know what would happen to them in future.

Case 2

Ballav Jana is a middle aged man who owned 3 acres of paddy field and one acre of land for vegetable cultivation. All his paddy fields have been acquired for Tata Metaliks. He belonged to Tanti Caste and was an active participant in the movement against land acquisition. He also spent the compensation money in his daughter's marriage. He thinks that his one acre of vegetable land is a blessing for him, because this land has not been acquired. He cultivates potato, onion, tomato, cauliflower, lady's finger etc. and sells them in the market. His two sons, who read upto Classes V and VIII respectively, help him in the cultivation and selling of those vegetables.

Case 3

Dhiren Choudhury is a Sadgope cultivator of the Gokulpur village. He owned one acre of paddy land which was fully acquired by the government for Tata Metaliks. When he first heard from the villagers that agricultural land would be acquired for an industry, he could not believe that his land would also be acquired. He discussed the matter with his elder brother whose land was already acquired. Finally, he received the notice and attended a meeting of the landlosers organised by the local leaders. Dhirenbabu received his compensation money from the Bank of Baroda at Kharagpur. With the compensation money he purchased seven *kathas* of land and he did not sell out his pair of bullocks and plough. He already had some vegetable land (*kalajami*) in which he cultivates green vegetables which he sells in the market.

The other cases from Gokulpur reveal almost the same pattern. The case studies narrated above show that the affected persons had hopes that they would be getting jobs in the company and even participated in the movement to press their demand for a job and higher rates of compensation. The case studies also reveal that the landlosers, who had some vegetable land of their own, continued with agriculture, one person even purchased some land with the compensation money.

Land Acquisition *Versus* Land Reforms: The Case of Kalaikunda Gram Panchayat

Like land acquisition, land reforms is basically a legal and administrative procedure. Through land reforms, the State Government updates the various types of ownership rights according to the Land and Land Reforms Act, 1955 and its further amendments in 1981 and 1986. One of the major objectives of land reforms is to confiscate land beyond the limits of ceiling stipulated under section 14M of the Act held by any particular family having a specified size (W.B.L.R. Act and Rules, 1984). Another objective of the Act is to distribute land to the landless by following certain administrative steps. Recording of the rights of sharecroppers is also a vital part of the land reforms process. Under the Land Reforms Act, 1955 the above-mentioned tasks are lengthy, complicated and vulnerable to various kinds of litigation. Essentially, land reform empowers the poor landless peasants in two ways, of which one is indirect and the other direct. When the government confiscates the land from a farmer who has kept land beyond the limits of ceiling, there is a likelihood that this surplus land would be distributed in future to the landless families. The confiscated land becomes the property of the government through an administrative procedure called vesting. So confiscation of land beyond ceiling limits and its subsequent vesting is an essential prerequisite for the distribution of land to the landless. This definitely encourages the landless peasants. The distribution of vest land (*patta* distribution) to the poor and landless is a direct means of empowering them. By this procedure the landless gets land for the sustenance of his/her family.

The differences between land reforms and land acquisition can be noticed quite easily. By land acquisition, the government acquires legally owned private land for a public purpose. Land Acquisition Act cannot be employed to confiscate land beyond the limits of ceiling. This is specifically the job of the Land and Land Reforms Act. So one can say that while Land and Land Reforms Act empowers the poor and the landless, the Land Acquisition Act disempowers the individual farmers for a public purpose.

Secondly, Land Acquisition and Land Reforms Acts differ at the level of the government administration from which they begin their operation. The land reforms process starts at the district level and the major part of the lengthy procedure takes place at the block level where the updated records about ownership on land are preserved. The distribution of land to the landless is a purely block level phenomenon which only requires the approval of the sub-divisional officer (SDO).

The land acquisition on the other hand primarily starts at the highest level of the administrative structure i.e. at the level of the Ministerial Secretariat and sometimes at the Cabinet level at the state capital in Kolkata. The decision to acquire land comes from the highest level of the bureaucracy. From this perspective, it may be stated that land acquisition is a centralised and top-down administrative process while land reforms operate in a more decentralised manner.

Thirdly, land reforms and land acquisition processes deal with elected panchayats in a markedly different manner. The Land Acquisition Acts (both Acts I and II) do not have any provision on the part of the administration to consult the elected panchayats in connection with any kind of land acquisition for public purpose. In West Bengal, screening committees consisting of a member from the elected panchayat samity are formed to consider the proposals from the requiring bodies involving land acquisition. But in the screening committee majority of the members belong to the administration viz. the Collector, Additional District Magistrate and Land Acquisition Officer. Moreover, the screening committee does not have any statutory or legal backing, it is simply an administrative appendage of the office of the District Collector. In matters of hearing objections from landlosers and the fixation of rates of compensation, the District Collector holds the highest power which is conferred to him by the Land Acquisition Act.

The implementation of the various stages of land reforms requires not only the mere presence of panchayat members but also their active participation. One of the most vital affairs of the land reforms process is the distribution of government land through *patta* to the landless families. It has certain stages, which begins with the preparation of *Math Khasra. Math Khasra* is a kind of survey conducted by the Block Land and Land Reforms Officer to enquire into the actual possession of land by the cultivators which has to be distributed among the landless families. The Land and Land Reforms Act stipulates that *Math Khasra* has to be done jointly by the panchayat and the government employees of the Revenue Inspector's Office at the gram panchayat level. This survey, which is a necessary step towards the distribution of land to the landless cannot be done without involving the panchayat. In addition to this, the list of beneficiaries i.e. landless persons (to whom land would have to be distributed) is also prepared by the gram panchayat.

The foregoing comparison of land reforms and land acquisition clearly reveals crucial differences between them. It can be said that land acquisition is a centralised and bureaucratic procedure than land reforms through which the *eminent domain* of state acquires private land in India (Guha 2006 b:155-173). The implications of this comparison for the LFG in West Bengal are important. Because, when the Left Government came to power in 1977, it gave top priority to land reforms, which was linked with decentralised planning through the involvement of the elected panchayats. The Left Government in West Bengal claims its uniqueness among the Indian States not only in staying at office for the last 29 years through parliamentary democracy, but also for implementing a pro-people land reform programme with fair amount of success (Mukarji and Bandopadhyay 1993). The key to this success lies in involving the poor peasants of the vast rural areas in the execution of the government policies related to their empowerment. The three majors planks of the land reforms programme of the LFG were (i) confiscation of the agricultural land of the big landlords beyond the limits of ceiling, (ii) distribution of land to landless labourers and (iii) the recording of the rights of the *bargadars* through "operation barga". Another facet of this land reform programme was the empowerment and activation of the elected panchayats through which developmental programmes were implemented.

These socio-political developments undoubtedly raised the level of consciousness and aspirations among the poorer sections (landless labourers, small and marginal farmers, etc.) of the rural population in West Bengal. In erstwhile Medinipur district, the grassroots level approach of the left government crystallized into a politico-administartive movement which was officially phrased as *village based district planning process* during 1985-86, a few years before the adoption of the economic liberalisation policy by the then Central Government (ruled by the Congress Party which is regarded as a centrist party in India) in 1991. The major objective of the decentralised planning process was to unleash a movement of village based rural development programmes by the villagers and get a feedback primarily from the participants for further development.

It would be relevant here to mention that the district planning committee (the first of its kind in West Bengal) of erstwhile Medinipur visualised the whole process of development by putting the poor peasants at the centre of all kinds of planning process. The DPC published a small book entitled *Village based district planning process : an outline of methodology* in September 1985, that described and analysed in detail how relevant socio-economic information on every village could be collected by the panchayat workers for using them in this micro level planning process. Among many pro-people planning elements, the document gave much importance to the (i) identification of the nature and amount of agricultural land as well as their improvement through ecologically sustainable use and (ii) exploration of the possibilities of developing industries in terms of local demand, raw material and/or skill. To quote from the monograph:

> Apart from human beings, the most important wealth of the village is its land. It is used for locating residence, for cultivation, for planting trees, for forest, for ponds, and other water bodies, for roads, for school, markets etc. ... Again, it is crucially necessary to know whether, why and how much of cultivable land of your village have either been kept fallow or have not been properly cultivated. What type of families owned these land? (District Planning Committee 1985).

Within a few years, and particularly in the wake of liberalisation in India, the development policy of the West Bengal Government began to change. The government which was fully committed to land reform started to invite capital intensive and technologically sophisticated heavy industrial corporations. The success in land reform in the state was cited as one of the justifications for huge industrial investment in the state by the ministers of the LFG. In a recent publication of the WBIDC, the justifications for the changes in the policy of the government has been described in a precise manner:

> Since the Left Front Government was installed in the State in 1997, it embarked on a course of reconstruction of the economy. The sectors in which the State had the powers to act under the constitution naturally received priority attention. As a matter of conscious policy, the State Government focused on rural development, land reforms, agriculture, small scale industries and fisheries along with decentralisation through empowerment and involvement of the panchayats in all development works. The policy resulted not only in a major breakthrough in the rural agricultural sector but also an upsurge in agricultural production, creation of a fast expanding domestic market and a stable political environment (West Bengal: Industry News Update June 2000: 44)

In another important publication, entitled *Destination West Bengal* the *agricultural growth* rather than the *empowerment of the poor peasants* was highlighted to show the advantage of industrial investment in West Bengal. In the said publication it was argued that since West Bengal registered the highest growth in foodgrain production and yield during 1985-90 it has helped to "increase the overall purchasing power in the rural areas" (*Destination West Bengal* 1999).

Contrary to what has been said in the recent government reports which reflected the policy changes of the State Government, an earlier report of the government devoted to the evaluation of the panchayats in West Bengal observed quite emphatically that land reforms is still an incomplete programme. In the words of the authors of the report:

> Land reform is not yet a complete programme ... in the nearly eleven years till 30 September, 1992, only 94

> thousands acres were distributed. At this rate the remaining 2.6 lakh acres will take almost 30 years to be distributed (Mukarji and Bandopadhyay 1993).

The authors further stated:

> There is no sustained effort to help small and marginal farmers by converging rural development schemes on their households. Pattaholders are, more or less, left to fend for themselves, once land is allotted to them. So far this has been an area of neglect. (*Ibid.*).

The above observations made by Mukarji and Bandopadhyay seem to be very much pertinent to the field level situation at the Kalaikunda gram panchayat area within which land acquisition for Tata Metaliks and Century Textiles had taken place during the 1990s. The Annual Report of the Kalaikunda gram panchayat for the year 1994-95 contains statistics on the distribution of the land to the landless families during the period 1993-95.

The figures revealed that from 1993 to June 1995, at about 300 acres of land was distributed to 1500 landless families inhabiting within the Kalaikunda gram panchayat (*Smaranika*, Kalaikunda gram panchayat 1994-95). Interestingly, the Annual Report of the Kalaikunda Gram Panchayat for the year 1992-93 also gave statistics on land reform in its last page which published figures of land distribution during the period 1978-1992. The figures show the same number of families (i.e. 1500) who had been given land which simply means that during the period 1992-1995 no landless family in the Kalaikunda gram panchayat area has been given land (*Smaranika*, Kalaikunda Gram Panchayat 1992-93). The rate of land distribution in this area during 1978-1992 (i.e. 15 years) turns out to be 20 acres per year. Now if only the amount of land acquired, during 1986-2000 (i.e. 15 years) for Tata Metaliks and Century Textiles is considered then the pace of land acquisition *vis-à-vis* land distribution can be compared. Roughly, at about 759 acres (233 acres for Tata Metaliks and 526 acres for Century Textiles) of land has been acquired for the two afore mentioned industries under the Kalaikunda gram panchayat during 1986-2000. The rate of land acquisition comes out to be 50.6 acres per year i.e. more than 2½ times the rate of land distribution by the government. It should be remembered in this connection that a major portion of this land which was acquired for Century Textiles has remained unutilised for more than four years.[1]

Table 4.14 : A Comparison Between Land Distribution and Land Acquisition in Kalaikunda Gram Panchayat

Period	*Amount of land distributed (in acres)*	*Annual rate (acres/year)*
1978-1992	300	20
1986-2000	Amount of Land Acquired (in acres)	
	759	50.6

In the light of above comparison, the case of Kalaikunda gram panchayat brings out an important implication for the development programmes in the state. The distribution of land to the landless families in this area, which operated through the involvement of the elected panchayat was a much slower process than land acquisition for large industries. Moreover, land acquisition caused dispossession of small and marginal farmers and disempowered the *bargadars* and *pattaholders* who despite all their efforts and resistances ultimately failed to achieve empowerment.

During the fieldwork, when the elected panchayat members as well as employees of the Kalaikunda gram panchayat were asked whether the panchayat had any rehabilitation plan for the dispossessed farmers in the area, the only answer was : "It is not the business of the panchayat. It is the duty of the government". The panchayat members were not even interested to conduct any household level survey to find out the number of families (including scheduled tribes) who had lost all of their land, and the number of *bargadars* and *pattaholders* who also lost their rights over land owing to acquisition for the two big industries, within their jurisdiction.

The empowerment of small peasants achieved through land reforms in the Kalaikunda area was reversed owing to the acquisition of huge chunks of farmland for large industries.

At the end of this chapter an anecdote from the field may be narrated. The event occurred near Kantapal village from where the huge chunk of land acquired for Century Textiles could be seen. A discussion was going on about the condition of the small dykes ('*Ail*' in the local parlance) raised by the farmers to demarcate the plots of land possessed by different owners within the acquired area. Since no cultivation could be taken up for three successive seasons in the whole area, which had turned into a grazing field, the dykes had started to crumble. Two consequences followed. Firstly, the farmers who still had unacquired land in the vicinity of the acquired area were facing a lot of difficulties in the agricultural plots from the grazing cattle. Earlier there were other farmers who also shared the responsibility of driving out the cattle from the fields during agricultural season. Driving out cattles is always a collective affair in rural areas. After acquisition, the number of farmers have decreased in this area. Moreover, cows and buffaloes of the milkmen of the urban areas of Kharagpur town have also ventured to exploit this huge chunk of land.

Secondly, after the breakdown of dykes the poor people (mainly women) of the area who used to collect a good quantity of small fishes of various types from those agricultural plots as a common pool resource, are not getting any fish in those plots. In the discussion four persons including one middle-aged women and an old man were present. All of them were denouncing the government for the takeover of the fertile agricultural land for Century Company which had not yet been established. When the question arose that if people of this area had started to dislike the ruling party and the government then why did they cast their votes at the panchayat and assembly elections to the same party every year? An interesting reply came from the old man which is reproduced here in verbatim: "Look babu, we poor people always have to ride on some animal almost blindfolded. After the ride for some time we start to realise whether it is a tiger or a bullock. But very often we have to twist its tail in order to keep it in proper direction" (translated freely from Bengali). All of us laughed at the old man, but we soon realised his sense of political humor about the Left Front Government in West Bengal.

The case of land acquisition for Century Textiles in Kalaikunda gram panchayat and the disempowerment of the peasants coupled with the inaction of the panchayat has clearly revealed the ground realities in a land scarce agricultural area of West Bengal where large scale industrialisation is in the offing.

NOTE

1. In the Annual Report for the year 1993-94 and 1994-95 of Kalaikunda G.P. it was mentioned that 75 acres (25 per cent of the total land distributed in this G.P.) of vested land could not be distributed due to litigation at the High Court. The Annual Report for the period 1997-98 does not contain any figure on the distribution of land to the landless family by the State Government.

FIVE

Conclusion

A humane notion of "displacement" must go beyond cash compensation, beyond even land for land, and extend to compensate all opportunity - costs of uprooting from habitats, i.e. complex social, religious, cultural and material ways of life.

Upendra Baxi quoted by Walter Fernandes (1989)

In this empirical research an attempt has been made to study the various dimensions of land acquisition in West Bengal. This is neither a work in contemporary history based solely on official documents nor a typical anthropological village study which usually depends almost entirely on data collected through fieldwork. The study is rather a combination of methods from both the areas of investigation, using various types of documentry evidences (gazette notifications, letters, memoranda, unpublished government report and results of surveys, proceedings of the legislative assembly, news items etc.) and quantitative as well as qualitative data collected through personal observations, household surveys, interviews and case studies conducted in the villages affected by land acquisition for pig-iron industries in Kharagpur I block of the Paschim Medinipur district in West Bengal.

In recent times, development induced displacement and rehabilitation of project affected people have gained considerable importance in the academic field as well as in popular literature. A substantial portion of this literature, however, lies somewhere between the *academic-popular continuum* and is produced by a good number of action-oriented NGOs in India. The international funding agencies, like World Bank and Asian Development Bank, are also playing a crucial role in managing affairs connected with displacement in India caused by development projects through their continued insistence on rehabilitation in the bank financed projects.

A careful reading of the literature on displacement produced by academicians, NGOs and international funding agencies has revealed that there is a dearth of description and analysis on the ground realities of the land acquisition laws and its close relationship with the empowering institutions like Land Reforms Act and the panchayats which function within the jurisdiction of Stae power. Typical empirical studies on displacement dealt only with its socio-economic consequences which occasionally ended with some policy recommendations containing suggestive measures for radical changes in the Land Acquisition Act of 1894. None of the works, however, made any serious attempt to study land acquisition process within a particular administrative unit (a block or a district) from administrative, legal and policy perspectives. In addition to this, studies on displacement in India have not yet ventured into the policy significance of the interrelationship among displacement of peasants, land reforms and the panchayati raj. Another neglected issue in the displacement research in India is the impact of land acquisition on sharecroppers. In fact, West Bengal offers a unique situation for studying displacement, land acquisition, land reforms, panchayats and the dispossession of sharecroppers by pinpointing development projects within a single framework. This research is an attempt towards that endeavour.

Against this background, it has been assumed that displacement of peasants through the acquisition of land at any place in India cannot take place in a political vacuum. Because, acquisition of land in the Indian states has to be a decision of the government and whenever the government takes agricultural land of the peasants for development projects, it tries to justify the decision at different levels and institutionalised fora by taking advantage of the democratic set up. Since the basic thrust of the development policy of the LFG in West Bengal is empowerment of the poor peasants through land reforms and decentralised planning, the acquisition of agricultural land for large-scale private industries in the wake of economic liberalisation bears special significance. The policy makers of the Government of West Bengal developed their rationale for justifying capital-intensive industrialisation involving land acquisition in the context of an agricultural economy where distribution of land to the landless and recording of the rights of the sharecroppers formed the core of the development policy of the government even up to the mid-1980s. The success story in the implementation of land reforms measures has repeatedly been told to the common people with the idea to justify the establishment of large and medium scale industries in the state. The argument is basically theoretical and involves a macro-economic logic that since land reforms have considerably ameliorated the economic condition of the rural mass, the state is now prepared to take on industrialisation for which a strong domestic market has already been created. The recent slogan of the LFG in West Bengal which says 'Agriculture is our foundation and the future lies in industry' nicely epitomises this macro-economic logic.

In this study an attempt has been made to test the afore mentioned macro-economic argument of the policy makers of the LFG in the context of Kharagpur block I in Paschim Medinipur district by using methods of anthropology and history. The findings have revealed that the establishment of industries through acquisition of private agricultural land primarily caused dispossession and disempowerment of the peasantry who initially put up resistances against the decision of the government. Furthermore, it is observed that land acquisition has deeper political consequences besides causing landlessness. It has not only pauperised the peasantry but also dampened the spirit of success achieved through land reforms by the dispossession of *pattaholders* and *bargadars*. The failure of the elected panchayat at the village as well as block levels to adopt any measure for mitigating the hardships encountered by the project affected persons has created a sense of helplessness and despondency among them. The case of the Century Textiles Company provides a glaring example. About 525 acres of fertile agricultural land was acquired in ten mouzas for this industry in April 1996. But no industry has been established till August 2001. The total failure of the panchayat leaders to re-establish the rights of the farmers on their land has further deteriorated their trust and faith upon the elected panchayats.

The detailed findings regarding the execution of the Land Acquisition Acts by the government administrastion at the district level revealed a basic contradiction between policy and practice. With the change of the policy of Government of West Bengal in the context of liberalisation, the demand for land has been increasing at a much faster rate, but there is little likelihood that the LA Department of Medinipur with its stupendous amount of pending work, poor infrastructural facilities and understaffed condition would be able to catch up with the ambition of the policy makers of the government operating from the modernised offices of the West Bengal Industrial Development Corporation at the state capital.

The debates and discussions in the State Assembly also exposed the poor condition of the Land Acquisiton Department particularly in the context of the unusual delay towards the payment of compensation to the landlosers. The Assembly proceedings brought out another interesting feature of land acquisition in West Bengal. No elected people's representative of West Bengal, irrespective of political affiliation has yet raised the issue of the impoverishment of peasants by land acquisition who were the direct beneficiaries of the land reforms process. For the elected members of the Legislative Assembly, debates around land acquisition for development projects was a routinised ritual. The members in opposition invariably criticised the West Bengal Land (Requisition and Acquisition) Act, 1948 at the time of its extension although never in the history of West Bengal had any political party placed a proposal of rehabilitation for project affected people for its incorporation in the Land Acquisition Act. The vibrant political culture of West Bengal still maintains a silence regarding modifications and/or radical changes in the colonial Land Acquisition Act.

With the above analysis and interpretation on the land acquisition process and the overall disempowerment of the poor peasants in Paschim Medinipur, we may now proceed to propose some policy recommendations regarding land acquisition in West Bengal. The recommendations are as follows:

1. Any generalised macro-level hypothesis regarding economic development should take into consideration the micro-level realities of the field of its application. That

land reform prepares the ground for industrialisation may be true in some specific situations but industrialisation without a down-to earth policy of rehabilitation through the generation of employment and skill development could be a self-defeating endeavour. The case of industrialisation in the Kalaikunda area has clearly demonstrated this self-defeating process.

2. The West Bengal Government should have a clear-cut policy regarding the acquisition of fertile agricultural land (whether monocrop or multicrop) for the establishment of industries. The government should explore all the possibilities of the establishment of industries on non-agricultural land and mention this with reasons in the Gazette notification, if acquisition of agricultural land becomes unavoidable. The gazette notification for land acquisition must mention the type of land (agricultural, non-agricultural wasteland, orchard, pond etc.) acquired for a particular project. And the State Government should publish a book from the Land and Land Reforms Department every year which would give the statistics on the type of land acquired by the government in each district for development projects. This would enable the government to evaluate its policy towards development.
3. Every case of land acquisition should be preceded by a socio-economic survey of the would-be affected people in collaboration with the local gram panchayat before the preparation of the preliminary enquiry report by the Land Acquisition Department. This survey should be specifically aimed to make a socio-economic impact assessment (SEIA) of the concerned development project (Ramanathan and Geetha 1999). The socio-economic impact assessment survey should first be cleared by the gram panchayat(s) and then forwarded to the District Land Acquisition Department for its placement in the screening committee. And this procedure should be made mandatory and incorporated in the LA Act by making necessary amendments in the State Legislative Assembly.

The gram panchayat and the panchayat samity should be legally empowered to reject any proposal for land acquisition within their jurisdiction by showing sufficient reasons. This amendment would also be well in line with the 73rd Amendment of the Indian Constitution which empowered the panchayats to the level of a self-government.

4. There should be a provision in the West Bengal Panchayat Act which would make it mandatory for the elected panchayats to give priority to PAPs within its area at the time of implementation of various poverty alleviation schemes by the panchayat. Here the project affected scheduled tribe and scheduled caste families should be given priority among all the DPs.
5. The existing method of calculation of monetary compensation for *bargadars* should be changed.The *bargadars* must be compensated by following the same principles of compensation calculation as it is being done in case of the owner of the land. The *bargadars* may be given 75 per cent or 50 per cent (as the specific case may be) of the compensation money awarded to the owner of the land. This would also considerably reduce the time which is now being taken by the LA Department to make payment to the *bargadars*. The payment of the landowner and the *bargadar* should be made at the same time (Guha 2006 a: 219-233).
6. There should be an arrangement for the payment of compensation to the unrecorded *bargadars* affected by land acquisition. If a genuine *bargadar* loses his/ her rights of cultivation over *barga* land due to acquisition, then it should be the responsibility of the government to arrange for the payment of compensation, since recording of the *bargadar* is the joint responsibility of the Block Land and Land Reforms Office and panchayat. Non-recording should not be regarded as a fault on the part of the *bargadar.*

7. Specific amendments in the LA Act should immediately be made with regard to cases of land acquisition where the acquired land has remained unutilised by the RB for more than one year. The rights of the owners of this type of land should be re-established without taking back the money which they had received as compensation. As they have failed to utilise the land, there is no point in paying back the money deposited by the RB (out of which compensation payment is made) in all these cases.
8. Since it is very difficult to identify all the persons and families who derive some benefits in terms of CPR from the acquired agricultural land, it would be better to make an approximate estimate of the said amount in monetary terms. For example, one can roughly calculate with the help of the villagers, the amount of straw eaten by the cattle through grazing in the agricultural fields during the post-harvest season when it becomes a CPR. The market price of this straw should be taken into consideration in the calculation of compensation after acquisition. But since this compensation cannot be paid to any individual landowner, it should be paid to the gram panchayat which would decide in its grassroots level meetings about the mode of expenditure of that money received as compensation for the destruction of its CPRs owing to the acquisition of land for development projects. Accordingly, the Land Acquisition Act should be amended to include the provision for the payment of *collective compensation* to the gram panchayat to be calculated in terms of the market value of the CPRs produced in the agricultural fields.The calculation of market value of various types of CPR should be a part of the planning process to be undertaken by the gram panchayats. If a gram panchayat in collaboration with the DPC, conducts surveys on the market value of CPRs produced in the agricultural fields under its jurisdiction, then it would be of use for the calculation of *collective compensation* at the time of their acquisition.

The foregoing discussion and policy recommendations which have emerged out of the last four chapters clearly reveal that an anthropological study of land acquisition in the context of West Bengal has theoretical, methodological and policy relevance.

The theoretical relevance of the study lies in examining the depeasantisation process in a macro-level perspective. With the help of this kind of study, one may look into the process of depeasantisation by incorporating documentary evidences from the legal and administrative wings of the state power along with field level data within a single framework.

The methodological relevance of this research follows from its theoretical orientation. In this study, micro-level field data have been combined with a variety of documentary evidences collected from the District Collectorate of erstwhile Medinipur and the library of West Bengal State Assembly to understand the constraints and dynamics of the land acquisition process. This kind of combination of archival materials for a short period (say 10-20 years) with that of first hand field data can also be made in the study of various policy related issues like forest management, land management, agricultural marketing etc.

The policy relevance of this study brings us to the frontier areas of applied anthropology wherein the researcher can start a fruitful dialogue with the policy makers and administrators. Unless the researcher is equipped with all the details and nuances of land acquisition, the mere collection of data on displacement from the field may not pave the way towards a constructive and meaningful exchange with the administrators and policy makers. The suggested recommendations on the reforms about land acquisition process could be a begining towards that exchange.

Appendices

APPENDIX—A

Patriculars of Gazette Notification for Land Acquisition in Erstwhile Medinipur District During 1991-97

Sl. No.	*Notice/ Declaration Nos.*	*Date*	*Location*	*Amount (in acre)*	*Section(s) of the Act*	*Purpose*	*Gazette publ. date*
Midnapore							
1.	6908L.A./ 5C-51/91/C& I	4 Nov. 1991	Latibpur, J.L.-113, P.S. KGP, Mid	6.30	Requisitioned under Sub-sec.3 of the W.B. Land(Req. and Acq.)Act, 1948 by the persons authorised under section 3(1A) of the Act.	Establishment of Commercial and industrial estates for setting up Pig-Iron project.	7 Nov. 1991
2.	6907 LA(II)/ 5C-50/91/C& I	-do-	Latibpur 113	7.01	-do-	-do-	-do-
3.	6909 LA(II)/ 5C-49/91/ C&I	-do-	-do-	5.85	-do-	-do-	-do-
4.	6905 LA(II)/ 5C-48/91/ C&I	-do-	-do-	6.26	-do-	-do-	-do-
5.	6904 LA(II)/ 5C-47/91/ C&I	-do-	-do-	6.32	-do-	-do-	-do-
6.	6903 LA(II)/ 51-46/91/ C&I	-do-	-do-	6.45	-do-	-do-	-do-
7.	6902 LA(II)/ 5C-43/91/ C&I	-do-	-do-	5.78	-do-	-do-	-do-

Contd.....

Sl. No.	Notice/ Declaration Nos.	Date	Location	Amount (in acre)	Section(s) of the Act	Purpose	Gazette publ. date
8.	6901 LA(II)/ 5C-44/91/ C&I	-do-	-do-	6.49	-do-	-do-	-do-
9.	6900 LA(II)/ 5C-43/91/ C&I	-do-	-do-	6.04	-do-	-do-	-do-
10.	7024 LA(II)/ 5C-52/91/C&I	18 Nov. 1991	Prithimpur 117 P.S. KGP, Mid	5.97	-do-	-do-	19 Nov. 1991
11.	7023 LA(II)/ 5C-61/91/ C&I	-do-	Ashapur 118 P.S. KGP Mid.	6.41	-do-	-do-	-do-
12.	7022 LA(II)/ 5C-60/91/ C&I	-do-	-do-	5.92	-do-	-do-	-do-
13.	7021 LA(II)/ 5C-59/91/ C&I	-do-	-do-	6.19	-do-	-do-	-do-
14.	7020 LA(II)/ 5C-58/91/ C&I	-do-	-do-	7.32	-do-	-do-	-do-
15.	7019 LA(II)/ 5C-57/91/ C&I	-do-	-do-	6.14	-do-	-do-	-do-
16.	7018 LA(II)/ 5C-56/91/ C&I	-do-	Amba 115 P.S. KGP	5.21	-do-	-do-	-do-
17.	7017 LA(II)/ 5C-55/91/ C&I	-do-	-do-	5.25	-do-	-do-	-do-
18.	7016 LA(II)/ 5C-54/91/ C&I	-do-	Prithimpur 117	5.91	-do-	-do-	-do-
19.	7015 LA(II)/ 5C-53/91/ C&I	-do-	-do-	5.88	-do-	-do-	-do-

Contd....

Sl. No.	*Notice/ Declaration Nos.*	*Date*	*Location*	*Amount (in acre)*	*Section(s) of the Act*	*Purpose*	*Gazette publ. date*
20.	5167 LA(II)/ 1M-97/91	27 Aug. 1991	Kasbera J.L.146, P.S. Sutahata, Mid.	4.06	Sub-sec (1) of section 3 of W.B. Land (Req and Acq.) Act, 1948 by the person etc. under sec. 3(1A)	Establishment of industrial and commercial estates setting of small, medium and large scale industries.	-do-
21.	5582 LA(PW)/ II-77/91/I&W	17 Sept. 1991	Jagannath-bati 129	0.735	-do-	Providing proper facilities for irrigation and drainage namely relieving the drainage problem of Anchal 3 of Daspur I Block.	-do-
22.	5588 LA(II)/2R-14/91/Transport	-do-	Brajalalchak 81 Nandigram PS, Mid.	9.27	-do-	Providing facilities for transport and communication namely for construction of Tamluk-Digha Broad gauge (B.G.) Railway Line.	-do-
23.	6708 LA(II)/2R-15/91/Transport	26 Sept. 1991	Saripur 92	5.64	-do-	-do-	-do-

Contd....

Sl. No.	Notice/ Declaration Nos.	Date	Location	Amount (in acre)	Section(s) of the Act	Purpose	Gazette publ. date
24.	6858LA (P.W)	30 Oct. 1991	Bhabanipur 150, P.S.Sutahata, Mid.	0.79	-do-	Providing facilities for transport and communication namely for construction of Link Road from NH6 to Haldia Port (NH41).	-do-
25.	6977 LA (P.W)/ 11-125/91/I&W	12 Nov. 1991	Natsal 157, P.S. Mahisadal, Mid.	4.58	-do-	Providing facilities for irrigation and drainage, namely, for strenghtening the Doro Schedule 'D' embankment.	-do-
26.	8280 LA(II)/ 5C-80/91/C&I	23 Dec.1991	Amba 115, P.S. KGP, Mid.	5.39	-do-	Industrial estate for setting up pig-iron project.	26 Dec. 1991
27.	8282 LA(II)/ 5C-79/91/C&I	-do-	Amba 115	5.42	-do-	-do-	-do-
28.	8284 LA(II)/ 5C-78/91/C&I	-do-	Prithimpur 117	5.53	-do-	-do-	-do-
29.	8286 LA(II)/ 5C-77/91/C&I	-do-	Latibpur 113	6.75	-do-	-do-	-do-
30.	8288 LA(II)/ 5C-76/91/C&I	-do-	Mathura-Kismat 114 P.S. KGP, Mid.	6.40	-do-	-do-	-do-

Contd....

Sl. No.	Notice/ Declaration Nos.	Date	Location	Amount (in acre)	Section(s) of the Act	Purpose	Gazette publ. date
31.	8290 LA(II)/ 5C-47/91/C&I	-do-	Mathura-Kismat	7.74	-do-	-do-	-do-
32.	8292 LA(II)/ 5C-73/91/C&I	-do-	Mathura-Kismat	6.57	-do-	-do-	-do-
33.	8294 LA(II0)/ 5C-72/91/C&I	-do-	Prithimpur, 117 P.S. KGP Mid.	6.07	-do-	-do-	-do-
34.	5586 LA(II)/2R-12/91/Transport	17 Sept. 1991	Thakurnagar 134, Khejuri PS, Mid.	6.695	-do-	Provinding facilities for transport and communication namely for Const. of Tamluk Digha B.G. Rail Line.	-do-
35.	6706 LA(II)/2R-11/91/Transport	26 Sept. 1991	Thakurnagar 134, Khejuri PS.,Mid.	6.26	-do-	-do-	-do-
36.	162-LA(II)/3M-1/92/Dec. and Planning	17 Jan. 1992	Jagibasan 93, Maitrapur 94, Mirjapur,95, Mukundapur 211, Begundiha 221, Digha 213, Jhawa-216, Nilpur 223, Chota Balarampur 214, Roypur 215, in P.S. Digha, Mid. And Jhangerya 207,	2027.64 + 3139.35 = 5166.99	Sec. 4 of the L.A. Act, 1894— (Act I of 1894)	Development of Tourist infrastructure	1 Feb. 1992

Contd....

Sl. No.	Notice/ Declaration Nos.	Date	Location	Amount (in acre)	Section(s) of the Act	Purpose	Gazette publ. date
			Kiageria 217, Balarampur 222, Joshipur 228, Birampur 225, Bodhora 234, Tengramdri 235, Bherichauli 239, Jaldha 242, Sankarpur 224, Dalbaldya 220, Panch Daria 221, Lachhimpur 219, Kaema 236, Jamra Shyampur 218, Chandpur 237, P.S. Ramnagar, Mid.				
37.	245LA(II)/ 5C-87/91/C&I	22 Jan. 1992	Mathurakismat 114, P.S. KGP, Mid.	6.03	Sub-sec(1) of Sec. 3 of W.B	Pig Iron Project	3 Feb. 1992
38.	244 LA(II)/ 5C-86/91/C&I	-do-	-do-	6.26	-do-	-do-	-do-
39.	243 LA(II)/ 5C-84/91/C&I	-do-	-do-	6.36	-do-	-do-	-do-
40.	242 LA(II)/ 5C-85/91/C&I	-do-	-do-	6.31	-do-	-do-	-do-

Contd....

Sl. No.	Notice/ Declaration Nos.	Date	Location	Amount (in acre)	Section(s) of the Act	Purpose	Gazette publ. date
41.	241 LA(II)/ 5C-41/91/C&I	22 Jan. 1992	-do-	6.56	-do-	-do-	3 Feb. 1992
42.	106 LA(II)/ 1M-137/91/ Dec. and Planning T and CP	10 Jan. 1992	Kasbere 146, P.S. Sutahata, Mid.	1.35	-do-	Comm. and Indus. estate setting up of small, middle and large industries (Haldia Petro Chemical down stream industries).	10 Feb. 1992
43.	8350 LA(PW)/ 11-105/91/I&W	31 Dec. 1991	Kishoripur, 339, P.S. Binpur, Mid.	6.74	-do-	Providing facilities for irrigation and drainage, namely, for Excavation of Minor 4 of D-IR of Tarafani South Main Canal	-do-
44.	5592 LA(PW)/ 11-106/11/I&W	17 Sept. 1991	Sealdanga, 416, P.S. Binpur, Mid.	4.505	-do-	Providing facilities for irrigation and drainage, namely for excavation of water-course.	-do-
45.	5580 LA(PW)/ 11-107/91/I&W	-do-	Jambdahri,123 P.S. Binpur, Mid.	6.205	-do-	Providing facilities for irrigation and drainage.	-do-

Contd....

Sl. No.	Notice/ Declaration Nos.	Date	Location	Amount (in acre)	Section(s) of the Act	Purpose	Gazette publ. date
46.	239 LA(PW)/ 11-52/91/I&W	22 Jan. 1992	Jamrasuli 331, P.S. Binpur, Mid.	13.91	-do-	-do-	-do-
47.	5594 LA(PW)/ MDP/11-108/ 91/I&W	17 Sept. 1991	Belda, 210	0.415	-do-	Providing facilities for irrigation and drainage, namely for Telkarai Minor irrigation scheme DPAP	21 March 1992
48.	8352 LA(II)/ 4B-16/91/ Transport	31 Dec.1991	Mahatabpur, 178, P.S. Mid. Dist. Mid.	0.31	-do-	Providing facilities for transport and communication namely for construction of Bus-Depot.-cum-Bus Terminus by S.B.S.T.C.	-do-
49.	670 LA(II)/2R-1/ 92/Transport	6 March 1992	Khagda, 107, P.S. Nandigram, Mid.	21.89	-do-	Providing facilities for transport and communication namely, for construction of Tamluk Digha B.G. Rly. Line.	27 April 1992

Contd....

Sl. No.	Notice/ Declaration Nos.	Date	Location	Amount (in acre)	Section(s) of the Act	Purpose	Gazette publ. date
50.	5 LA(II)/Spl/I&W	27 April 1992	Gopalchak, 167, P.S.Mahisadal, Mid.	0.20	-do-	Maintain supplies and services essential to the life of the construction of Haldia water supply scheme.	29 April 1992
51.	7 LA(II)/Spl/ Transport	-do-	Jalpai, 70, P.S. Mahisadal, Mid.	2.22	-do-	Transport and communication for const. & Tamluk Digha B.G. Rly. Line.	-do-
52.	9 LA(II)/Spl/ Transport	-do-	-do-	12.65	-do-	-do-	-do-
53.	11LA(II)/Spl/ Transport	-do-	-do-	0.995	-do-	-do-	-do-
54.	13 LA(II)/Spl/ Transport	-do-	-do-	0.48	-do-	-do-	-do-
55.	15 LA(II)/Spl/ Transport	-do-	Kandapasra, 42 P.S. Nandigram, Mid.	8.76	-do-	-do-	-do-
56.	17 LA(II)/Spl/ Transport	-do-	Jalpai, 70 R.S. Mahisadal, Mid.	0.71	-do-	Const. of Tamluk-Digha B.G. Rly. Line	-do-

Contd....

Sl. No.	*Notice/ Declaration Nos.*	*Date*	*Location*	*Amount (in acre)*	*Section(s) of the Act*	*Purpose*	*Gazette publ. date*
57.	19 LA(II)/Spl/ I&W	-do-	Betkundu 164, P.S. Mahisadal, Mid.	0.24	-do-	Supplies and services essential to the life of the community namely, for const. & Haldia water supply scheme.	-do-
58.	21 LA(II)/Spl/ I & W	-do-	Bajitpur, 43, P.S. Sutahata, Mid.	0.17	-do-	-do-	-do-
59.	23 LA(II)Spl/ I&W	-do-	Gopalchak, 167, P.S. Mahisadal, Mid.	0.70	-do-	-do-	-do-
60.	25 LA(II)/Spl/ Transport	-do-	Kandapasra, 42	9.335	-do-	Transport and communication for const. of Tamluk-Digha B.G. Rly. Line.	-do-
61.	27 LA(II)/Spl/ Transport	-do-	Chandipur, 96	4.5825	-do-	-do-	-do-
62.	6630 LA(PW)/ II-89/91/I&W	19.9.91	Harirampur, 183	3.75	-do-	Irrigation and drainage namely, for the upper reaches of Kherai Khal in connection with Kherai Boxi Bashin drainage scheme.	15.5.92

Contd....

Sl. No.	*Notice/ Declaration Nos.*	*Date*	*Location*	*Amount (in acre)*	*Section(s) of the Act*	*Purpose*	*Gazette publ. date*
63.	221/LA/Spl/ Transport	28.4.92	Mahatabpur, 178, P.S. Mid. (Sadar), Mid.	0.39	-do-	Maintenance of supplies and services essential to the life of the community namely, setting up a depot-cum-terminal for long dist. buses of S.B.S.T.C.	13.8.92
64.	59 LA(II)/ Spl/PHE	27.4.92	Simul Kundu 227	0.10	-do-	Maintaining of suppiles and services essential to the life of the community namely, for construction of pump house sinking of 2nd tubewell etc.	13.8.92
65.	1563 LA(II)/2R-5/ 92/Tr. Deptt.	30.5.92	Thakur Nagar 134, P.S. Khejuri, Mid.	6.17	-do-	Const. of Tamluk-Digha Rly. Line.	4.9.92
66.	2149L A(II)2R-13/92/Transport	27.7.92	Kismat-Bajkul, 156, P.S. Bhagwanpur, Mid.	5.77	-do-	-do-	-do-
67.	2208 LA(II)/2R-8/ 92/Transport	30.7.92	Dakshin Gobindachak, 129	9.98	-do-	-do-	2.9.92

Contd....

Sl. No.	Notice/ Declaration Nos.	Date	Location	Amount (in acre)	Section(s) of the Act	Purpose	Gazette publ. date
68.	8348 LA(II)/2R-22/91/Transport	31.12.91	Bikramnagar, 132, P.S. Khejuri	9.42	Sub-sec.(1) of Sec. 3 of W.B.(Req. and Acq.) Act, 1948	Const. of Tamluk Digha B.G. Rly. Line.	4.9.92
69.	169 LA(II)/ SPL/I&W	28.4.92	Dubdi, 191, PS. Egra, Mid.	12.69	-do-	Irrigation, drainage namely, re-excavation of Ropper Kudi of inner channel of Dubda-Swamp.	15.9.92
70.	171 LA(II)/ Spl/I&W	-do-	Dubda, 191, P.S. Egra, Mid.	13.41	-do-	Facilities for drainage namely, re-excavation of Balighai Khal in connection with Dubda basin drainage scheme	-do-
71.	2364 LA(II)/2R-16/92/Transport	18.8.92	Maklasi, 232, P.S. Bhagwanpur, Mid.	4.95	-do-	Const. of Tamluk Digha B.G. Rly. Line.	30.9.92
72.	2366 LA(II)/2R-II/92/Transport Deptt.	-do-	Tethibari, 153, P.S. Bhagwanpur	12.11	-do-	-do-	-do-
73.	2368 LA(II)/2R-15/92/Transport	-do-	Narayanbari, 152, P.S. Bhagwanpur	0.63	-do-	-do-	-do-

Contd....

Sl. No.	Notice/ Declaration Nos.	Date	Location	Amount (in acre)	Section(s) of the Act	Purpose	Gazette publ. date
74.	2360 LA(II)/ 2R-17/92/Tr.	18.8.92	Tethibari, 153, P.S. Bhagwanpur Mid.	1.89	-do-	-do-	30.9.92
75.	2354 LA(II)/ 24-9/92/Tr.	-do-	Jaranagar, 128, P.S. Khejuri, Mid.	10.59	-do-	-do-	30.9.92
76.	105 LA(II)/ Spl/(Power)	28.4.92	Purbabahala 302, P.S. Panskura, Mid.	4.87	-do-	Maintaining supplies and services essential to the life of the community namely, Const. of Ash Pond No. 4 for K.T.P.P.	16.11.92
77.	2720 LA(II)/ IM-110/92	15.9.92	Bardhanyaghata, 172, P.S. Sutahata	8.57	-do-	Small, medium and large industries (Haldia Petro-chemical) Downstream industries.	-do-
78.	2362 LA(II)/ 2R-19/92/Tr.	18.8.92	Chakbasudevpur 45	16.715	-do-	Facilities for transport and communication, namely, for construction of Tamluk-Digha B.G. Rly. Line.	-do-
79.	97 LA(II)/Spl/ (Power)	28.4.92	Amalnara, 291, P.S. Panskura	0.26	-do-	Const. of Rly. Infrastructure for KTPP stage II	-do-

Contd....

Sl. No.	*Notice/ Declaration Nos.*	*Date*	*Location*	*Amount (in acre)*	*Section(s) of the Act*	*Purpose*	*Gazette publ. date*
80.	2819 LA(PW)/ IM-128/92	24.9.92	Inda, 232, P.S. Kharagpur	0.7135	-do-	Kharagpur Water Supply Augmention scheme.	27.11.92
81.	3194 LA(II)/ SC-21/92/C&I	17.11.92	Latibpur 113, P.S. KGP	0.42	-do-	Increasing employment opportunities by establishing industrial estates and purpose connected therewith and incidental thereto namely, for setting up of pig-iron project.	1.12.92
82.	201 LA(II)/Spl./ Transport	28.4.92	Sarifabad, 145, P.S. Panskura	0.615	-do-	Providing proper facilities for transport viz. Const. of Ratulia to Gobardhanpur Road via Haur Rly. Stn. Rd.	8.1.93
83.	2356 LA(II)/2R-10/92/Transport	18.8.92	Tethibari, 153, P.S. Bhagwanpur	8.22	-do-	Tamluk-Digha B.G. Rly. Line.	30.1.93
84.	119 LA(II)/SC-23/ 92/C&I	13.1.93	Mathura Kismat 114, P.S.KGP	7.02	-do-	Pig-Iron Project.	-do-

Contd....

Sl. No.	Notice/ Declaration Nos.	Date	Location	Amount (in acre)	Section(s) of the Act	Purpose	Gazette publ. date
85.	3410 LA(PW)/ IIM-B4/92	17.12.92	Sonamukhi, 188	0.88	-do-	Augmention of water supply scheme for KGP municipality.	24.2.93
86.	470 LA(II)/SC-22/92/C&I	17.2.93	Mathura Kismat, 114	9.065	-do-	Pig-Iron project.	16.3.93
87.	2358 LA(II)/2R-12/92/Transport	18.8.92	Jarar Nagar, 128	8.775	-do-	Tamluk Digha, B.G Rly. Line.	12.7.93
88.	1401 LA(II)/ 4B-3/88	7.5.93	Keranitola, 171, P.S. Mid.	1.84	Sec.4 of LA Act 1894	Const. of Settlement Head qtrs. Office at Midnapore in the village of Keranitola.	30.9.93
89.	1945 LA(II)/IM-39/93/UD	6.7.93	Bardhanyaghata 172, Sutahata PS	0.08	Sub-sec.(I) of Sec. 3 of W.B. Land (Req. and Acq.) Act, 1948.	Comm. and indus estates in diff. areas namely, for Haldia Petro-chemicals projects.	-do-
90.	1941 LA(II)/PW-IM-37/93/UD	-do-	Paranchak, 145, Sutahata PS	0.39	-do-	-do-	-do-
91.	1943 LA(II)/ IM-39/93/UD	-do-	Kismat Dhanya Ghata 173 Sutahata	0.255	-do-	-do-	-do-
92.	1939 LA(II)/ IM-36/93/UD	-do-	Bardhanyaghata 172 P.S. Sutahata	0.52	-do-	-do-	-do-

Contd....

Sl. No.	Notice/ Declaration Nos.	Date	Location	Amount (in acre)	Section(s) of the Act	Purpose	Gazette publ. date
93.	748 LA(II)/IM-164/92/C&I	11.3.93	Debhog, 149, Sutahata PS, Mid	1.7425	-do-	Commercial estates and industrial estates for setting up small, medium and large industries, Haldia Petro-chemical/Down stream industries.	30.7.93
94.	2097 LA(PW)/ IM-49/97/Power	26.7.93	Torapara 189 Mid. PS	22.20	-do-	Const. of 220/132KV power sub-station of W.B.S.E.B.	-do-
95.	1846LA(II)	29.6.93	Dogechhya 446	2.98	-do-	Const. of 33/11KV sub-station of W.B.S.E.B.	-do-
96.	31 LA(II)/ Spl/I&W	27.4.92	Nandigram 180	6.00	-do-	Establishment of a P.H.C. at Nandigram-I Block, Mid by conversion of Zilla Parishad dispensary.	4.8.93
97.	53 LA(II)/Spl/ Transport	-do-	Nor, 39 Nandigram	0.49	-do-	Const. of Rd. from Narghat to Gokhari Health Centre, P.S. Nandakumar.	-do-

Contd....

Sl. No.	Notice/ Declaration Nos.	Date	Location	Amount (in acre)	Section(s) of the Act	Purpose	Gazette publ. date
98.	1947 LA (PW)/ IM-40/93/VD	6.7.93	Tentul Bere 170 Sutahata	0.46	-do-	Comm. and Indust. estates namely, for Haldia Petro-chemicals Project.	4.8.93
99.	209 LA(II)/Spl/ H & FW	28.4.92	Anantapur, 108, P.S. Tamluk, Mid.	3.225	-do-	Establishmnt of P.H.C.	20.8.93
100.	1449 LA(II)/ IM28/93/C&I	7.5.93	Debhog, 149, P.S. Sutahata	6.4475	-do-	Comm. and indust. estates for setting up small, medium and large industries (HPC down streamn Indus.).	-do-
101.	1455 LA(II)/ IM-23/93/C&I	-do-	-do-	6.56	-do-	-do-	-do-
102.	2019 LA(PW)/ IM-53/93/MA	23.7.93	Padumbasan, 144, P.S.Tamluk	0.68	-do-	Water Supply augmentation scheme	23.8.93
103.	2101 LA(PW)/ IM-60/93/UD	26.7.93	Brajanathchak, 196, PS Sutahata	13.18	-do-	Establishment of housing and comme-rcial zone within the Haldia Notified area.	-do-
104.	2188 LA(PW)/ IM-62/92/UD	4.8.93	-do-	10.96	-do-	-do-	-do-
105.	2099 LA(PW)/ IM-58/93/UD	26.7.93	-do-	15.87	-do-	-do-	-d0-

Contd....

Sl. No.	Notice/ Declaration Nos.	Date	Location	Amount (in acre)	Section(s) of the Act	Purpose	Gazette publ. date
106.	2186 LA(PW)/ IM-53/93/UD	4.8.93	-do-	13.54	-do-	-do-	23.8.93
107.	91 LA(Spl)/I&W	28.4.92	Doyarkhal, 45, P.S. KGP Mid.	20.73	-do-	Proper facilities for irrigation, drainage of Tarafeni south main canal (South).	26.8.93
108.	223 LA(II)/ Spl/Tr.	-do-	Sekhpura, 172, P.S. Mid.	0.02	-do-	Const. of Narendralal Khan Rd. at the Junction of Keranitola PS	-do-
109.	59 LA(PW)/II-89/92/I&W	7.1.93	Barmritberia, 55	0.75	-do-	Irrigation and drainage viz. for strenghtening of Rup. Right Embankment.	3.9.93
110.	2425 LA(II)/4B-18/91/Board of Rev.	30.8.93	Changsole, 427 and Bhalkuri, 428	7.59	-do-	Const. of state level Analysis Research and Training Centre.	10.9.93
111.	2543 LA(II)/5C-25/93/C&I	13.9.93	Sadatpur, 89, PS KGP	2.85	-do-	Establishment of Indust. Estates.	15.9.93
112.	756 LA(PW)/ II-14/93/I&W	11.3.93	Nekragudri 18, Gopiballavpur	6.32	-do-	Irrigation and drainage viz. for Jhil Khal irrigation scheme.	-do-

Contd....

Sl. No.	Notice/ Declaration Nos.	Date	Location	Amount (in acre)	Section(s) of the Act	Purpose	Gazette publ. date
113.	2216 LA(PW)/ II-53/93/I&W	4.8.93	Uttar Dalhara, 80, P.S. Tamluk	1.39	-do-	Irrigation and drainage viz. for making ring Bundh.	15.9.93
114.	121 LA(II)/ PHE	13.1.93	Dipa, 84, Keshiary	0.39	-do-	Const. of Keshiary Kulboni O.D.R.	24.9.93
115.	2393 LA(II)/PHE	25.8.93	Khoridanagar 266, P.S. Tamluk	0.10	-do-	For 2nd tubewell site under piped water supply scheme for Simulia and its adjoining mouza.	30.9.93
116.	141 LA(II)/Spl/Tr	28.4.92	Amlatania, 241, P.S. KGP	2.785	-do-	Transport/Communication viz. Jhapatapur Kashijora.	12.10.93
117.	3408 LA(PW)/II-39/92/I&W	15.12.92	Dengasole, 343, P.S. Jhargram	4.39	-do-	Irrigation and drainage viz. for excavation of minor and for Kangsabati Reservoir Project	-do-
118.	147 LA(PW)/II-45/92/I&W	15.1.93	Jangalkhar 395 Jhargram P.S.	0.10	-do-	Making banking in connection with Kangsabati Reservoir project.	-do-

Contd....

Sl. No.	*Notice/ Declaration Nos.*	*Date*	*Location*	*Amount (in acre)*	*Section(s) of the Act*	*Purpose*	*Gazette publ. date*
119.	89 LA(II)/ Spl/I&W	28.4.92	Chandipur, 222 P.S. Pingla	4.16	W.B.Act 1948	Irrigation and drainage for E.D.R. and breach closing to Gokulnagar Moyna embankment	21.10.93
120.	2578 LA(PW)/ IM-65/93/Power	14.9.93	Rakshachak 293, P.S. Panskura	1.565	-do-	Const. of Ash pipeline of KTPP stage II.	-do-
121.	2190 LA(PW)/ IM-21/93/UD	4.8.93	Debhog, 149, P.S. Sutahata	10.13	-do-	Transport, viz. for establishment of Truck Terminal at Haldia.	5.11.93
122.	2192 LA(PW)	-do-	Keshpore, 148, Sutahata	1.43	-do-	Comm. and Indus. Estates for setting up small, medium and large scale industries.	-do-
123.	2811 LA(II)/ IM-112/92	24.9.92	Debhog, 149	9.11	-do-	Small, medium and large scale industries, Haldia Petro-chemicals/ Down stream industries.	-do-
124.	744 LA(II)/ IM-163/92/C&I	11.3.93	Bordhanyaghata Part I, 172, P.S. Sutahata	0.35	-do-	-do-	-do-

Contd....

Sl. No.	*Notice/ Declaration Nos.*	*Date*	*Location*	*Amount (in acre)*	*Section(s) of the Act*	*Purpose*	*Gazette publ. date*
125.	921 LA(PW)/ II-19/93/I&W	24.3.93	Posda, 348, P.S. Binpur	1.355	-do-	Irrigation and drainage for Kangsabati Reservoir Project.	12.11.93
126.	1444 LA(PW)/ II-17/93/I&W	7.5.93	Baramechhua, 205, P.S. Binpur	5.525	-do-	-do-	-do-
127.	1620 LA(PW)/ II-24/93/I&W	31.5.93	Ghagra, 718, P.S. Binpur	6.44	-do-	Irrigation and drainage	-do-
128.	861 LA(PW)/ II-62/91	19.3.93	Jhingasol, 267, P.S. Binpur	12.735	-do-	-do-	-do-
129.	1055 LA(PW)/ II-20/81/I&W	15.4.93	Bhalaidiha, 218, P.S.Binpur	1.70	-do-	Irrigation in connection with Kangsbati Reservoir Project.	-do-
130.	3049 LA(PW)/ II-99/92/I&W	19.10.93	Jagul, 281, P.S. Midnapore	7.215	-do-	Irrigation and drainage for Kalai Chandi Khal Drainage scheme.	-do-.
131.	2580 LA(PW)/ II-27/93/I&W	14.9.93	Kalikapur, 256, P.S. Tamluk	0.555	-do-	Irrigation and drainage for re-excavation of Sankararah Khal in conn with drainage scheme of Tamluk Aru.	-do-

Contd....

Sl. No.	Notice/ Declaration Nos.	Date	Location	Amount (in acre)	Section(s) of the Act	Purpose	Gazette publ. date
132.	211 LA(II)/ Spl/Tr.	28.4.92	Kushalpur, 24, P.S. Nandigram	4.935	-do-	Transport and communication const. of road from Narghat-Gokuri Health Centre in P.S. Nandigram.	3.12.93
133. PHE	63 LA(II)/Spl/	27.4.92 P.S.Tamluk	Kulberia, 274,	0.055	-do- tubewell and pump	Const. of 1 No. 93 house under Uttar Sonamukhi W/S Scheme.	17.12.93
134.	3109 LA(PW)	3.11.93	Khodambari. 131, P.S.Nandigram	0.76	-do-	Const. 8 Nandigram Chandipur Rd. Via Reyapara.	29.12.93
135.	83 LA(II)/ Spl/I&W	28.4.92	Dakshin Kuchaipur	1.93	-do-	Irrigation Embankment in P.S. Moyna and Pingla.	-do-
136.	2986 LA(PW)/ IM-100/93	12.10.93	Jharia, 208, P.S.KGP	3.05	-do-	Augmentation of water supply scheme KGP municipality.	7.1.94
137.	2862 LA(PW)/ II-90/93/I&W	4.10.93	Naichanpur, 250, P.S.Moyna	1.22	-do-	Irrigation and drainage in connection with Moyna Basin Scheme.	13.1.94

Contd....

Sl. No.	Notice/ Declaration Nos.	Date	Location	Amount (in acre)	Section(s) of the Act	Purpose	Gazette publ. date
138.	3579 LA(PW)/ II-103/93/I&W	17.12.93	Bar Amritberia, 55 P.S. Mahisadal	0.40	-do-	M/R to Rup. R.E. Scheme Embktt.	28.1.94
139.	3251 LA(II)/ 2R-13/93/Tr.	22.11.93	Bikramnagar, 132, P.S. Khejuri	8.89	-do-	Const. of Tamluk Digha, B.G. Rly. Line.	-do-
140.	2964 LA(II)/ Tr. /2R-3/93	4.10.93	Krishnanagar, 123, P.S. Khejuri	10.87	-do-	-do-	-do-
141.	3577 LA(PW)/ II/101/93/I&W	17.12.93	Dinabandhupur, 165, P.S.Nandigram	1.38	-do-	Irrigation and drainage Cnst. of retired embankment.	10.2.94
142.	3571 LA(PW)/ II-99/93/I&W	-do-	Kendamarijalpai, 189, P.S. Nandigram	0.51	-do-	Irrigation and drainage for Kendamari Sonachura Reclamation scheme	-do-
143.	3498 LA9(II)/ 2R-12/93/Trans.	15.12.93	Jararnagar, 128, P.S. Khejuri	0.96	-do-	Const. of Tamluk Digha, Rly. Line.	-do-
144.	3575LA(PW)/ II/100/93/I&W	17.12.93	Jalpai, Part-I, 111, P.S. Nandigram	2.93	-do-	Irrigation and drainage for Doniakhal	
145.	5584 LA(PW)/	17.9.91	Erashol, 90, P.S. Nandigram	8.315	-do-	Const. of Nandigram Chandipur Rd. via Reyapara	-do-
146.	3410 LA(PW)/ IM-134/92	17.12.92	Sonamukhi, 188, P.S. KGP	0.88	-do-	Augmentation of water supply scheme for KGP municipality.	30.1.93

Contd....

Sl. No.	Notice/ Declaration Nos.	Date	Location	Amount (in acre)	Section(s) of the Act	Purpose	Gazette publ. date
147.	241 LA(PW)/ IM-46/93/Power	28.1.94	Maldah, 25, P.S. Khejuri	4.41	-do-	Const. of 33 KV sub station of W.B.S.E.B.	11.3.94
148.	659 LA(PW)/ IM-18/94/C&I	11.3.94	Kismatdhanya ghata, 173, P.S. Sutahata	0.18	-do-	Comm. and Indus. estates for Haldia Petro-chemical Project	18.3.94
149.	657 LA(PW)/ IM-16/94/C&I	11.3.94	Tentulberia, 170 P.S.Sutahata	0.78	-do-	Comm. and Indus. estates viz. for Haldia Petrochem Project.	-do-
150.	668 LA(PW)/ IM-136/91/PHE	6.3.92	Jangalkhas, 390, P.S. Jhargram	0.79	-do-	Jhargram Comprehensive water supply scheme.	-do-
151.	777 LA(PW)/ IM-17/94/C&I	22.3.94	Poranchak 145, Sutahata P.S.	18.7.05	-do-	Comm. and Indus. estates for setting up Haldia Petrochem Complex.	25.3.94
152.	313 LA(II)/ 4F-7/93	31.1.94	Sarda, 381, P.S. Contai	2.01	-do-	Establishment of Block seed Fram at P.S. Contai II Dev Block.	31.3.94
153.	627 LA(PW)/ Power	9.3.94	Rampur, 115, P.S.Bhangwanpur	3.30	-do-	Const. of 33/11KV sub-station of Bhagwanpur.	21.4.94

Contd....

Sl. No.	Notice/ Declaration Nos.	Date	Location	Amount (in acre)	Section(s) of the Act	Purpose	Gazette publ. date
154.	774 LA(PW)/ 2R-14/94	22.3.94	Padumbasan, 144, P.S. Tamluk	0.01	-do-	Const. of a link road from Tamluk to NH 41 along the bank of Sankarara Khal.	-do-
155.	629 LA(II)/ 5C-36/93/C&I	9.3.94	Dhekia, 135, P.S. KGP	11.615 (waste and arable land)	L.A. Act by 1894 (I of 1894) Sec. R	Const. of Housing Complex for the Employees of Tata Metaliks.	-do-
156.	918 LA(PW)/ IM-40/94	31.3.94	Bardhanyaghata, 172	0.41	W.B. Land (Req. Acq.) Act, 1948	Haldia Petrochem project.	-do-
157.	205 LA(II)/ SPL/I&W	28.4.92	Purusattampur, 24, P.S. Egra	0.79	-do-	Water supply scheme for Kasba, Egra and adjoining mouzas	2.5.94
158.	195 LA(II)/ Spl/I&W	28.4.92	Mohanpur, 191, P.S. Panškura	0.39	-do-	Proper facilities for drainage of viz. for Kharai Buxi basin Drainage scheme in P.S.Panskura.	-do-
159.	187 LA(II)/ SPL/I&W	28.4.92	Purul 143, P.S. Panskura	0.03	-do-	Const. of Ratulia Gobordhanpur Rd.	13.5.94
160.	2206 LA(PW)/ II-35/92/I&W	30.7.92	Nekragudri, 18, P.S.Gopiballavpur	0.56	-do-	Irrigation and drainage viz. for Jhilikhal irrigation scheme.	-do-

Contd....

Sl. No.	Notice/ Declaration Nos.	Date	Location	Amount (in acre)	Section(s) of the Act	Purpose	Gazette publ. date
161.	1453 LA(PW)/ LR-30/91	7.5.93	Agarpara, 105, P.S. Keshiary	6.505	-do-	Trans. and Comm. viz Const of Keshiary Kulboni O.D.R	18.5.94
162.	229 LA(II)/ SPL/SI&W	28.4.92	Durlavganj, 465, P.S. Garbeta	0.44	-do-	Establishment of milk chilling plant	-do-
163.	1215 LA(II)/ IM-66/94/Power	13.5.94	Bastia, 35, P.S. Egra	1.32	-do-	Installation of 132 KV sub-station of W.B.S.E.B.	-do-
164.	219 LA(II)/ Spl/I&W	28.4.92	Kalai, 190, P.S. Panskura	0.86	-do-	For drainage of Kharai Buxi Basin Drainage scheme	-do-
165.	49 LA(II)/Spl/ Transport	27.4.92	Santeswarpur, 8, P.S. Ramnagar	2.23	-do-	Const. of Depal-Juki (Mirgoda Market) on Egra-Ramnagar Road in P.S. Ramangar.	-do-
166.	145 LA(II)/Spl/ Transport	28.4.92	Bastia, 35, P.S. Egra	6.935	-do-	Proper facilities for trans. and comm. viz. for establishment of a stacking ward.	-do-
167.	3 LA(II)/Spl/ Hand F.W.	27.4.92	Chakgobindaberia, 486, P.S. Contai	3.855	-do-	Primary health centre Contai II Dev. Block	-do-
168.	161LA(II)/ Spl/I&W	28.4.92	Sarsa, 532, P.S. Contai	16.39	-do-	Irri. and drainage viz. Mirjapur Khal in conn with Contai Basin Dra. scheme Phase-II.	27.5.94

Contd....

Sl. No.	Notice/ Declaration Nos.	Date	Location	Amount (in acre)	Section(s) of the Act	Purpose	Gazette publ. date
169	1 LA(II)/Spl/ Trans.	27.4.92	Baliharpur, 20, P.S. Ramnagar	3.375	-do-	Depal Jaki (Mirgoda Market) Egra Ramnagar Rd.	27.5.94
170	41 LA(II)/Spl/ Water Supply	-do-	Purbamakundapur, 1/88, P.S. Contai	0.49	-do-	Approach Rd. to the Pump house under Contai Municipality water scheme.	-do-
171	225 LA(II)/Spl/ I&W	28.4.92	Pathra, 248, P.S. Midnapore	8.275	-do-	Irrigation and drainage in conection with Kalai Chandi Khal drainage scheme.	3.6.94
172	163 LA(II)/Spl/ I&W	-do-	Faridpur, 575, P.S. Contai	3.615	-do-	Drainage viz. for Mirzapur Khal in Con. with Contai Basin Drainage scheme Phase-II.	-do-
173	165 LA(II)/Spl/ I&W	-do-	Barasubarnanagar, 502, P.S. Contai	26.88	-do-	Mirjapur Khal -do-	-do-
174	57 LA(II)/Spl/ I&W	27.4.92	Kendamarijalpai, 189, P.S. Nandigram	1.07	-do-	Irrigation and drainage viz. const. of Embankment round Kendamari Sonachura Reclamation scheme.	-do-

Contd....

Sl. No.	Notice/ Declaration Nos.	Date	Location	Amount (in acre)	Section(s) of the Act	Purpose	Gazette publ. date
175	231 LA(II)/Spl/ I&W	28.4.92	Metaldoba, 280, P.S. Garbeta	0.89	-do-	Providing power facilites for irrigation and drainage viz. of Garbeta Branch canal in connection with Kangsabati Reservoir project.	16.6.94
176	85 LA(II)/Spl/ I&W	-do-	Chakturia, 354 P.S. KGP	8.00	-do-	Irrigation and drainage	6.94
177	1370 LA(II)/ 4B-3/88	30.5.94	Keranitola, 171, P.S. Midnapore	0.55	Act I of 1894	Const. of settlement Head Qtrs. office.	20.6.94
178	1143LA(PW)/II-46/94/I&W/ Case40/76-77	6.5.94	Kendui, 381, P.S. Jhargram	4.95	Act of 1948	Irrigation and drainage	-do-
179	199 LA(II)/Spl/ I&W	28.4.92	Nauri Gopinathchak, 171, P.S. Panskura	1.47	-do-	Irrigation and drainage for breach close to Upalda, Jardai and Narui Gopinath Chak.	-do-
180	29 LA(II)/Spl/ I&W	27.4.92	Garesuli, 331	4.97	-do-	Irrigation in conn. with Kangsabati Reservoir project.	12.7.94

Contd....

Sl. No.	Notice/ Declaration Nos.	Date	Location	Amount (in acre)	Section(s) of the Act	Purpose	Gazette publ. date
181	47 LA(II)Spl/ I&W	27.4.92	Paldapara, 33, P.S.Jamboni	8.085	-do-	Irrigation and drainage.	-do-
182	37 LA(II)/Spl/ I&W	-do-	Murakati 116, P.S. Jamboni	4.715	-do-	Irrigation and drainage.	-do-
183	1604 LA(II)/IM-46/94/ Power	15.6.94	Kakdihi, 5 P.S. Tamluk	0.57	-do-	Const. of Rly. Infrastructure and drainage pond KTTP (Stage II).	-do-
184	1606 LA(PW)/II-58/94/I&W Case No. 53/82-83	-do-	Simli, 909, P.S.Jhargram	4.03	-do-	Irrigation for Kangsaboti Reservoir Project.	15.7.94
185	854 LA(FW)/II-34/94/I&W Case No. 202/73-74	28.3.94	Dhitpur, 304, P.S. KGP	14.6	-do-	Irrigation and drainage.	-do-
186	2898 LA(PW)/ LR-85-86	6.10.93	Kukrakhupi, 48, P.S. Sankrail	6.91	-do-	Const. of Road from Lodhasuli to Rogra.	-do-
187	1145 LA(PW)/II-45/94/I&W Case No. 21/74-80	6.5.94	Songramchak, 221, P.S.Pingla	4.65	-do-	Irrigation and drainage.	-do-
188	39 LA(II)/Spl/ I&W	27.4.92	Murakata 151, P.S.Sankrail	4.14	-do-	Irrigation and drainage.	5.8.94
189	35 LA(II)/Spl/ I&W	-do-	Shiyalya, 144, P.S. Sankrail	14.275	-do-	Irrigation and drainage.	-do-

Contd....

Sl. No.	Notice/ Declaration Nos.	Date	Location	Amount (in acre)	Section(s) of the Act	Purpose	Gazette publ. date
190	43 LA(II)Spl/ I&W	27.7.92	Tiakati, 175, P.S. Sankrail	0.21	-do-	Irrigation and drainage.	-do-
191	45 LA(II)Spl/ I&W	-do-	Chhelaberia,203, P.S. Sankrail	6.92	-do-	Irrigation and drainage	-do-
192	1565 LA(PW)/ 2R-21/90	30.5.92	Bajuaguri, 206, P.S. Gopiballavpur	7.50	-do-	Const. of bridge apporach road over Subarnarekha for stalking yard at Kutighat.	23.8.94
193	2386 LA(PW)/II-99/94/I&W Case No. 24/78-79	16.8.94	Koptipur, 324, P.S. Sadbong	3.49	-do-	Resuscitation of river Keliaghai and its tributaries in the Dist. of Midnapore.	7.9.94
194	2382 LA(PW)/ 3B-2194 /I&W Case No. 22/74-75	16.8.94	Sonamukhi, 183, P.S.KGP	1.60	-do-	Const. of rest house, section office-cum-quarters and Khalasi shed at Sonamukhi.	7.9.94
195	2262LA(II)/ 4F-4/92(Pt)/ Fisheries/ Case No.5/88-89	2.8.94	Talaria, 206, P.S. Ramnagar	79.66	-do-	Const. of Brackish water fish form at Digha.	15.9.94

Contd....

Sl. No.	Notice/ Declaration Nos.	Date	Location	Amount (in acre)	Section(s) of the Act	Purpose	Gazette publ. date
196	213 LA(II)/ Spl/ I&W	28.4.92	Panchgechia, 224 (Part II) P.S.Daspur Adampur 223, P.S.Daspur, Dakshinbar, 224, P.S.Daspur, Nischintapur 230, P.S. Daspur	4.83	-do-	Irrigation and drainage viz. remodelling of Kalmijole Khal under P.S. Daspur.	14.9.94
197	203 LA(II)/Spl/ Trans.	-do-	Ramdaspur, 19, P.S. Daspur	3.38	-do-	Const. of Daspur Narajole Road	-do-
198	197 LA(II)/Spl/ Trans.	-do-	Tajpur, 173, P.S. Daspur	0.285	-do-	Transport and communication const of Kalmijore-Gopiguing V.R. (5 th mile)	-do-
199	193 LA(II)/Spl/ Trans.	-do-	Chandrakona	0.295	-do-	Const. of the approach road of the market complex at Chandrakona.	-do-
200	189 LA(II)/Spl/ Power	-do-	Sultannagar, 69, P.S. Daspur	0.16	-do-	Erection of 33/11 KV sub-station at Sultannagar, P.S.Daspur.	-do-

Contd....

Sl. No.	Notice/ Declaration Nos.	Date	Location	Amount (in acre)	Section(s) of the Act	Purpose	Gazette publ. date
201	173 LA(II)/Spl/ Trans.	28.4.92	Tajpur, 173, P.S. Daspur, Chainpat 216, P.S. Daspur	10.475	-do-	Const. and Transporting Kalmijore-Gopiganj V.R. (5th mile) P.S.Daspur.	-do-
202	157 LA(II)/Spl/ I&W	-do-	Sangaprasad, 107, P.S. Daspur	4.91	-do-	Drainage viz. for restoration by setting back the Dursapur Circuit Embankment.	-do-
203	153 LA(II)/Spl/ I&W	-do-	Srirampur, 117, P.S. Daspur	4.84	-do-	-do-	-do-
204	151 LA(II)/Spl/ I&W	-do-	Kasinathpur 236, P.S. Daspur	0.15	-do-	Irri. and drainage viz. re-excavation of Solatopa Khal in P.S.Daspur.	-do-
205	149 LA(II)/Spl/ I&W	-do-	Gokulnagar 23, P.S. Daspur, Paikandarjyachan 32, P.S. Daspur, Jadpur 27, P.S. Daspur, Srirampur, 117, P.S. Daspur	9.075	-do-	Drainage viz. for remodelling the chetue circuit embankment.	-do-

Contd....

Sl. No.	Notice/ Declaration Nos.	Date	Location	Amount (in acre)	Section(s) of the Act	Purpose	Gazette publ. date
206	147 LA(II)/Spl/ Trans.	-do-	Uttarbar, 222, P.S. Daspur	2.725	-do-	Transport viz. stackyard in connection with const. of Kolmijor Gopigang V.R.	-do-
207	135 LA(II)/Spl/ Trans.	-do-	Krishnapur ,35, P.S. Chandrakona	0.95	-do-	Const. of Kalyanchak Srinagar Rd. (7th to 18th km.) under P.S. Chandrakona.	-do-
208	133 LA(II)/Spl/ I&W	-do-	Ghola, 155, Chandrakona P.S.	7.565	-do-	Irrigation viz. for excavation of distributory No. 26 of Ghatal Branch Canal.	-do-
209	131 LA(II)/Spl/ I&W	-do-	Begurgram, 179, P.S. Chandrakona	8.07	-do-	Irrigation, drainage viz. excavation of distributory No. 33R of Ghatal Branch canal in connection with Kangsabati Reservoir Project.	-do-
210	129LA(II)/Spl/ I&W	-do-	Ghola, 155, P.S Chandrakona	2.31	-do-	Irrigation viz. excavation of Ghatal Branch Canal.	-do-

Contd....

Sl. No.	Notice/ Declaration Nos.	Date	Location	Amount (in acre)	Section(s) of the Act	Purpose	Gazette publ. date
211	127 LA(II)/Spl/ I&W	-do-	Ramjibanpur, 16, P.S. Chandrakona	0.68	-do-	Irrigation and drainage viz. const. of Zilladar's office at Ramjibanpur, in connection with Kangsabati reservoir project.	-do-
212	125 LA(II)/Spl/ I&W	-do-	Srinagar, 27, P.S. Chandrakona	0.86	-do-	Irrigation and drainage viz. for excavation of Ghatal Branch Canal.	-do-
213	123 LA(II)/Spl/ I&W	-do-	Jadupur, 27, P.S. Daspur	1.36	-do-	Irrigation, drainage viz. emergent flood damage repairs to Chatna embankment at 34th mile.	-do-
214	121 LA(II)/Spl/ I&W	-do-	Nonanrayanchak 248, P.S. Daspur	0.265	-do-	Irrigation and drainage viz. strenghtening Mohan Khali circuit embankment, P.S. Daspur.	-do-

Contd....

Sl. No.	Notice/ Declaration Nos.	Date	Location	Amount (in acre)	Section(s) of the Act	Purpose	Gazette publ. date
215	119 LA(II)/Spl/ Trans.	-do-	Uttarbar, 222, P.S. Daspur	4.50	-do-	Transport and communication, const. of Kalmijore-Gopigung V.R 9th mile.	-do-
216	117 LA(II)/Spl/ I&W	-do-	Suratpur, 41, P.S. Daspur	0.06	-do-	Irrigation and drainage viz. for closing breach in Chetua circuit at Suratpur.	-do-
217	115 LA(II)/Spl/ I&W	-do-	Raghunathpur, 51, P.S. Daspur	0.35	-do-	Irrigation drainage for same as above at Raghunathpur, P.S. Daspur.	-do-
218	113 LA(II)/Spl/ I&W	-do-	Bara,203, P.S. Chandrakona	0.16	-do-	Irrigation viz. for excavation of Distributory No. 28-R of Ghatal Branch Canal.	-do-
219	111 LA(II)/Spl/ Trans.	-do-	Konnagar, 147, P.S.Ghatal	0.035	-do-	Const. of approach road to the Silabati Bridge at Ghatal.	-do-

Contd....

Sl. No.	*Notice/ Declaration Nos.*	*Date*	*Location*	*Amount (in acre)*	*Section(s) of the Act*	*Purpose*	*Gazette publ. date*
220	107 LA(II)/Spl/ I&W	-do-	Jotekanurangarh 212, P.S. Daspur	2.04	do	Drainage for restoration by setting back the Chetua circuit embankment at 9th mile.	-do-
221	103 LA(II)/Spl/ I&W	-do-	Jayantipur, 109, P.S. Chandrakona	4.58	do	Irrigation, drainage, viz. excavation of minor 'A' of Distributory No. 31of the Garbeta Br. Canal	-do-
222	101 LA(II)/Spl/ I&W	-do-	Purshuri, 181, P.S.Chandra	8.08	do	Irrigation and drainage viz. excavation of distributory No. 33-R of Ghatal Branch Canal in connection with Kangsabati Reservoir Project.	-do-
223	99 LA(II)/Spl/ PHE	-do-	Gombhirnagar, 32, P.S. Ghatal	0.08	do	Water supply scheme for Ghatal Municipality.	-do-

Contd....

Sl. No.	*Notice/ Declaration Nos.*	*Date*	*Location*	*Amount (in acre)*	*Section(s) of the Act*	*Purpose*	*Gazette publ. date*
224	2555 LA(II)/ 5C-36/93/C&I	31.8.94	Dhekia, 135, P.S. KGP	11.615	-do-	Const. of Housing complex for employees of Tata Metaliks.	-do-
225	2264 LA(PW)	2.8.94	Bishnubarh, 102, P.S. Tamluk	0.0262	-do-	Const. of 2nd tube-well site under piped water supply scheme for providing drinking water to the society.	-do-
226	2583 LA(PW)/ 2R-64/94	2.9.94	Khadalgobra, 86, P.S. Digha	0.37	-do-	Trans. and communication for const. of internal road at Digha.	-do-
227	2948 LA(PW)/II-47/94/I&W Case No.97/72-73	31.10.94	Mokarbinda, 70, P.S. KGP Hariatara, P.S.KGP, Deyerkhal 45, P.S.KGP	9.75	-do-	Irrigation and drainage for excavation of minor IL of Disty No. 22-R of Tarafeni South Main Canal (South).	17.11.94
228	175LA(II)/Spl/ I&W	28.4.92	Santra, 46, P.S. Ramnagar	4.73	-do-	Drainage, namely Hinari Nardanda, drainage scheme.	-do-

Contd....

Sl. No.	Notice/ Declaration Nos.	Date	Location	Amount (in acre)	Section(s) of the Act	Purpose	Gazette publ. date
229	2226 LA(PW)/2R-12/94/ Housing	2.8.94	Salgachhia, 278	0.08	-do-	Apporach road to housing complex at Tamluk.	17.11.94
230	13 LA(II)/Spl I&W	22.11.94	Amritberia, 93, Bemanpur, 96, P.S. Mahisadal	3.65	-do-	Irrigation and drainage for the strengthening the marginal embknt of Bholsara Khal.	17.12.94
231	15 LA(II)/Spl I&W	-do-	Lansha, 151, P.S. Mohisadal	0.58	-do-	Irrigation and drainage viz. for const of Natsal Laksha piped water supply scheme.	-do-
232	75 LA/Spl/ PHE	-do-	Bargedagudar, 7, P.S. Mahisadal	1.035	-do-	Const. SRCC elevated reservoir.	-do-
233	17 LA/SPL/ PWD/(Rds)	-do-	Muradpur, 128, P.S. Nandigram, Kulbari 129, P.S. Nandigram.	7.575	-do-	Const. Nandigram Chandipur via Reyapara Road.	-do-
234	11 LA/Spl/ PWD/ (Rds)	-do-	Groshel, 90, P.S. Nandigram, Muradpur, 128, P.S. Nandigram	10.405	-do-	-do-	-do-

Contd....

Sl. No.	Notice/ Declaration Nos.	Date	Location	Amount (in acre)	Section(s) of the Act	Purpose	Gazette publ. date
235	11 LA/Spl/ PWD/ (Rds.)	-do-	Salikadhani Chak 122, P.S. Tamluk, Laichanpur,123. P.S. do, Rajnagar, Bharjola, 161, P.S. do.	3.00	do	Const. of Rd. from Haridaspur to Srirampur.	9.12.94
236	5 LA/Spl/ PWD/ (Rds.)	-do-	Dinabandhupur, 165, P.S. Nandigram	9.195	do	Irri. and drain. viz. for excavation of Tengakhal.	-do-
237	9 LA/Spl/ I&W	-do-	Putputiza, 163, P.S. Tamluk	6.395	do	Const. of Rd. from Haridaspur to Srirampur	-do-
238	1 LA/Spl/ PWD/ (Rds.)	-do-	Uttarsantanchak 271, P.S.Tamluk Baichherya, 17, P.S. Mahisadal, Chakchakandpira 18, P.S. Mahisadal	0.595	do	Trans.and comm. viz. const.of Tamluk Moyna O.D.R.(5th Mile).	-do-
239	7 LA/Spl/ I&W	-do-	Uttar Charasankarara, 142	4.525	do	Const. of a sluice of the outfall of Sankarara Khal in P.S.Tamluk.	-do-

Contd....

Sl. No.	Notice/ Declaration Nos.	Date	Location	Amount (in acre)	Section(s) of the Act	Purpose	Gazette publ. date
240	41 LA/Spl/ PWD/ (Rds.)	-do-	Dakshin Rampur 539, P.S. Contai. Benpur, 543, P.S do. Khikina,542, P.S. do, Subdi, 547, P.S. do.	5.345	-do-	Trans.and comm. viz for const. of contai Junput ODR.	19.12.94
241	63 LA/Spl/ PWD/ (Rds.)	-do-	Nayabasan, 154, P.S. Gopiballavpur	2.04	-do-	Const. of Gopiballavpur Hatibari Rd. in 3rd Km.	-do-
242	65 LA/Spl/ I&W	-do-	Phuldihi, 17, Moubhandar 16, P.S. Gopiballavpur	5.06	-do-	Irri.and drainage viz. for submerged area of Jhilu Khal irri. sche.	-do-
243	61 LA/Spl/ PWD/ (Rds.)	-do-	Jhili, 11, P.S. Gopiballavpur	4.47	-do-	Const. of Gopi-Hatibari Rd. in P.S.Gopi.	-do-
244	25 LA/Spl/ I&W	-do-	Kendugeria, 239, P.S. Gopi	8.155	-do-	Irri. and drain viz. for Kendugeria Minor Irri. scheme in Gopi.	-do-
245	31 LA/Spl/ PWD/ (Rds.)	-do-	Santrapur, 114, P.S. Gopi Suk Amrasol, 116 P.S. do, Gurpukuria, 68, P.S. do, Bandhgore Math Raghunathpur 110, P.S. do.	30.69	-do-	Const. of Gopi Hati Rd.	-do-

Contd....

Sl. No.	Notice/ Declaration Nos.	Date	Location	Amount (in acre)	Section(s) of the Act	Purpose	Gazette publ. date
246	19 LA/Spl/ PWD/ (Rds.)	-do-	Sarsa, 52, P.S. Gopi	11.84	-do-	Const. of Gopi Hati Rd.	-do-
247	71 LA/Spl/ PWD/ (Rds.)	-do-	Panchkhalia, 66, P.S. Gopi	0.48	-do-	-do-	-do-
248	69 LA/Spl/ PWD/ (Rds.)	-do-	Nayabasan, 154, P.S. Gopi	4.93	-do-	-do-	-do-
249	21 LA/Spl/ PWD/ (Rds.)	-do-	Chourmundi, 207, P.S. Gopi, Beldihia, 205, P.S. do.	5.97	-do-	Const. of Bridge approach Rd. at Khutighat	-do-
250	23 LA/Spl/ I&W	-do-	Panisole 15, P.S. Gopi	6.51	-do-	Irri. and drain viz. Jhilikhal irri. scheme	-do-
251	73 LA/Spl/ PWD/ (Rds.)	-do-	Jamboni, 109, Kanoha Arrasol, 118, Dhoba Bahi, 147, Raiband, 148, Asud, 151, P.S. Gopi	9.651	-do-	Gopi Hati Rd.	-do-
252	27 LA/Spl/ I&W	-do-	Suk Amrasole, 116, P.S.Gopi Kancha Amrasole 118, P.S. do, Jagannathpur, 117, P.S. do.	2.80	-do-	Irri. and drain. viz. for Left Bank Canal of Amrasole Khal Irri. Scheme.	-do-
253	29LA/Spl/ I&W	-do-	Nohamolia, 259, P.S.Gopi	0.20	-do-	Irri. and drain. viz. Kendugari Minor Irrigation scheme.	-do-

Contd....

Sl. No.	Notice/ Declaration Nos.	Date	Location	Amount (in acre)	Section(s) of the Act	Purpose	Gazette publ. date
254	79 LA/Spl/ I&W	-do-	Kendboni, 127, P.S. Binpur	2.29	-do-	Irrigation and drain. excavation of Kangsabati Reservoir project.	21.12.94
255	81 LA/Spl/ I&W	-do-	Barajharimura, 960, P.S. Binpur Dahijuri, 970, P.S. do.	5.49	-do-	Irri. and drain. excavation of minor IR of Disty. No. 10L in connec. with the acquisition of land for Kangsabati Reservoir project.	-do-
256	83 LA/Spl/ I&W	-do-	Khamar, 216, P.S.Binpur, Suknapahari, 120, P.S. do	11.375	-do-	Irrigation and drainage	-do-
257	85 LA/Spl/ I&W	-do-	Ergoda, 401,P.S. Binpur, Bijrabandh 52, P.S. Jamboni	4.90	-do-	Irrigation and drainage for Kangsabati Reservoir project.	-do-
258	87 LA/Spl/ I&W	-do-	Bahadurpur, 460, P.S. Binpur	2.70	-do-	Irri. and drain.	-do-

Contd....

Sl. No.	Notice/ Declaration Nos.	Date	Location	Amount (in acre)	Section(s) of the Act	Purpose	Gazette publ. date
259	89 LA/Spl/ I&W	-do-	Dighisol, 972, P.S. Binpur, Lakshmisagar, 973, P.S. do, Nakraduba, 345, P.S.Jhargram.	5.04	-do-	Irrigation and drainage for Kangsabati Reservoir project.	-do-
260	91 LA/Spl/ I&W	-do-	Dumuria, 173, P.S. Binpur, Pukuriapara, 254, P.S. do, Barajamsole 255, P.S. do, Chhotojamusole, 257, P.S. do	4.355	-do-	Irri. in connec. with Rangametia Irri. scheme.	-do-
261	93 LA/Spl/ I&W	-do-	Rangamatia, 171, P.S. Binpur, Kendapara, 179, P.S. Binpur	1.7025	-do-	Irrigation scheme of Rangamatia.	-do-
262	95 LA/Spl/ I&W	-do-	Panchiara 912, P.S. Binpur	0.77	-do-	Irrigation viz. excavation of DY No.101.	-do-
263	99 LA/Spl/ I&W	-do-	Jeyetyara, 325, P.S. Binpur Korkora, 36, P.S. do Laksmanpur, 380, P.S. do	8.44	-do-	Irri. viz. excavation of Distri. No. 3AL.	-do-

Contd....

Sl. No.	Notice/ Declaration Nos.	Date	Location	Amount (in acre)	Section(s) of the Act	Purpose	Gazette publ. date
264	103 LA/Spl/ IR&W	-do-	Belpahari, 136, P.S. Binpur, Krishnapur, 133, P.S. do	4.19	-do-	Irri. and drainage viz. for Belpahari Silda Water Supply Scheme.	-do-
265	69 LA/Spl/ I&W	27.4.92	Manikara ,355, P.S. Sabong	1.07	-do-	Irri. and drainage viz. for const. of sluices on ex-zamindary embankment in P.S. Sabong.	-do-
266	77 LA/Spl/ PWD/ (Rd.)	22.11.94	Ramdevpur ,26, P.S.Daspur, Rajnagar, 25, P.S. do	10.165	-do-	Trans. comm. viz. for approaches of river Kanki on Narajole-Daspur Rd.	9.1.95
267	754 LA(PW)/ II-16/93/I&W/ Case no. 144/77-78	11.3.95	Jamidardanga 334, P.S. Jhargram Kayma, 333, P.S. Jamboni	4.03	-do-	Irr. drain. viz. for excavation of escape channel.	-do-
268	3034 LA(PW)/ 2R/ 77/94/PW(Rds.)	10.11.94	Bhagwanpur ,35, P.S. Bhagwanpur, Benadia, 741, P.S. do	0.685	-do-	Const. of Prajabar Bhagwanpur Rd.	-do-
269	45 LA/Spl/ I&W	22.11.94	Barurbheri, 36 , P.S. Bhagwanpur Nalda, 89, P.S. do, Aktazpur, 39, P.S. do	4.595	-do-	Irri. drain. excavation of Thakurchak Khal in conn. with Dariadighi Vabadal khal drainage scheme.	-do-

Contd....

Sl. No.	Notice/ Declaration Nos.	Date	Location	Amount (in acre)	Section(s) of the Act	Purpose	Gazette publ. date
270	39 LA/Spl/ PHE	-do-	Tikashi, 138, P.S. Khejuri	0.84	-do-	Sinking of tubewell No. 1 under Tikashi W/s scheme.	-do-
271	37 LA/Spl/ I&W	-do-	Durgapur , 48, P.S.Ramnagar	0.54	-do-	Irri. drain viz. Hinari Nasdanga drain. scheme in conn. with Dubdo basin drain scheme.	-do-
272	47 LA/Spl/ Fisheries	-do-	Talaria, 206, P.S. Ramnagar	101.19	-do-	Const. of brackish water Fish Farm at Digha.	-do-
273	43 LA/Spl/ I&W	-do-	Gobindabasan, 89, P.S. Ramnagar	2.01	-do-	Protection of Digha township.	-do-
274	49 LA/Spl/ Fisheries	-do-	Jalgachani, 108, P.S. Ramnagar	9.83	-do-	Const. of brackish water Fish Farm at Digha.	-do-
275	53 LA/Spl/ Fisheries	-do-	Kuliata, 227, P.S. Ramnagar	8.04	-do-	-do-	-do-
276	55 LA/Spl/ Fisheries	-do-	Ramnagar, 208, P.S. Ramnagar	6.80	-do-	-do-	-do-
277	35 LA/Spl/ Fisheries	-do-	Deul Botla, 208, P.S. Ramnagar	0.45	-do-	-do-	-do-
278	33 LA/Spl/ Fisheries	-do-	Nilpur, 223, P.S. Ramnagar	24.35	-do-	-do-	-do-

Contd....

Sl. No.	Notice/ Declaration Nos.	Date	Location	Amount (in acre)	Section(s) of the Act	Purpose	Gazette publ. date
279	101 LA/ Spl/ I&W	-do-	Guimara , 549, P.S. Jhargram	2.39	-do-	Irri. and drain. viz. for flood protection work at Lalgeria Minor Irrigation scheme.	-do-
280	97 LA/Spl	-do-	Chenchurgerya, 712, P.S. Jhargram, Bansol, 711, P.S. do, Jangalkhas, 731, P.S. do	13.33	-do-	Irr. and drain. viz. for excavation of disty. in conn. with Kangsabati Reservoir project.	-do-
281	105 LA/Spl/ IR&W	-do-	Vronsal, 411, P.S Jhargram, Rangidas, 88, P.S. Keshiary, Janikata, 413, P.S. Jhargram	8.93	-do-	Irr. drain. excavation of disty. in conn. with Kangsabati Reservoir project.	-do-
282	2691 LA(II)/ 2R-5/94/ Trans	16.9.94	Kismat-Bajkul, 156, P.S. Bhagwanpur	5.55	-do-	Const. of Tamluk-Digha B.G. Rail line.	12.1.95
283	33 LA(II)/Spl/ I&W	27.4.09	Muradpur, 128, P.S. Nandigram	0.13	-do-	Irri. and drainage viz. silt clearance of Daniakhal.	-do-
284	4238 LA (PW)/ 2R-47/ 93 PW(Rds.)	6.12.94	Kayalchak, 41	0.36	-do-	Const. of Contai side app. Rd. of Haldi Bridge on Tamluk Contai Rd.	-do-

Contd....

Sl. No.	Notice/ Declaration Nos.	Date	Location	Amount (in acre)	Section(s) of the Act	Purpose	Gazette publ. date
285	183 LA(II)/ Spl/ I&W (Rds.)	2.4.92	Motaghata, 258, P.S. Egra	0.20	-do-	Restoration of flood damages due to flood of 1971 on marginal embankment of Khal and L.R. embankment repairs.	-do-
286	4290 LA(PW)/ 2R/70/94/ PW	8.12.94	Kasba-Patashpur, 49, P.S. Patashpur	0.275	-do-	Const. of Patashpur Bhagwanpur ODR.	-do-
287	(Rds.) 2790 LA(PW) /II-106/94/ I&W Case No. 57/	28.9.94	Kudi, 39, P.S. Egra, Naraharepur, 40, P.S. do, Rasan, 128, P.S. do	0.90	-do-	Dubdra basin drainage scheme.	-do-
288	75-76 2904 LA(PW) /II-108/94/ I&W Case No.200/	25.9.94	Khagda, 208, P.S. Egra	8.18	-do-	Drainage re-excavation of Balighai Khal in conn. with Dubda Basin Drainage.	-do-
289	80-81 SILA/SPL/	22.11.94	Purba Mukundapur, 211, P.S. Ramnagar	37.65	-do-	Brackish Water Fish Farm at Digha.	6.2.95
290	Fishery 107 LA/Spl/ I&W	-do-	Bhabaninagar, 249, P.S. Midnapore	5.08	-do-	Irri. and drain. Inz. for flood embankment (from outfall Kaliachandi Khal upto Kalinagar) in connec. with Kalaichandi Khal drainage scheme.	10.2.95

Contd....

Sl. No.	Notice/ Declaration Nos.	Date	Location	Amount (in acre)	Section(s) of the Act	Purpose	Gazette publ. date
291	109 L.A/Spl/ I&W	-do-	Khasjangal, 937, P.S. Jhargram	0.03	-do-	Irri. and drain. exca. of Disty in conn. with Kang. Reser. Proj.	-do-
292	111 LA/Spl/ CSSE	-do-	Balaramdihi, 309, P.S. Jhargram	0.344	-do-	Commer. estates and industrial estates.	-do-
293	113 LA/Spl /PHE	-do-	Brojolalchak, 57, P.S. Sutahata	0.76	do	Const. of head work struct. and sinking of 2 nos. tubewell under Dakshinchak water supply scheme.	-do-
294	115 LA/Spl./ I&W	-do-	Banaskhana Jalpai, 55 P.S. Sutahata	2.49	do	For protection of Jalpai sch. 'D' embankment.	-do-
295	117 LA/Spl./ I&W	-do-	Gobindnagar, 209, P.S. Mid. Paikarapore, 211, P.S. Mid. Juarhati, 208, P.S. Midnapore.	12.74	do	Irri. drain. exca. of Kalaichandi drain scheme.	-do-
296	149 LA(PW)/ 2R-101/94	13.1.95	Keshiary, 105, P.S. Keshiary	1.77	do	Kulboni ODR.	17.2.95
297	343 LA/5C-14/ 94/ C&I	3.2.95	Rayranachak P.S. Sutahata	11.46	do	For Haldia Petro-chemical Proj.	-do-

Contd....

Sl. No.	Notice/ Declaration Nos.	Date	Location	Amount (in acre)	Section(s) of the Act	Purpose	Gazette publ. date
298	4397 LA(PW) 2R-88/94	15.12.94	Badalpur ,212, P.S. Contai	0.60	-do-	For the purpose of app. Rd. for the work const. of foot bridge over Pichabani Khal.	-do-
299	67 LA/PI/ PWD/ (Rds.)	21.11.94	Betkala ,63, P.S. Gopiballavpur, Talpada, 64, P.S. do. Panchakahalia, 65, P.S. do	8.105	-do-	Const. of Gopi-Hatibari Rd.	10.3.95
300	4246 LA(PW) 2R-64/94/ PW (Rds.)	6.12.94	Gobardhanpur, 79, P.S. Patashpur, Lachhubar ,93, P.S. Pataspur Chandan-pur, 103, P.S. Pataspur Rautara, 92, P.S.Pataspur	4.85	-do-	Gobardhanpur-Itaberia Rd.	-do-
301	999 LA/SC- 10/ 94	10.2.95	Chiranjibpur, 168, P.S. Sutahata	6.85	Act I of 1894	Development work of Calcutta Port Trust (Haldia Dock Complex).	-do-
302	1107 LA(II)/ 4P-7/95/ Power	14.2.95	Bargachia, 1, P.S.Tamluk	6.81	-do- -do-	Const. of Ash Pond No. 5 of K.T.P.S.	-do-
303	1046 LA(II) 4P-18/95/ Power	13.2.95	-do-	9.67	-do-	-do-	-do-

Contd....

Sl. No.	Notice/ Declaration Nos.	Date	Location	Amount (in acre)	Section(s) of the Act	Purpose	Gazette publ. date
304	1104 LA(II)/ 4P/ 6/95/ Power	14.2.95	-do-	9.21	-do-	-do-	10.3.95
305	4240 LA (PW) / 1M-146/34/ PHE	6.12.94	Basudebpur, 85 P.S. Mahisadal	0.02	W.B. Act of 1948	Const. of head work structure under Khejurberia W/S scheme	-do-
306	339 LA/(PW)/ I1-158/94/ I&W	3.2.95	Chengnageria, 77, Ghorabandha Chati, 170, Porapara, 172	20.16	-do-	Irri. drain for exca. of disty. No. 22R of Tarafeni South main Canal.	-do-
307	305 LA(II)/6p-2/94	31.1.95	Kishorenagar, 265, P.S. Contai	0.62	-do-	Development of Contai Telephone Network system.	16.3.95
308	1116 LA(II)/ 4P-9/95/ Power	14.2.95	Baragachia, 1, P.S.Tamluk	9.48	Act I of 1894	Ash pond No.5 of KTPS.	-do-
309	1135 LA(II)/ 4P-8/95/ Power	16.2.95	do	8.74	-do-	-do-	-do-
310	1141 LA/(II)/ 4P-10/95/ Power	-do-	do	2.98	-do-	-do-	-do-
311	1186 LA/2R-12/95	17.2.95	Kusba, 245 P.S. KGP, Arasini, 244, P.S. KGP	3.09	W.B. Act of 1948	Const. of Jhapatapur Kashijora Road via Abhoy Ashram.	-do-
312	1243 LA/IW/1/95	21.2.95	Baramathakapur, 316, P.S.Belda (Narayangarh)	0.25	Act I of 1894	Belda Water Supply scheme.	-do-

Contd....

Sl. No.	Notice/ Declaration Nos.	Date	Location	Amount (in acre)	Section(s) of the Act	Purpose	Gazette publ. date
313	1138 LA(I)/ 4P-11/95/ Power	16.2.95	Bargachia, 1, P.S.Tamluk	NA	-do-	NA	NA
314	1174 LA/IW/ (1274)-2/95/I and W/Case No. 11/ 86-87	17.2.95	Radhaban, 185, P.S. Panskura	3.01	W.B. Act of 1948	Kherai Suki Basin drainage scheme.	31.3.95
315	1176 LA//11/ (379)-7/95/ I and W /Case No.186/ 76-77	-do-	Rajarbagan 244, P.S.Midnapore	3.74	-do-	Flood embankment from Midnapore anti-cut to outfall of Kalaichandi Khal	-do-
316	1598 LA/5I-8/95/ I and SI	16.3.95	Rayraynachak, 161, P.S. Sutahata	65.85	-do-	Haldia Petro-chem. Project.	-do-
317	1611 LA(II)/ 4P-30/95// Power	-do-	Purbabahala, 302, P.S. Panskura	2.48	Act I of 1894	Ash pond Praket No.5 of K.T.P.P.	-do-
318	742 LA(II)/1M-165/92/ C and I	11.3.93	Bardhanyaghata Part I, 172, P.S. Sutahata	1.03	W.B. Act of 1948	Small, medium and large, industries of Haldia Pet Chem./ Down Stream Industries.	18.4.95
319	746 LA(II)/1M-8/ 93/ C&I	-do-	do	4.82	-do-	-do-	-do-
320	1738 LA(II)/ 4P-16/95/ Power	27.3.95	Bargachia, 1, P.S.Tamluk	5.78	Act I of 1894	Ash pond No.5 of KTPP.	-do-

Contd....

Sl. No.	Notice/ Declaration Nos.	Date	Location	Amount (in acre	Section(s) of the Act	Purpose	Gazette publ. date
321	1741 LA(II)/ 4P-17/98/ Power	-do-	-do-	8.03	-do-	-do-	18.4.95
322	2784 LA(II)/ 3M-28/94	28.9.94	Maroberia, 278 P.S. Panskura	1.90	-do-	Rehabilitation of erosion affected people on the abandoned embankment of Rupnarayan river.	-do-
323	1758 LA(PW)/ 19/59/92	11.3.93	Parihati, 50, P.S. Jamboni	1.42	W.B. Act of 1948	Irri. and drain. viz. for excav. of M-4/ DIR/T.S.M. C(N).	19.4.95
324	1898 LA(PW)/II-107/94/ I&W/ Case No. 198/	6.3.95	Dalkuchi, 44 P.S. Egra	3.2.45	-do-	Kudi diversion channel in con. with Subda.	-do-
325	7374 1491 LA(PW)11-70/94/I.W.D/Case No. 24/93-94	9.3.95	Barbasudevpur, 62, P.S. Sutahata	2.115	Act I of 1894	Const. of canal connecting the Ananda Khali Canal for the Deulpota Canal for the purpose of extending Irri. facilities.	-do-
326	1565 LA(II)/ 4F-3/ 92/ Fisheries/ Case No. 11/88-89	15.3.95	Sankarpur 224, P.S. Ramnagar	17.58	W.B. Act of 1948	Const. of brackish water Fish Farm at Digha.	-do-

Contd....

Sl. No.	Notice/ Declaration Nos.	Date	Location	Amount (in acre)	Section(s) of the Act	Purpose	Gazette publ. date
327	1698 LA(PW)/ 11-67/94/ I&W/ Case No. 89/79-80	28.3.95	Kunjabera, 29, P.S. Patashpur	0.07	-do-	Const. of right embankment of river Baghai in conn. with remodelling of Balighai drain scheme	-do-
328	1700 LA(PW)/11-65/94/I&W/Case No.192/75-76	23.3.95	Erenda, 155 P.S. Egra, Chakbhabani, 254, P.S. Patashpur	4.44	-do-	Re-excavation of Balighai Main Drain in conne. with Balighai Basin drain Scheme	-do-
329	2718 LA(II)	15.9.92	Bardhanyaghata Part I, 172, P.S. Sutahata	6.99	-do-	Small, medium and large, industries of Haldia Petrochem./ Down Stream Industries.	24.4.95
330	2140 LA/5I-12/95 Canal P	3.5.95	Ramgopalchak, 163, P.S. Sutahata	128.097	Act I of 1894	Housing complex of Haldia Petrochem Ltd.	18.5.95
331	2009 LA(II) 4P-34/95/ Power	21.4.95	Bargachia, 1, P.S.Tamluk	8.10	Act I of 1894	Ash Pond project No.5 of KTPP.	19.5.95
332	1997 LA(II)/ 4P-28/95/ Power	20.4.95	Manderpacha, 301, P.S. Panskura	8.98	-do-	-do-	-do-
333	2000 LA(II)/ 4P-37/95/ Power	-do-	-do-	3.72	-do-	-do-	-do-

Contd....

Sl. No.	Notice/ Declaration Nos.	Date	Location	Amount (in acre)	Section(s) of the Act	Purpose	Gazette publ. date
334	1954 LA(II)/ 4P-33/95/ Power	17.4.95	Bargachia, 1, P.S.Tamluk	8.81	-do-	-do-	19.5.95
335	1803 LA(PW) 1M-43/94/ M.A.	30.3.95	Deghashipur, 152, P.S. Sutahata	43.0125	Act I of 1894	Establishment of housing and commerical zone.	-do-
336	195 LA/1W (1280) 8/95/I and W Case No. 184/ 74-75	17.4.95	Nimakbar, 5, P.S. Bhagwanpur, Sribachhipur, 9 P.S.Bhagwanpur, Manoharpur, 10, P.S. Bhagwanpur, Haripur, 58, P.S. Bhagwanpur.	2.34	W.B. Act of 1948	Irri. and drain. viz. for Deriadighi Udaldal Khal drainage scheme.	-do-
337	2679 LA/4H-43/94	29.5.95	Baraghasipur, 156 P.S. Sutahata	43.7983	-do-	Est. of housing and comm. zone as well as to maintain and develop other essential service within Haldia notified area.	8.6.95
338	2676 LA(PW)/ M.A.	-do-	Barghasipur, 156 P.S. Sutahata.	31.57	Act I of 1894	-do-	-do-
339	2673 LA/4H-39/94	-do-	Brajanath Chak, P.S. Sutahata.	4.54	-do-	-do-	-do-

Contd....

Sl. No.	Notice/ Declaration Nos.	Date	Location	Amount (in acre)	Section(s) of the Act	Purpose	Gazette publ. date
340	2755 LA(II)/5I-40/95/UD	1.6.95	Joynagar ,123, P.S. Sutahata	40.185	-do-	Small, medium and large scale industries incl. approach Rd. and rehabilitation complex at Haldia.	-do-
341	2746 LA(II)/5I-37/95/UD	-do-	Bhuyanraychak,122, P.S. Sutahata	90.01	-do-	-do-	-do-
342	2743 LA(II)/5I-36/95/UD	-do-	-do-	93.104	-do-	-do-	-do-
343	2752 LA(II)/ 5C-42/95/UD	-do-	Baneswarchak, 120, P.S. Sutahata	81.35	-do-	Small, med. and large scale industries.	9.6.96
344	2749 LA(II)/5I-41/95/UD	-do-	-do-	62.62	-do-	-do-	9.6.95
345	2740 LA(II)/ 5I-39/95/UD	-do-	-do-	71.92	-do-	Small, med. and large scale industries and rehabilitation complex.	-do-
346	2737 LA(II)/ 5I-45/95/UD	-do-	Bhayarochak, 122, P.S. Sutahata, Ramnagar, 124, P.S. Sutahata, Purbaraghunathchak, 127, P.S. Sutahata	5.385	Act I of 1894	Small, med. and large scale indust. and rehabilitation complex.	-do-

Contd....

Sl. No.	Notice/ Declaration Nos.	Date	Location	Amount (in acre)	Section(s) of the Act	Purpose	Gazette publ. date
347	2734 LA(II)/5I-43/95/LID	-do-	Patherberia, 113, P.S. Sutahata	19.95	-do-	-do-	-do-
348	2731 LA(II)/5I-44/95/LID	-do-	Ramnagar, 124, P.S. Sutahata Jagannathchak, 125, P.S. Sutahata Purba, Raghunathchak, 127	42.525	-do-	-do-	-do-
349	2750 LA(PW) / 2R-71/91	17.9.92	Nimakbarc, 5, P.S.Bhagwanpur	0.55	W.B. Act of 1948	Const. of Prajabar Bhagwanpur Rd.	16.6.95
350	2577 LA(II)/56-33/95/UP	22.5.95	Baneswarchak, 120, P.S. Sutahata	84.39	Act I of 1894	Small, med. and large scale industries and rehabilitation complex.	-do-
351	2580 LA(II)/ 5I-34/95/UP	-do-	-do-	92.97	-do-	-do-	-do-
352	2574 LA(II)/ ID/ 6/95/U.P.	-do-	Debhog, 149, P.S. Sutahata	231.09	-do-	Small, medium, and large industries for Haldia down stream industries.	-do-
353	2583 LA(II)/ 5I-31/95/UP	-do-	Bhuyanroychak, 122, P.S. Sutahata	85.41	-do-	Small, medium and large scale industries incl. app. Rd. and Rehabi complex.	-do-

Contd....

Sl. No.	Notice/ Declaration Nos.	Date	Location	Amount (in acre)	Section(s) of the Act	Purpose	Gazette publ. date
354	2611 LA/1M-152/94/L and I	29.5.95	Chakrarayan, 193, P.S. Sutahata	0.96	-do-	Dev. Work Cal. Port Trust (Haldia Dock Complex).	19.6.95
355	2612 LA/1M / 152/94/ L and I	-do-	-do-	0.45	-do-	-do-	-do-
356	7613 LA/1M - 152/94/ L and I	-do-	-do-	3.60	-do-	-do-	-do-
357	2614 LA/1M - 152/94/ L and I	-do-	Bishnuram Chak, 217, P.S. Sutahata	1.89	Section 4 of Act I, 1894	Development work of CPI	-do-
358	2615 LA/1M - 152/94/ L and I	-do-	Kumarchak,133 P.S. Sutahata	0.42	-do-	-do-	-do-
359	2616 LA/1M -52/ 94/ L and I	-do-	Hatibari, 167, P.S. Sutahata	0.37	-do-	-do-	-do-
360	2605 LA(II)/ 5I-30/95/UP	-do-	Ramnagar ,124 P.S. Sutahata	15.895	-do-	Small, medium and large scale indus. incl. app.rd. and rehabi. complex.	-do-
361	2571 LA(II)/ 5I-32/95/UP	-do-	Bhuniroychak, 122, P.S. Sutahata	64.90	-do-	-do-	23.6.95
362	2110 LA/2R-8/ 94/S.E. Rly.	2.5.95	Dakshin ,203 P.S.-Ramnagar	1.28	W.B. Act of 1948	Const. of Tamluk Digha B.G. Rly. from Digha Eng.	-do-
363	2085LA/2R-22/ 95	28.4.95	Itaberia, 178 P.S.Bhagwanpur	0.954	-do-	Const.of Mugberia-Itaberia V. Rd.	-do-

Contd....

Sl. No.	*Notice/ Declaration Nos.*	*Date*	*Location*	*Amount (in acre*	*Section(s) of the Act*	*Purpose*	*Gazette publ. date*
364	1864 LA/24-21	5.4.95	Baruipur, 193 P.S. Patashpur	0.17	-do-	Const. for Patashpur Bhagwanpur Rd.	-do-
365	2873 LA(II)/ 51-18/95/UD	7.6.95	Radhamadhab Chak, 130, P.S. Sutahata	10.90	Act I of 1894	Small, med. and large scale industries.	-do-
366	2867 LA(II)/ 51-13/95/U.D.	-do-	do	9.13	do	-do-	-do-
367	2870 LA(II)/ 51-24/95/U.D.	-do-	do	11.88	do	-do-	-do-
368	2876 LA(II)/ 5I-35/95/U.D.	-do-	Joynagar ,124, P.S. Sutahata	54.543	do	Small, med. and large scale indust. inc.app. rd. and rehab. complex.	17.7.95
369	3018 LA(II)/ 1D-8/95/U.D.	9.6.95	Radhamadhab Chak, 130, P.S. Sutahata	11.32	do	Small, med. and large scale indust.	-do-
370	2568 LA (PW)/ 1M-146/90	4.4.92	Kasbere, 146	0.19	W.B. Act of 1948	11 and HPC downstream indust.	-do-
371	2029 LA/4H-44/94	23.6.95	De-Ghasipur, 152, P.S. Sutahata	27.52	Act I of 1894	Est. of housing and commercial zone within Haldia notified area.	-do-
372	4057 LA(II)/5I-19/95/UD/ (Tandl-p)	-do-	Kasbere, 146 P.S.Sutahata	1.11	W.B. Act of 1948	Small, med. and large scale industries (H.P. downstream).	-do-

Contd....

Sl. No.	Notice/ Declaration Nos.	Date	Location	Amount (in acre)	Section(s) of the Act	Purpose	Gazette publ. date
373	2608 LA/11 (430)-58/95/ I&W/ Case No. 24/94-95	29.5.95	Bhabanipur, 2, P.S. Debra	0.78	Act I of 1894	Closing breach on Govt. Embankment of river Cosseye.	18.7.95
374	4341 LA/ID-7/95	13.7.95	Bhabanipur ,150, P.S. Sutahata	14.14	-do-	Est. of housing and Commercial zone within Haldia notified area	-do-
375	4052 LA	23.6.95	Solat, 151, P.S. Sutahata	30.04	-do-	-do-	-do-
376	2718 LA(II)	15.9.92	Bardhanyaghata 172, P.S. Sutahata	6.99	W.B. Act of 1948	Small, med. and large scale industries (HPC and downstream).	-do-
377	2759 LA/ PHE/ IM/ 11/95	1.6.95	Kismat-Bajkul, 156, P.S. Bhagwanpur	1.065	Act I of 1894	Rural piped water supply scheme.	-do-
378	3034 LA/PHE/ 1W/ (1284)-12/95	12.6.95	Paikpari, 286. P.S. Panskura	0.270	-do-	Head works site in connec. with Kolaghat and adjoining Mouzas W/S scheme.	-do-
379	4371 LA(II) 4P-11/95/ Power	17.7.95	Bargachia, 1, P.S.Tamluk	7.60	-do-	Const. of Ash Pond No. 5 of KTPP.	-do-
380	4365 LA(II) 4P-8/95/ Power	-do-	-do-	8.74	-do-	-do-	-do-

Contd....

Sl. No.	Notice/ Declaration Nos.	Date	Location	Amount (in acre	Section(s) of the Act	Purpose	Gazette publ. date
381	4280 LA/ 1W(1289)-17/95/ I&W/ Case No. 19/95-96	10.7.96	Amritberia, 93, P.S. Mahisadal, Bholsora, 95, P.S. Mahisadal	7.535	-do-	Const. of a sluice at the outfall of Bhalasora Khal in connec. with drainge scheme.	-do-
382	4047 (4)/LA/ 1W(128)-9/95/ I&W/Case No.141/76-77	23.6.95	Bishnupur, 53, P.S.Bhagwanpur	0.86	W.B. Act. II of 1948	Dariadighi-Udhadal Khal drainage scheme.	-do-
383	4277 LA/2R-17/95	10.7.95	Uttarsitala, 260, P.S. Ramnagar	4.42	Act I of 1894	Const. of R.C.C. Bridge over Pichaboni Khal	12.9.95
384	4368 LA(II)/ 4B-18/95/ DLROS	17.7.95	Keranitola, 171	0.50	-do-	Const. of offices of the L.R. Deptt.	-do-
385	5265 LA(II)/ 19-70/94/UD	1.9.95	Barbasudevpur, 62, P.S.Sutahata, Kumarpur, 53, P.S. Sutahata	2.115	-do-	Const. of canal for the purpose of extending irrigation facilities.	-do-
386	5508 LA(II)/ 1D 8/95/UD	14.9.95	Radhamadhab Chak, 130, P.S. Sutahata	11.32	Act I of 1894	Small, med., and large scale industries.	28.9.95
387	5485 LA(II)/ 5I-18/95/UD	-do-	-do-	10.19	-do-	-do-	-do-
388	5505 LA(II)/ 5I-13/95/UD	-do-	-do-	9.13	-do-	-do-	16.9.95

Contd....

Sl. No.	Notice/ Declaration Nos.	Date	Location	Amount (in acre)	Section(s) of the Act	Purpose	Gazette publ. date
389	5511 LA(II)/ 5I-24/95/UD	-do-	-do-	11.88	-do-	-do-	16.9.95
390	5559LA(II)/ 5I-54/95	18.9.95	Purbaraghunath Chak, 127, P.S. Sutahata	1.02	-do-	Creation of railway siding facilitites, for Hindusthan Petroleum Corpn. Ltd.	13.10.95
391	5103 LA/ 1R-5/ 95/ Transport	24.8.95	Narayandari, 152, P.S. Bhagwanpur	4.01	Act II of 1948	Const. of Tamluk-Digha B.G. Rly. Line.	-do-
392	5445 LA/1M-152/94/L&I	12.9.95	Royrayana Chak, 161, P.S. Sutahata	5.20	Act I of 1894	Development work of CPT in conn. with Haldia dock proj.	-do-
393	5656 LA(PW)/ 11-98/94/ I&W	21.9.95	Amadpurpal, 246, P.S. Midnapore, Hatihalka, 245	10.78	Act II of 1948	Embankment for flood from Mid. Anticut to outfall of Kalichandi Khal in connec. with Kalaichandi Khal Scheme.	-do-
394	5657 LA(II) (483)-11/95/ I&W	-do-	Bishnu Mishra Chak, 175, P.S. Moyna	0.13	Act I of 1894	Const. of sluice regarding kherai Boxi Basin Drainage Scheme.	12.10.95
395	5469 LA(II) /4P-17/95/ Power	14.9.95	Bargachia, 1, P.S.Tamluk	8.03	-do-	Const. of Ash Pond No. 5 of KTPS.	-do-

Contd....

Sl. No.	*Notice/ Declaration Nos.*	*Date*	*Location*	*Amount (in acre)*	*Section(s) of the Act*	*Purpose*	*Gazette publ. date*
396	5251 LA/4P-38/ 95/ Power	31.8.95	Manderpacha, 301, P.S. Panskura	8.98	-do-	-do-	12.10.95
397	4134 LA/1W-16/ 95/PHE	28.6.95	Bonnia, 223, P.S. Bhagwanpur	0.08	Act II of 1948	Sinking of bigger tube-well No. 2 under Madhakali W/S scheme.	-do-
398	5571 LA(II)/ 2R-10/94/ iiSE Rly.	19.9.95.	Shyamchak, 130, P.S. Khejury	7.01	-do-	Const. of Tamluk-Digha B.G. Rly. Line.	-do-
399	5571 LA(II)/ 2R-10/94/ SE Rly.	-do-	Shyamchak, 130, P.S. Khejury	7.01	-do-	Const. of Tamluk-Digha B.G. Rly. Line.	3.11.95
400	5967 LA(II)/ 5I-47/95/ C&I	17.10.95	Kalikapur, 137, Niranjanbar ,134, Chaksonadhar, 136, Tarabamri, 138, Rajpura, 130, Sujatpur, 139, Kantageria, 92, Panchrolya, 91, Dhekia, 135, Malancha, 131	526.71	Act I of 1894	Sponge and pig-iron project of Century Textiles.	-do-
401	5934 LA(II)/ 5I-30/95/UD	16.10.95	Ramnagar, 124	15.895	-do-	Small, med. and large scale industries incld. app. road and rehab. complex.	-do-

Contd....

Sl. No.	Notice/ Declaration Nos.	Date	Location	Amount (in acre)	Section(s) of the Act	Purpose	Gazette publ. date
402	5078 LA/PH-11/95	23.8.95	Kola, 287, P.S. Panskura	0.87	-do-	Needed by the Central Govt. for the expansion of Kola Union Jogendra Girls'High School.	6.11.95
403	5898 LA/ 5I-66/ 95/ L&I	12.10.95	Kasbere, 146, P.S. Sutahata	10.28	Act II of 1948	Small, med, and, large scale industries in conn. with HP chem. proj.	-do-
404	5931 LA(II)/ 5I-42/95/UD	16.10.95	Baneswarchak, 120, P.S. Sutahata	81.35	Act I of 1894	Small, med. and large scale industries.	-do-
405	5940 LA(II)/ 5I-33/95	-do-	-do-	84.39	-do-	Small, med., large indust. apprd, and rehab. complex.	-do-
406	5696 LA 1R-1/95	22.9.95	Tethibari, 153, P.S. Bhagwanpur	26.35	Act II of 1894	Const. of Tamluk-Digha B.G. Rail. Line.	-do-
407	5869 LA/ 5I-65/ 95/ L&I	10.10.95	Kasbere, 146, P.S. Sutahata	7.93	-do-	Small, med. and large indust. in conm, with Haldia Petro Chem. Downstream, indus.	-do-
408	5875 LA(II)/ 5I-10/94/ L&I	17.10.95	Chiranjibpur, 168, P.S. Sutahata	6.85	Act I of 1894	Dev. work. CPT (Haldia Dock Complex).	9.11.95

Contd....

Sl. No.	Notice/ Declaration Nos.	Date	Location	Amount (in acre)	Section(s) of the Act	Purpose	Gazette publ. date
409	2722 LA(II)	15.9.92	Bardhanyaghata, Part I, 172 P.S. Sutahata, Kasbere, 145, P.S. Sutahata	6.40	Act II of 1948	Small, med., and large industries (Haldia Petro Chem. Downstream).	-do-
410	1722 LA/1M-45/93	27.3.95	Kasbere, 145, P.S. Sutahata	0.80	-do-	-do-	-do-
411	5973 LA(II)/5I-43/95/LID	16.10.95	Patherberia, 113, P.S. Sutahata	19.95	Act I of 1894	Small med. and large indust. incl. app. rd. and rehab. complex.	-do-
412	6111 LA(II)/1M-152/94(D) C&I	24.10.95	Kumarchak,133, P.S. Sutahata	0.42	-do-	Dev. work of CPT (Haldia).	-do-
413	6108 LA(II)/1M-152/94(E)/ C&I	-do-	Bishnuramchak, 217, P.S. Sutahata	1.89	-do-	-do-	10.11.95
414	5950 LA(II)/1M-152/94(I)/ L&I	16.10.95	Chaktarayan, 193, P.S. Sutahata	3.60	-do-	-do-	-do-
415	5988 LA(II)/1M-152/94(A)/ L&I	17.10.95	Hatibari, 167 P.S. Sutahata	0.37	-do-	-do-	-do-
416	6170 LA/2R-24/90	27.10.95	Hirapur, 60, P.S. Ramnagar	0.695	Act II of 1948	Const. of Tamluk-Digha Rly. Line.	-do-
417	5953 LA/1M/ 152/94/L&I	16.10.95	Chaktarayan, 193, P.S. Sutahata	0.96	Act I of 1894	Dev. of work of CPT.	-do-
418	5900 LA/1M-47/94	12.10.95	Barghasipur, 156 P.S. Sutahata	31.57	-do-	Est. of commercial zone	-do-

Contd....

Sl. No.	Notice/ Declaration Nos.	Date	Location	Amount (in acre)	Section(s) of the Act	Purpose	Gazette publ. date
419	5758 LA(II)/ 4P-6/95/ Power	26.9.95	Bargachia, 1, P.S.Tamluk	9.21	-do-	Ash pond, KTPP	-do-
420	320 LA(PW)/11-81/92 I&W/Case No.91/71-72	18.11.92	Baghunasole, 958 P.S. Binpur Uddhabpur, 961 P.S. Binpur Chhota Jhariamura 962	11.93	Act II of 1948	Excavation of Disty. No. IDL in conn. with Kangsabati Res. Proj.	-do-
421	6229 LA/5I-2/ 95(Part)/ L and I	31.10.95	Ramgopalchak, 163, P.S. Sutahata	5.47	Act I of 1894	Housing complex of Haldia Petrochem Ltd.	15.11.95
422	6230 LA/5I-12/ 95(Part)/ C and I	-do-	-do-	5.50	-do-	-do-	-do-
423	6231 LA/5I-12/ 95(Part)/ L and I	-do-	-do-	6.99	-do-	-do-	-do-
424	6232 LA/5I-12/ 95(Part)/ L and I	-do-	-do-	5.63	-do-	-do-	-do-
425	6233 LA/5I-12/ 95(Part)/ L and I	-do-	-do-	4.90	-do-	-do-	-do-
426	6234 LA/5I-12/ 95(Part)/ L and I	-do-	-do-	5.08	-do-	-do-	-do-
427	6235 LA/5I-12/ 95(Part)/ L and I	-do-	-do-	4.99	-do-	-do-	-do-
428	6236 LA/5I-12/ 95(Part)/ L and I	-do-	-do-	6.43	-do-	-do-	-do-

Contd....

Sl. No.	Notice/ Declaration Nos.	Date	Location	Amount (in acre)	Section(s) of the Act	Purpose	Gazette publ. date
429	6237 LA/5I-12/ 95(Part)/ L and I	-do-	-do-	4.78	-do-	-do-	-do-
430	6238 LA/5I-12/ 95(Part)/ L and I	-do-	-do-	6.08	-do-	-do-	-do-
431	6239 LA/5I-12/ 95(Part)/ L and I	-do-	-do-	8.35	-do-	-do-	-do-
432	6292 LA(II)/ SL47/95/(III)/ L and I	1.11.95	Srirampurjia, 97, Radhanagar, 98, Matharakismat, 114, Amba, 115, Dhulyarchak, 126, Kantapal, 127, Mollachak, 128, Khosalchak, 129 P.S. Khargagpur.	283.77	-do-	Sponge and pig-iron Project of Century Textiles.	16.11.95
433	6217 LA/ 5I-12/ 95/Land I	31.10.95	Ramgopal Chak, 163, P.S. Sutahata	5.93	-do-	Housing complex of HPC Ltd.	28.11.95
434	6218 LA/ 5I-12/ 95/Land I	31.10.90	-do-	5.97	-do-	-do-	-do-
435	6219 LA/ 5I-12/ 95/Land I	-do-	-do-	5.23	-do-	-do-	-do-
436	6220 LA/ 5I-12/ 95/L and I	-do-	-do-	3.59	-do-	-do-	-do-

Contd....

Sl. No.	*Notice/ Declaration Nos.*	*Date*	*Location*	*Amount (in acre*	*Section(s) of the Act*	*Purpose*	*Gazette publ. date*
437	6221 LA/ 5I-12/ 95/Land I	-do-	-do-	9.15	-do-	-do-	-do-
438	6222 LA/ 5I-12/ 95/Land I	-do-	-do-	7.50	-do-	-do-	-do-
439	6223 LA/ 5I-12/ 95/Land I	-do-	-do-	6.197	-do-	-do-	-do-
440	6224 LA/ 5I-12/ 95/Land I	-do-	-do-	6.32	-do-	-do-	-do-
441	6225 LA/ 5I-12/ 95/Land I	-do-	-do-	7.84	-do-	-do-	-do-
442	6226 LA/ 5I-12/ 95/Land I	-do-	-do-	6.17	-do-	-do-	-do-
443	6655 LA/1W (1289)-17/95/ I and W	20.11.95	Amrit Berya, 93 Bholsara, 95 P.S. Mahisadal	6.985	-do-	Const. of sluice at the outfall of Bholsora Khal in conn. with drainage scheme	7.12.95
444	6298LA(II)/ Agri/ 1F-5/95	1.11.95	Karasai, 10 P.S. Garbeta	0.56	Act II of 1948	Const. of Block Seed Farm in Garbeta Block II.	18.12.95
445	4439 LA/ 4B-19/95	19.7.95	Kharagpur, Khasjangle, 142, P.S. KGP	0.70	Act I of 1894	Est. of Children's Park for KGP Municipality.	-do-

Contd....

Sl. No.	Notice/ Declaration Nos.	Date	Location	Amount (in acre)	Section(s) of the Act	Purpose	Gazette publ. date
446	6752 LA/(II)/ 5I-34/95/UD	24.11.95	Baneswarchak, 120, P.S. Sutahata	92.97	-do-	Small, med. large indus, app. rd. and rehab. complex.	-do-
447	6755 LA(II)/ 1D/ 47/95/LID (Toud CP)	-do-	Bardhanyaghata, 172, P.S. Sutahata	8.05	Act II of 1948	Small, med. and large indust. (HPC and down stream indust.).	-do-
448	6746LA/2R-50/95	-do-	Baisnab Chak, 275, P.S. KGP Hemtikri, 276, P.S. KGP, Banpatra, 340. P.S. KGP	11.66	-do-	Const. of Shyamalpur Achimouli Rd.	-do-
449	145 LA(PW)/ 99-46/92	15.1.93	Darpasila, 100, P.S. Jamboni, Bhorbani, 99 P.S. Jamboni.	11.84	-do-	Irrigation and draninage for Bhorbani minor irrigation scheme	8.1.96
450	6835 LA(II)/ 5I-31/95/UD	29.11.95	Bhuniaryachak, 122, P.S. Sutahata	85.41	Act I of 1894	Small, med. and large industries incld. app. road and rehab. complex.	-do-
451	6942 LA(II)/ 5I-32/95/UD	5.12.95	-do-	64.90	-do-	-do-	-do-
452	335 LA/ 4H-39/94	18.1.96	Brajamatt Chak	4.54	-do-	Housing and commercial zone	24.1.96

Contd....

Sl. No.	Notice/ Declaration Nos.	Date	Location	Amount (in acre)	Section(s) of the Act	Purpose	Gazette publ. date
453	358 LA/ 4H-45/94	-do-	Sotat, 151, P.S. Sutahata	30.04	-do-	Housing and commercial zone	-do-
454	6533 LA/ LR-46/91	13.11.95	Uttarbar, 1, P.S. Bhagwanpur	10.81	-do-	Providing proper faciliities for trans. and commu. No. 3 const. of Projabar Bhwanpur Rd. and Bhwanpur section.	-do-
455	7076 LA(II) (461)- 89/85/ I and W	11.2.95	Mohammodpur, 7, P.S. Bhagwanpur	0.25	Act II of 1948	Dariadighi-Udbadal Khal drainage scheme.	-do-
456	4378 LA/2R-20/95	17.7.95	Baradabar, 298, P.S. Panskura, Kodali, 230, P.S. Panskura, Chandpur, 232, P.S. Panskura, Pudumpur, 233, P.S. Panskura	6.30	-do-	Const. of link rd from NH 6 to Bhogpur	-do-
457	7343 LA/ 4P-37/95/ Power	26.12.95	Mandergacha, 301, P.S. Panskura	3.72	Act I of 1894	NH 6 of Bhogpur Const. of Ash pond No. 5 of KTPP.	-do-

Contd....

Sl. No.	Notice/ Declaration Nos.	Date	Location	Amount (in acre)	Section(s) of the Act	Purpose	Gazette publ. date
458	345 LA/IW (1289)-17/95/ I and W sec. Sl. No. (391)	18.1.96	Amritberya 43, Bholsara, 95, P.S. Mahisadal	6.975	Act I of 1894	Const. & sluice at the outfall of Bholsara Khal in connc. with drainage scheme for Tamluk areas	29.1.96
459	7297 LA(II)/ 5I-37/95/UD	22.12.95	Bhuyanroychak, 122, P.S. Sutahata	90.01	-do-	Small, med, and large scale indust. incld. app. rd. and rehab. complex.	-do-
460	7081 LA(II)/5I-40/95/UD	11.12.95	Joynagar, 123, P.S. Sutahata	40.185	-do-	-do-	-do-
461	408 LA(II)/ 5I-81/95/ L and I	22.1.96	Radhanagar, 98, Mathurakismat, 114, Amba, 115, P.S. KGP	91.065	-do-	Coke oven project and link road of Tata Metaliks Ltd.	12.2.96
462	145 LA/PW/ 19-26/92 LA Case No. 10882-83	7.5.95	Jarulia, 723, P.S. Jhargram, Khasijangal, 725 P.S Jhargram Ghatidubai, 726, Chukua, 827	14.735	Act II of 1948	Irrigation and drainage of Kangsbati Reservoir Project.	-do-
463	367 LA(II) 4P-7/ 95/ Power	19.1.96	Bargachia, 1, P.S.Tamluk	6.81	Act I of 1894	Ash pond No. 5 of KTPP.	-do-
464	409 LA/ 4P-93/95/ Power	22.1.96	Khandal Gobra, 86, P.S. Ramnagar	4.665	-do-	Const. of 33/11 K.V. Sub-stn.	-do-

Contd....

Sl. No.	Notice/. Declaration Nos.	Date	Location	Amount (in acre)	Section(s) of the Act	Purpose	Gazette publ. date
465	625 LA/4P-30/95/ Power (Dcelaration)	5.2.96	Purbabohala, 302, P.S. Panskura	2.48	-do-	Ash pond No.5 of KTPP.	-do-
466	643 LA/411-44/ 94/ (Declaration)	-do-	Deghashipur, 152, P.S. Sutahata	27.62	-do-	-do-	-do-
467	640 LA/1D/95	-do-	Bhabanipur, 150, P.S. Sutahata	14.14	-do-	Housing and comm. zone.	27.3.96
468	5021 LA(II)/ 2R-41/95	18.8.95	Anadapur, 378, P.S. Keshpur	21.11	Act II of 1948	Estd. of Potato and veg. seed production farm under five year plan.	-do-
469	1158 LA/2R-4/94	28.2.96	Marisda, 393	5.68	-do-	Const. of Tamluk-Digha B.G. Rly. Line.	—
470	1337 LA/2R-2/93	4.3.96	Narayandari, 152,	6.43	-do-	-do-	27.3.96
471	1608 LA/1W-45/95	19.3.96	Mianbazar, 173, P.S Midnapore	1.725	Act I of 1894	Const. of water reservoir for water supply.	20.5.95
472	1887 LA/2R-25/96	3.4.96	Chongra, 186, P.S. Moyna Banki, 187, P.S. Moyna, Garmoyna, 207, P.S. Moyna	20.915	Act II of 1948	Const. of Prajubarh Bhagwanpur rd.	24.5.96

Contd....

Sl. No.	Notice/ Declaration Nos.	Date	Location	Amount (in acre)	Section(s) of the Act	Purpose	Gazette publ. date
473	1687 LA(II)/5I-35/95/UD	25.3.96	Joynagar ,123, P.S. Sutahata	54.545	Act I of 1894	Small, med., large indus. incld. app. rd. rch. complete at Haldia.	-do-
474	2297 LA(II)/ 1D-4/96/ LID (Declaration)	17.4.96	Debhog, 149, P.S. Sutahata	11.67	do	Small, med, large indust.	-do-
475	2289 LA(II)/1D-12/96/ UD (Declaration)	-do-	-do-	12.63	do	-do-	27.5.96
476	2294 LA(II)/1D-9/96/ LID (Declaration)	-do-	-do-	12.70	do	-do-	-do-
477	2449 LA(II)/1D-27/96/ UD (Declaration)	24.4.96	-do-	11.00	do	-do-	-do-
478	953 LA(II)/ (427) 55/95/I/ I and W	20.2.96	Guripukur, 729, P.S. Jhargram, Brindabanpur, 730	16.035	Act II of 1948	Excavation of Disty. No. 13R in conn. with Kang. Res. Project.	-do-
479	2408 LA(II)/10-24/96/UD (Declaration)	23.4.96	Debhog, 149, P.S. Sutahata	11.28	Act I of 1894	Small, med, large indus.Haldia downstream.	-do-

Contd....

Sl. No.	Notice/ Declaration Nos.	Date	Location	Amount (in acre)	Section(s) of the Act	Purpose	Gazette publ. date
480	1519 LA/ PHE/ 1W-10/95	13.3.96	Kismat Bajkul, 156, P.S. Bhagwanpur	0.875	-do-	Rural piped W/S scheme (MNP).	-do-
481	2369 LA(II)/1D-23/96/ UD (Declaration)	19.4.96	Debhog, 149, P.S. Sutahata	8.74	-do-	Small, med. and large indust.	-do-
482	2300 WA(II)/1D-8/96/ UD (Declaration)	17.4.96	-do-	9.92	-do-	-do-	12.6.96
483	2303 LA(II)/1D-13/96/ UD (Declaration)	-do-	-do-	18.00	-do-	-do-	-do-
484	2306 LA(II)/1D-18/96/ UD (Declaration)	-do-	-do-	6.97	Act I of 1894	Small, med, indust.	-do-
485	2347 LA(II)/10/96/ UD (Declaration)	19.4.96	-do-	16.13	-do-	-do-	-do-
486	2309 LA(II)/1D-19/96/ UD (Declaration)	17.4.96	-do-	9.94	-do-	-do-	-do-
487	2403 LA(II)/1D-26/96/ UD (Declaration)	23.4.96	-do-	12.23	-do-	-do-	-do-

Contd....

Sl. No.	Notice/ Declaration Nos.	Date	Location	Amount (in acre	Section(s) of the Act	Purpose	Gazette publ. date
488	1801 LA/11 (430)/ 58/95/ I&W (Declaration)	28.3.96	Bhabanipur, 2, P.S. Debra	0.78	-do-	Housing breach on govt. embankment of river Cosseye.	-do-
489	2836 LA/ PHE/ AW-11/95/ (Declaration)	24.5.96	Kismat Bajkul, 156, P.S. Bhagwanpur	1.065	-do-	Implementation of rural piped w/s scheme (MNP).	-do-
490	2928 LA(II)/ 5C-54/95/ T and C.P. (Declaration)	4.6.96	Purbaraghunath Chak, 127 and Kumarchak 133, P.S. Sutahata	1.02	-do-	Creation of railway siding facilitites, for HPC.	19.6.96
491	1860 LA/ 1E-11/ 95/ (Declaration)	2.4.96	Kolo, 287, P.S. Panskura (Lolaghat)	0.87	-do-	Kola Union Jogendra Girls' School	-do-
492	2365 LA/1M/ 152/94/ C and I (Declaration)	19.4.96	Ohaktarayan, 193, P.S. Sutahata	0.45	-do-	Dev. work of CPT (Haldia Dock Complex)	-do-
493	2405 LA(II)/ 1D-29/96/ UD (Declaration)	23.4.96	Debhog, 149, P.S. Sutahata	13.90	-do-	Small, med., large indust.	-do-
494	2593 LA(II)/ 5I-36/95/UD (Declaration)	13.5.96	Bhuyanroy Chak, 122, P.S. Sutahata	93.104	-do-	-do-	-do-
495	2334 LA/ 4P-9/ 95/Power/ (Declaration)	21.6.95	Bargachia, 1, P.S.Tamluk	9.48	-do-	Ash pond No. 5 of KTPP.	24.6.96

Contd....

Sl. No.	Notice/ Declaration Nos.	Date	Location	Amount (in acre	Section(s) of the Act	Purpose	Gazette publ. date
496	2452 LA(II)/ 1D-28/96/UD (Declaration)	24.4.96	Debhog, 149, P.S. Sutahata	22.15	-do-	Small, med., large	25.6.96
497	2446 LA(II)/ 1D-25/96/UD (Declaration)	-do-	-do-	14.35	-do-	-do-	-do-
498	2400 LA(II)/ 1D-22/96/UD (Declaration)	23.4.96	-do-	16.17	-do-	-do-	-do-
499	2394 LA(II)/ 1D-21/96/UD (Declaration)	22.4.96	-do-	13.19	-do-	-do-	-do-
500	966 LA/ 4P-16/ 95/ Power	20.2.96	Bargachia, 1, P.S.Tamluk	5.78	Act I of 1894	Ash pond No. 5 of KTPP.	-do-
501	2557 LA(II)/ 5C-44/95/UD	2.5.96	Ramnagar ,124, P.S. Sutahata, Jagannath Chak, 125, P.S. Sutahata, Basudebpur, 126. P.S. Sutahata	42.525	-do-	Small, med., large indus. incld. app. rd. and rehab. complex.	-do-
502	3546 LA/4P-93/95/ Power	8.7.96	Khadal Gorba ,86 P.S. Ramnagar (Digha)	4.665	-do-	Const. of 33/11 K.V. Sub-stn.	19.7.96
503	3137 LA/ 1F(2511)-2/95 Fisheries	19.6.96	Kuliato, 227, P.S. Ramnagar	11.93	Act II of 1948	Const. of brackish water fish farm.	-do-

Contd....

Sl. No.	Notice/ Declaration Nos.	Date	Location	Amount (in acre)	Section(s) of the Act	Purpose	Gazette publ. date
504	3089 LA/2R-17/95	14.6.96	Uttarsitala, 260, P.S. Ramnagar Nimadasbar, 215, P.S. Contai	4.12	Act I of 1894	Const. of RCC bridge over Pichaboni Khal.	-do-
505	3334 LA/4P-9/95/ Power	21.6.96	Bargachia, 1, P.S.Tamluk	9.48	-do-	KTPP Ash Pond No. 5	-do-
506	2661 LA(II)/ 1W-12/96 H and FW	15.5.96	Bagpara, 202, P.S. Ramnagar, Saiyadpur, 204, P.S. Ramnagar	1.16	Act II of 1948	Const. of elevated reservoir, IE plant CW and pump house.	-do-
507	1703 LA/11-111/ 94/ I and W	25.3.96	Dubda, 191, P.S. Egra	15.33	-do-	Re-excavation of Balighai Khal in connec. with Dubda basin drainage scheme.	-do-
508	3826 LA/2R-1/96	22.7.96	Dudakhali 489, P.S. Salboni, Durbagere, 491, P.S. Salboni	3.31	-do-	Const. of one box culvert on 141 Km of R.M. Road.	18.9.96
509	3683 LA/2R-2/94	12.7.96	Thikra, 107, P.S. Ramnagar	0.235	-do-	Tamluk Digha B.G. Rly. Line.	-do-
510	22 LA/Cell/ HDA/ 12/26-91	22.8.96	Sobharampur, 147, P.S. Sutahata	81.06	Act I of 1894	Small, med and large indust.	-do-

Contd....

Sl. No.	Notice/ Declaration Nos.	Date	Location	Amount (in acre)	Section(s) of the Act	Purpose	Gazette publ. date
511	3-H/LA/96	11.10.96	Rajarampur, 102, P.S. Sutahata, Basudevpur, 126, P.S. Sutahata	224.545	Sub-section (3) of section 27 of the West Bengal Industrial Infrastructure Dev. Corp. Act, 1974.	Dev. of trade, commer. and industries on well planned basis.	11.10.96
512	4150 LA/2R-37/96	2.8.96	Kuturia, 505, P.S. Salboni	1.07	Const. of RCC Bridge over river Kalaichandi at 147 Km of MR Road.	Act II, 1948	-do-
513	5097 LA/2R-9/94	19.9.96	Marishda, 393, P.S. Contai	7.41	Act II of 1948	Tamluk Digha B.G. Rly. Line.	-do-
514	6209 LA/4P-34/ 95/ Power	1.10.96	Bargachia, 1, P.S.Tamluk	8.10	Act I of 1894	KTPP Ash Pond No. 5.	-do-
515	6482 LA/11 (483)-III/95/ I and W	15.10.96	Bishnu Mishra Chak, 175, P.S. Mayna	0.13	-do-	Const. of sluice in Kherai Buxi basin drainage scheme.	-do-
516	91 LA (Cell)/ HDA/39/96-97	30.10.96	Baneswar Chak, 120, P.S. Sutahata	71.92	-do-	Small med., and large scale indust. incl. app. rd. rehab. complex.	-do-

Contd....

Sl. No.	*Notice/ Declaration Nos.*	*Date*	*Location*	*Amount (in acre)*	*Section(s) of the Act*	*Purpose*	*Gazette publ. date*
517	6793 LA/11-(950)-88/96	6.11.96	Purnapani, 879, P.S. Jhargram, Barasuli, 880, P.S. Jhargram Bankati, 881, P.S. Jhargram	4.24	Act II of 1948	Excavation of Minor 2L/Disty No. 13R in conn. with Kangasaboti Proj.	1.1.97
518	168 LA(cell)/ HDA /97/96-97	23.12.96	Keshbere, 146, P.S. Sutahata	0.42	Act I of 1894	Small, med and large scale indus.	-do-
519	166 LA/cell/ HDA/90/96-97	-do-	Bhabanipur, 150, P.S. Sutahata	150.1975	-do-	Est. of urban complex.	-do-
520	6788 LA(II)/ WI Dev/1M-154/92	6.11.96	Sinduria, 81, P.S. Binpur, Barighati, 92, P.S. Binpur, Bamni, 108, P.S. Binpur	9.175	Act II of 1948	Barighati M.I Scheme.	-do-
521	181 LA(cell)/ HDA/20/96-97	31.12.96	Tentulbere, 170, P.S. Sutahata	63.185	Act I of 1894	Small, med., large indus.	13.1.97
522	183 LA/(Cell)/ HDA/21/96-97	-do-	-do-	92.76	-do-	-do-	-do-
523	185 LA (Cell)/ HDA/70/96-97	-do-	Bhagyabantapur, 104, P.S. Sutahata	55.38	-do-	Rehabilitation of evictees, due to acquisition of land at Haldia.	-do-
524	10 LA (Cell)/ HDA/79/96-97	14.1.97	Paranchak, 145, P.S. Sutahata	73.0125	-do-	Small, med., large indust.	-do-

Contd....

Sl. No.	*Notice/ Declaration Nos.*	*Date*	*Location*	*Amount (in acre)*	*Section(s) of the Act*	*Purpose*	*Gazette publ. date*
525	8 LA(Cell)/ HDA/69/96-97	-do-	Radhaballav Chak, 165, P.S. Sutahata Chaitaitanya Pajarir Chak, 162, Bhabanipur, 150, P.S. Sutahata, Barghashipur 156, P.S. Sutahata, Banbishnupur, 158, P.S. Sutahata	23.0555	Act I of 1894	Extn. of Haldia Petro-chem. link road upto river Haldia.	22.1.97
526	24 LA (Cell)/ HDA/100/ 96-97	20.1.97	Basudebpur, 126, P.S. Sutahata	31.13	-do-	Small, med. and large indust.	-do-
527	29 LA (Cell)/ HDA/81/ 96-97	27.1.97	Purba Srikrishnapur 103, P.S. Sutahata	70.60	-do-	Rehabilitation of evictees, due to acquisition of land at Haldia	-do-
528	30A LA (Cell)/ HDA/1/ 96-97	29.1.97	Kismat Shibramnagar, 94, P.S. Sutahata	82.20	-do-	Small, med. and large indust.	4.2.97
529	32 LA (Cell)/ HDA/54/ 96-97	-do-	Sovarampur, 147, P.S. Sutahata	34.72	-do-	-do-	-do-
530	34 LA (Cell)/ HDA/55/ 96-97	-do-	-do-	51.41	-do-	-do-	-do-
531	36 LA (Cell)/ HDA/56/ 96-97	-do-	-do-	45.41	-do-	-do-	5.2.97

Contd....

Sl. No.	Notice/ Declaration Nos.	Date	Location	Amount (in acre)	Section(s) of the Act	Purpose	Gazette publ. date
532	38 LA (Cell)/ HDA/60/ 96-97	-do-	-do-	25.90	-do-	-do-	-do-
533	561 LA/11-1/97/ I and W	22.1.97	Joykrishnapur, 257, P.S. Tamluk	0.22	-do-	Excav. of Sankarara Khal in conn. with drainage scheme for Tamluk Area.	-do-
534	564 LA/4B-28/ 96/ Panchayat	-do-	Keshpur, 338, P.S. Keshpur	1.91	-do-	Const. of Thana Market Complex.	-do-
535	68 LA/ (Cell)/ HDA/99/96-97	3.3.97	Purba Srikrishnapur, 103, P.S. Sutahata	81.04	-do-	Rehabili. of evictees due to acquisition of land at Haldia.	-do-
536	1390 LA/2R/ (1559)-124/90/ I and W	24.2.97	Hazipur, 152, Godalipur, 155, Arangabad, 151, Hasimpur, 148, P.S. Keshairy	35.64	-do-	Const. of diversion road from Belda to Bhasraghat for Subaranarekha barrage project.	17.3.97
537	66 LA (Cell)/ HDA/ 98/96-97	3.3.97	Purba Srikrishnapur, 103, P.S. Sutahata	68.69	-do-	Rehabilitation of evictees due to acquisition of land at Haldia.	18.3.97
538	75 LA (Cell)/ HDA/ 101/96-97	5.3.97	Kashberia, 146, P.S. Sutahata	76.92	-do-	Small, med and latge scale indust.	19.3.97
539	89 LA/ (Cell)/ HDA/ 93/96-97	7.3.97	Tentulbere, 170, P.S. Sutahata	79.0775	-do-	-do-	-do-

Contd....

Sl. No.	Notice/ Declaration Nos.	Date	Location	Amount (in acre)	Section(s) of the Act	Purpose	Gazette publ. date
540	81 LA (Cell)/ HDA/ 4/96-97	-do-	Kashberia, 146, P.S. Sutahata	53.80	-do-	-do-	-do-
541	87 LA (Cell)/ HDA/78/96-97	-do-	Purba Srikrishnapur ,103, P.S. Sutahata	87.49	-do-	Rehab. of evictees due to acq. of land.	-do-
542	351 LA/19-89/96	13.1.97	Sonamuri, 824, P.S. Jhargram	3.13	-do-	Excav. of Minor 5 of Disty. No. 13 RI in conn. with Kangsaboti reservoir project.	26.3.97
543	6255 LA/19-63/ 96/ I and W	3.10.96	Khashjangle, 725, P.S. Jhargram	1.02	Act II of 1948	Excav. of M-2 Disty 13.	-do-
544	6272 LA (II)/19-17/96	4.10.96	Bhorbani , 99, P.S. Jamboni, Bangabandhi, 103, P.S. Jamboni	9.09	-do-	Excav. of Bhorbani canal under Minor Irrigation scheme.	-do-
545	1138 LA (Cell)/ HDA /108/96-97	4.4.97	Debhog, 149, P.S. Sutahata	0.94	Act I of 1894	Small, med., large indust. (for Haldia downstream).	16.4.97
546	136LA (Cell)/ HDA/102/96-97	-do-	Joynagar, 123, Patharberia, 113, P.S. Sutahata	16.55	-do-	-do-	-do-
547	2444 LA/4P- 9/ 95/ Power	2.4.97	Bargachia, 1, P.S.Tamluk	9.48	-do-	Const. of Ash pond No. 5 of KTPP.	-do-

Contd....

Sl. No.	Notice/ Declaration Nos.	Date	Location	Amount (in acre)	Section(s) of the Act	Purpose	Gazette publ. date
548	2329 LA/1W-45/ 95 (Declaration)	31.3.97	Miabazar, 173, P.S Midnapore	1.725	-do-	Const. of water reservoir.	-do-
549	2430 LA/4P-29/ 97/ Power	2.4.97	Baithapur, 64, P.S. Daspur	9.69	-do-	Const. of 132/33 KV s/stn. of W.B.S.E.B.	-do-
550	153 LA (cell)/ HDA/110/97-98	15.4.97	Kasbere, 146, P.S.Sutahata	0.55	-do-	Small, med., large industries (Haldia downstream).	17.4.97
551	1788 LA/2Q-37/97	10.3.97	Purba Dobandhi Patna, 209, P.S. Moyna	0.75	-do-	Const. of Srirampore side approach rd. for the bridge over Kansai	-do-
552	2235 (Declaration)	26.3.97	Kismat Bajkul, 156, P.S. Bhagwanpur	0.875	-do-	Implementation of rural piped W/S Scheme (MNP).	-do-
553	161 LA (Cell)/ HDA/40/96-97 / LAP/ 14/93-94	16.4.97	Bhuyaroy Chak, 122, P.S. Sutahata. Ramnagar ,124, P.S. Sutahata Purbaraghunath Chak, 127, P.S. Sutahata	5.385	-do-	Small, med., large indust. incl. app rd. and rehab. complex.	26.5.97

Contd....

Sl. No.	Notice/ Declaration Nos.	Date	Location	Amount (in acre)	Section(s) of the Act	Purpose	Gazette publ. date
554	170 LA (Cell)/ HDA/ 69/96-97/ 2LA P-2/95-96 (Declaration)	28.5.97	Bhabanipur, 150, Barghasipur, 156, Radhaballavpur 165, Barbishnupur, 158	23.055	-do-	Extn. of Haldia Petro-chem link rd. upto river Haldia.	28.5.97
555	2670 LA/4P-83/ 95/ Power	8.4.97	Dharinda, 279 P.S. Tamluk	3.97	-do-	Const. of 132 KV. S./Stn. of WBSEB.	-do-
556	509 LA/11-2/97/ I and W	21.1.97	Gathra, 25, P.S. Tamluk	0.05	-do-	For Mirzapur Khal.	-do-
557	202 LA (Cell)/ HDA/100/96-97/LAP-15/96-97 (Declaration)	28.5.97	Basudebpur, 126, P.S. Tamluk	31.13	-do-	Small, med., large indust.	-do-
558	207 LA (Cell)/ HDA/41/96-97/ LAP-6/93-94	-do-	Baneswar Chak, 120, P.S. Sutahata	62.62	-do-	Small, med., large indust.	29.5.97
559	205 LA (Cell)/ HDA/70/96-97/ LAP-5/96-97	-do-	Bhagyabantapore, 104, P.S. Sutahata	55.38	-do-	Rehab. of evictees due to land acqui. at Haldia.	-do-
560	209 LA/ (Cell)/ HDA/19/96-97/ LAP-2/96-97	-do-	Sobharampur, 147, P.S. Sutahata	75.65	-do-	Small, med. and large indust.	-do-
561	231 LA (Cell)/ HDA/116/97-98/ LAP-7/4/96-97	18.6.97	Purba Srikrishnapur, 103, P.S. Sutahata	39.61	-do-	Rehab, of evicted eamilies at Haldia.	24.6.97

Contd....

Sl. No.	Notice/ Declaration Nos.	Date	Location	Amount (in acre)	Section(s) of the Act	Purpose	Gazette publ. date
562	5072 LA/43 (18) 18/95	13.5.97	Keranitola, 171, Thana Mid.	0.50	-do-	Const. of offices of LR Dept.	29.5.97
563	6060 LA/4P-9/ 95/ Power	6.6.97	Bargachia, 1, P.S. Tamluk	9.48	-do-	Const. of Ash pond for KTPP.	24.6.97
564	6318 LA/ 2R-69/97	13.6.97	Nischindipur 31 P.S. Ghatal	0.004	-do-	Widening and imporving of the existing.	-do-
565	233 LA (Cell)/ HDA/2/96-97 LAP 12-96-97	18.6.97	Kismat Shibram Nagar, 94, P.S. Sutahata	85.60	-do-	Small med., large indust.	-do-
566	267 LA (Cell)/ HDA/123/97-98/ LAP-1/4/97-98	30.6.97	Bhabanipur, 150 P.S. Sutahata	21.53	-do-	Est. of urban complex at Haldia.	1.7.97
567	257/LA9 (Cell) HDA/115/97-98/ LAP-7/2/96-97	24.6.97	Purba Srikrishnapur, 103, P.S. Sutahata	31.28	-do-	Reh. of evicted family	-do-
568	271 LA (Cell)/ HDA/125-97/98/ LAP-1/6/97-98	30.6.97	Bhabanipur, 150, P.S. Sutahata	12.80	-do-	Est. of urban complex	-do-
569	269/LA (Cell)/ HDA/124/97/98/ LAP-1/5/97-98	-do-	-do-	18.04	-do-	-do-	-do-
570	263 LA (Cell)/ HDA/121/97-98/ LAP/2/97-98	-do-	-do-	26.04	-do-	-do-	-do-

Contd....

Sl. No.	*Notice/ Declaration Nos.*	*Date*	*Location*	*Amount (in acre)*	*Section(s) of the Act*	*Purpose*	*Gazette publ. date*
571	261 LA (Cell)/ HDA/1120/ 97-98/LAP/1/1/ 97-98	-do-	-do-	12.48	-do-	-do-	-do-
572	265 LA (Cell)/ HDA/122/97-98/ LAP1/3/97-98	-do-	-do-	10.5925	-do-	-do-	-do-
573	273 LA (Cell)/ HDA/126/97-98/ LAP 1/7/97-98	-do-	Bhabanipur, 150, P.S. Sutahata	5.695	-do-	Est. of Urban Complex.	7.7.97
574	279/LA (Cell)/ HDA/129/97-98 LAP-1/10/97-98	-do-	-do-	14.14	-do-	-do-	-do-
575	281/LA/ (Cell)/ HDA/130/97-98/ LAP-1/11/97-98	-do-	-do-	11.79	-do-	-do-	-do-
576	275/LA (Cell)/ HDA/127/97-98 LAP-1/8/97-98	-do-	-do-	8.01	-do-	-do-	-do-
577	277 LA (Cell)/ HDA/128/97-98 LAP-1/9/97-98	-do-	-do-	9.08	-do-	-do-	-do-

Contd....

Sl. No.	Notice/ Declaration Nos.	Date	Location	Amount (in acre)	Section(s) of the Act	Purpose	Gazette publ. date
578	6163 LA/II-86/97/ I & W/LAP Case No. 8 of 96-97	11.6.97	Bhasraghat, 139, P.S. Keshiary	34.165	-do-	Const. of Canal Head Regulator and Subarnarekha barrage project.	-do-
579	310 LA (Cell)/ HDA/20/96-97 LAP-11/96-97	11.7.97	Tentulbere, 170, P.S. Sutahata	60.345	-do-	Small, med. and large industries	21.7.97
580	318 LA (Cell)/ HDA/21/96-97 LAP-10/96-97	-do-	-do-	89.33	-do-	-do-	-do-
581	6811 LA/ PHEW-24 97 LAPNo.13/96-97	7.7.97	Shalikadhani Chak, 122, P.S. Tamluk	0.315	-do-	Water supply scheme.	30.7.97
582	6726 LA/ Panchayat/ 4B-28/96	1.7.97	Keshpur, 338, P.S. Keshpur	1.91	-do-	Const. of Thana Market complex.	-do-
583	6643 LA/11-1-97/ I and W	27.6.97	Joykrishnapur, 257, P.S. Tamluk	0.22	-do-	Excavation of Sankararah Khal	-do-
584	326 LA (Cell)/ HDA/98/96-97/ LAP-8/96-97	28.7.97	Purba Srikrishnapur 103, P.S. Sutahata	59.05	-do-	Reh. of evicted families.	-do-
585	6935 LA/ 2R-73/97	9.7.97	Srirampur, 253, P.S. Tamluk	1.35	-do-	Const. of Temp. bridge approach road.	-do-

Contd....

Sl. No.	Notice/ Declaration Nos.	Date	Location	Amount (in acre)	Section(s) of the Act	Purpose	Gazette publ. date
586	6885 LA/ 2R-72/97/PWD (R) LAP18/96-97	8.7.97	-do-	3.99	-do-	-do-	-d-
587	7134 LA/5C-6/97/C and I	21.7.97	Bhubaneswarpur, 146, P.S. Tamluk	0.4525	-do-	Communication repeater-cum-cathodic protection unit for Haldia Barauni crude pipeline project.	-do-
588	1/HAD/VIII-M-3/97	15.7.97	Anandachak and Krishna Chak, 129, P.S. Sutahata	4.995	Notice under sub-sec (3) of-sec 27 of the WBI/DC Act, 1974	Dev. of trade comm. and indust.	12.8.97
589	1/HAD/VII-M-3/97	-do-	Jhikurkhali, 121, P.S. Sutahata	9.335	-do-	-do-	-do-
590	1/HAD/VII-M-3/97	-do-	Bhuniaraichak	15.81	-do-	-do-	-do-
591	2/HAD/VII-M-3/97	28.7.97	-do-	43.42	-do-	-do-	13.8.97
592	2/HAD/VII-M-3/97	-do-	-do-	43.42	-do-	-do-	-do-
593	1/HAD/VII-M-3/97	15.7.97	Anandachak and Krishnachak, 129, P.S. Sutahata	18.415	-do-	-do-	-do-

Contd....

Sl. No.	Notice/ Declaration Nos.	Date	Location	Amount (in acre)	Section(s) of the Act	Purpose	Gazette publ. date
594	1/HDA/VII-M-3/97	-do-	Bhuriarai Chak 122, P.S. Sutahata	64.635	-do-	-do-	-do-
595	1/HDA/VII-M-3/97	-do-	Jhikurkhali, 121, P.S. Sutahata	52.115	-do-	-do-	-do-
596	338 LA (Cell)/ HDA/93/96-97/ LAP-51/94-95	5.8.97	Tetulbere, 170 P.S. Sutahata	77.165	Act I of 1894	Small, med. and large indust.	18.8.97
597	379 LA (Cell)/ HDA/108/96-97/ LAP-40/96-97	19.8.97	Debhog, 149, P.S. Sutahata	0.94	-do-	-do-	1.9.97
598	364 LA/Cell/ HDA/81/96-97/ LAP-996-97	-do-	Purba Srikrishnapur, 103, P.S. Sutahata	46.55	-do-	Rch. of evictees due to acq. of land at Haldia for industries.	-do-
599	403 LA (Cell)/ HDA/110/97-98/ LAP-38/96-97	1.9.97	Kasbere, 146, P.S. Sutahata	0.55	-do-	Small, med., large indust.	-do-
600	687 LA/4 P-29/97/ Power	8.7.97	Baikunthapur. 64, P.S. Daspur	9.69	-do-	Const. of 132/133 KV Sub-stn. of WBSEB.	22.9.97
601	9243 LA/ 2R-37/97	29.9.97	Purba Dobandhi Patna, 209, P.S. Moyna	0.75	-do-	Const. of side opp. road.	7.11.97
602	9121 LA/11-2/ 97/ I and W	25.9.97	Gathra, 25, P.S. Tamluk	0.05	-do-	Earth strengthening of Mirzapur Khal.	-do-

Contd....

Sl. No.	*Notice/ Declaration Nos.*	*Date*	*Location*	*Amount (in acre)*	*Section(s) of the Act*	*Purpose*	*Gazette publ. date*
603	7080 LA/ 2R-79/97	24.9.97	Amgechia 236, P.S. Nandigram	0.08	-do-	Const. of Nandigram Maldaha Road.	-do-
604	9917 LA/(II)/5 C-6/97 (pt)/C and I Case No. 21/96-97	13.11.97	Bhubaneswarpur, 146, P.S. Tamluk	0.4525	-do-	Comm. Repeater.	4.12.97
605	9914 LA/2R-73/ 97 Case No. 19/96-97	-do-	Srirampur, 253, P.S. Tamluk	1.35	-do-	Const. of temp. side bridge app. road.	-do-
606	546 LA/Cell/ HDA/139/97-98 LAP No. 2/97-98	4.12.97	Rayrany Chak, 161, P.S. Sutahata	1.38	-do-	Housing complex of Haldia Petro-Chemicals.	17.12.97
607	544 LA (Cell)/ HDA/140/97-98 LAP No. 3/97-98	-do-	Ramgopal Chak, 163, P.S. Sutahata	7.01	-do-	-do-	-do-
608	1038 LA/ 2R-69/97	25.11.97	Nischindipur, 31, P.S. Ghatal	0.004	-do-	Widening and improving of link road leading market complex.	-do-
609	553 LA (Cell)/ HDA/102/96-97/ LAP-14/96-97	11.12.97	Joynagar, 123, P.S. Sutahata Patherberia, 113, P.S. Sutahata	16.55	-do-	Small, med., large industries.	-do-

Contd....

Sl. No.	Notice/ Declaration Nos.	Date	Location	Amount (in acre)	Section(s) of the Act	Purpose	Gazette publ. date
610	11313 LA/11/86/ 97/ I and W LAP Case No. 8/96-97	30.12.97	Jotikrishnapur, P.S. Keshiary J.L. No. 130, Bhansra, 139, P.S. Keshiary	34.165	Act I, of 1894	Const. of canal Head Regulator guide Bandh and project complex of Subarnarekha Barrage.	16.1.97
611	11343 LA/ 2R (1559)/124/ 96/I and W LAP Case No.28/ 95-96	-do-	Hazipur, 152, P.S. Keshiary, Godalipur, 155, Arangabad, 151, Hasimpur, 148	35.64	-do-	Const. of diversion road for Subarnarekha Barrage Project.	16.1.98
612	11140 LA/ 46-45/97	22.12.97	Mobarak Chak 210, Ruisanda, 211, P.S. KGP	15.06	-do-	Const. of Adam. Building and Housing complex of various sub. divn. offices.	-do-
613	2 LA (Cell)/HDA/ 1/96-97LAP Case No.13/96-97	1.1.98	Kismat Sibramnagar, 94, P.S. Sutahata	82.20	-do-	Setting up of small, med. and large scale industries at Haldia.	-do-
614	11312 LA/ 2R-80	30.12.97	Garmoyna, 207, Anandapur, 212, P.S. Moyna	0.20	-do-	Const. of Road	6.3.98
615	11131 LA/ 11-144/97/I&W	22.12.97	Natsal 157, P.S. Mahisada	3.066	-do-	Strengthening of embankment in the bank of river Rupnarayan.	-do-

Contd....

Sl. No.	Notice/ Declaration Nos.	Date	Location	Amount (in acre)	Section(s) of the Act	Purpose	Gazette publ. date
616	3/HDA/VII-M-3/97	3.1.98	Srirampur, 147, P.S. Sutahata	6.65	Section 27 Sub-sec. 1 of WBIID Corp Act, 1974 (WB Act XXV of 1974)	Trade, commerce and industries on well planned basis.	24.3.98
617	4/HDA/VII-M-3/97	3.1.98	Sovarampur, 147, P.S. Sutahata	46.8266	-do-	-do-	-do-
618	76 LA (Cell)/ HDA/2/96-97 LAP-12/96-97	18.3.98	Kismat sibramnagar	85.60	Act I of 1894	Small, med. large scale industries.	25.3.98
619	1011 LA/ 2R-4/98	18.2.98	Garmoyna, 207, P.S. Moyna	0.10	-do-	Road construction.	30.3.98
620	No.6/HDA/VI I-M-3/97LA Case No. HDA-004/96-97	25.3.98	Sovarampur, 147, P.S. Sutahata	67.19	Sub-sec. (3) of sec. 27 of the WBIID Corp Act, 1974	Development of trade, commerce and industries on well planned basis.	-do-
621	No.7/HDA/VII-M-3/97 LA Case No. HDA/ 005/96-97	-do-	-do-	72.80	-do-	-do-	-do-
622	No.8 HDA/VII-M-3/97 LA Case No.HDA/ 006/97-97	-do-	-do-	32.56	-do-	-do-	-do-

Contd....

Sl. No.	*Notice/ Declaration Nos.*	*Date*	*Location*	*Amount (in acre)*	*Section(s) of the Act*	*Purpose*	*Gazette publ. date*
623	No.9/HDA/VI-1 M-3/97 LA Case No. HDA/ 007/96-97	-do-	-do-	24.13	-do-	-do-	-do-
624	No.10/HDA/VII-M-3/97 LA Case HDA/008/96-97	-do-	-do-	48.5025	-do-	-do-	-do-

APPENDIX—B

The Statesman, 24.08.1995

Dasgupta for free competition

Land reforms must for 'successful liberalization

By a Staff Correspondent

LAND reforms should form an important component of the liberalization process to improve the quality of life of the people for whom liberalization is meant. The essence of liberalization lies in unleasing the forces of competition, implying a movement from a less competitive to a more competitive situation.

Making these observations in Calcutta on Wednesday, Dr Asim Dasgupta, West Bengal Finance Minister, said that in agriculture moving towards more competition meant providing more equal access to land for working farmers, which could only be achieved through land reforms. Without land reforms, there could not be unleashing of competitive forces in agriculture which comprised the largest sector of the Indian economy.

In achieving this process, while a part is played by market forces, to make the process sustainable, collective action in an appropriate form is also necessary. This form could take the shape of a Government — at the Central, State or local level, Dr Dasgupta said.

The Finance Minister, who was delivering the inaugural address at the Seventh Annual Management Education Convention on the theme 'Liberalized economy and quality of life: challenges for management' organized by the Association of Indian Management Schools in collaboration with the Canadian Consortium of Management Schools at the Indian Institute of Management, Joka, said if we accepted that multinational monopolistic interests dominated the present pattern of international trade, then for a country like India, liberalization would require moving towards a core of achievable self-reliance and then participating in external trade.

Because, he said, this would basically mean acquiring more cially acceptable.

In view of such cirmstances. Dr Dasgupta said, to make liberalization a success, a reorientation of management education was necessary. Training for management in the small-scale sector as well as for decentalized collective action should also find a proper place in management education.

Dr Dasgupta said more than 80 per cent of the demand in India was for foodgrain, clothing, some kind of fuel and some medicines. Most of these items could be produced cheaply in India. In this context, he said that the land reforms in this State had led to a situation where West Bengal accounted for the highest rate of growth of foodgrains production in the country in recent years.

During this era of so-called liberalization, he said, the rate of growth of employment seekers was 2.5 per cent. But the rate of growth of employment generation was 2.3 per cent, and this rate was likely to fall further. Thus it was obvious that one of the major casualties of the so-called liberalization process was employment. However, the process cannot be sustained if such trends continue, according to him.

Mr R. P. Goenka, industrialist, who was the guest-of-honour at the function, said liberalization was not an end in itself. It was a means to an end. Underlining the need to quicken the growth of the agricultural sector, he said any reforms process that helped to improve the country's agricultural base was always welcome.

Mr Goenka said social responsibility should be an integral part of business administration and this should be incorporated in management studies.

The senior industrialist said West Bengal's position was second in the country today in terms of economic deve-

Midnapore farmers resist land survey

STATESMAN NEWS SERVICE

SADATPUR (Midnapore), Jan. 9. — Land survey and soil testing work in Mathura Kismat mouza in the Kalaikuna gram panchayat area of Kharagpur rural police station, undertaken by Century Textiles — a Birla Group of Industries — had to be abandoned following stiff resistance from villagers last week.

The engineer of the company had to leave when hundreds of farmers stormed his tent.

The farmers also blocked Sahachak Road far nine hours yesterday under the leadership of Mr Trilochan Rana, INTUC president of Kharagpur block. They also lodged a complaint with the police against the firm.

Survey and soil testing work began on January 1 after the State Government issued a notice to acquire 720 acres of agricultural land in 18 mouzas in Kalaikunda.

The acquired land would be distributed among industrialists on a 99-year lease through the West Bengal Financial Development Corporation.

Mr Nitai Karak, Mr Dilip Patra of Samraipur and others of adjoining villages told The Statesman that they were against agricultural land being acquired and surveyed surreptitiously.

Later, about 66 farmers of 18 mouzas in a memorandum to the SDO, Kharagpur, Mr Nilanjan Chatterjee, threatened they would not allow acquisition of land ignoring their demands.

Their nine-point charter of demands include compensation at the rate of Rs 3 lakh per acre and a job to each affected farmer's family or land against land besides supply of electricity to the villages.

They also demanded measures against liquor dens and pollution by industrial units set up in the Kharagpur industrial estate earlier.

Mr Rana said the farmers in the area had a bitter experience of being deprived of compensation and other benefits professed by Tata Metaliks, the coke oven unit of Wallman, and other concerns when 220 acres of farmland were acqired in the early 80s.

Of the 200 evicted farmers, only 20 were given jobs in these establishments while more than 50 per cent of the affected were yet to get their compensation, official sources confirmed.

Meanwhile, the Bansal Cement Company which had already acquired 12 acres paid Rs 75,000 as compensation against each acre, Mr Mohan Garulal of the company, said.

However, Mr Suresh Kumar, Additional District Magistrate, Midnapore, urged the farmers at a meeting not to disturb the survey and soil testing work as their grievances had been conveyed to the State Government.

But the farmers were adamant about continuing their agitatioon till an agreement was signed fulfilling their demands, Mr Patra and Mr Karak said.

Meanwhile, the State INTUC president, Mr Subrata Mukherjee, also asked the local leader of the INTUC not to budge an inch from his stand on the issue. This has heightened tension in the area.

The Statesman, 10 January 1996 (P.3)

THE STATESMAN, FRIDAY 28 FEBRUARY 1997

State to reclaim unused land leased to industries

STATESMAN NEWS SERVICE

CALCUTTA, Feb. 27. — Land leased out by the state government to industrial companies and which remain unutilised will be reclaimed for allotment to new industrial entrepreneurs.

The different municipalities have also been directed not to sanction any building plans on land belonging to owners of units which have subsequently closed down or have turned sick.

The owners will only be permitted to sell off the land for future industrial investment or for meeting the outstanding liabilities of the employees.

A special committee has been set up by the state government to identify land where industries can be set up without impinging on agricultural land.

The authorities were preparing a report on the basis of which planning for future industrial units will be made.

Announcing this at Writers' Buildings here today, the state's minister for land and land reforms, Mr Surjya Kanta Mishra, said that state departments had been instructed to relinquish land now in their possession which remains unutilised so that more plots can be made available for new industries.

For the industries requiring land in excess of the ceiling limit of 24.20 acres, the existing legislation has been amended to permit the entrepreneurs concerned to acquire the land.

The minister said that to expedite the process of acquisition of land for industries under the Land Acquisition Act steps have been taken to quicken the process.

In certain areas, collectors have been vested with the powers of the state government.

Financial powers of the collectors and divisional commissioners for the sanction of estimates and awards of land have been enhanced recently so that cases can be finalised at the field level, Mr Mishra added.

He also said that instructions had been issued to the district officers to assign priority to the applications by prospective entrepreneurs for mutation and conversion of land when they purchase the land directly from the owners.

Relevant rules are being amended to simplify the procedures for mutation and conversion, the minister said.

6 October 1997 (P.4)

Acquisition of land must be made simpler, says minister

STATESMAN NEWS SERVICE

CALCUTTA, Oct. 5. — the Urban Development and Municipal Affairs Minister today blamed lengthy land acquisition procedures for the lack of progress in West Bengal.

Mr Ashok Bhattacharya was speaking at the Salt Lake Stadium this afternoon after handing over cheques to 84 farmers who have sold land to the state government for the Rajarhat township.

The sale of land by farmers directly to the state government was yet another success of the Left Front government, the minister said.

Sonarpur, Dankuni and West Howrah have been identified for construction of the new townships.

Mr Dilip Gupta, chairman of the Bidhannagar Municipality, accused opponents of the government of trying to prevent development on the plea that the environment was being affected.

Neither iron nor rice for Midnapore tribals

12 March 1998 (P.3).

STATESMAN NEWS SERVICE

KALAIKUNDA (Midnapore), March 11. — Fertile agricultural land, acquired about two years ago for setting up a pig iron plant, is still lying unused here.

By a government notification, some 530 acres of agriculturally productive farm land falling under Kalaikunda gram panchayat area of Kharagpur subdivision, was given to a Mumbai-based company.

So far, nothing has been done to utilise these vast tracts. Neither have there been any moves to redistribute the land to other entrepreneurs, it is learnt.

The state land and land reforms minister, Dr Surya Kanta Mishra, had declared in Calcutta on 27 February, 1997, that government departments had been instructed "to reclaim unutilised land, earlier leased out to industrial companies by the state government, for their reallotment to new industrial entrepreneurs.

The conduct of the Mumbai-based company makes a mockery of the minister's statement, officials at Kharagpur say. The government has not initiated any steps against the firm. —

The loss of their land has caused widespread resentment among farmers here.

The acquisition has adversely affected the lives of hundreds of people, including tribals, who were primarily dependent upon agriculture in the area, a field survey by researchers from the department of anthropology, Vidyasagar University, revealed recently.

The anthropologists have demonstrated how the establishment of another pig iron plant in the area some four years ago had led to a further marginalisation of Kora tribals.

They had used their compensation money not in acquiring any assets, but had frittered it away for domestic needs and to repay loans. The land acquisition has, in fact, helped no one. If put to cultivation, the land could have yielded a minimum of 5,200 quintals of rice in the last two years, farmers point out.

Kalaikunda land unused

18 November 1999 (P. 4).

SHYAM SUNDER ROY
STATESMAN NEWS SERVICE

KALAIKUNDA, Nov. 17. — "Give us your land and we will give you jobs." Hundreds of farmers in Kalaikunda gram panchayat area were fed with this slogan by local CPI-M leaders and the state government.

Consequently, more than 526 acres of agricultural land ("Jal doem" in land reforms department's parlance) were acquired in April 1996 and offered to a Mumbai-based company, Century Textiles, to set up a Rs 400-crore sponge and pig iron unit.

But since then not a single brick has been laid on the land, near National Highway 6.

Mr BK Birla, the company MD, told The Statesman they will not proceed with the project as "the national market of pig iron has become very much competitive because of the entry of China and Australia in the field." This was conveyed to the state government long back, he added.

The fate of the huge chunk of fertile land now seems to hang in balance. It was the source of livelihood for several hundred farmers, including patta holders and sharecroppers.

Mr Surya Kanto Mishra, state Land and Land Reforms Minister, who also belongs to the district said: "We are not finding any taker for the land." About 420 farmers filed petitions to the district magistrate on 2 February '96 saying "the acquisition of the land will severely affect their livelihood in future."

A government report of 21 June '96 noted, "it is a fact that since large quantum of land is being acquired for the company and people chiefly subsist on agriculture many will be seriously affected in earning their livelihood and avocations."

The report further said: "The acquisition will affect at least 3,000 land owners, if not more. But ironically, all the objections of the farmers were overruled on the ground of setting up the industry as it would serve greater public interests."

Meanwhile, the region's economy has been affected.

There has been a loss of at least 20,000 quintal rice which could have been produced if the land were put to use, farmers say.

But most hard-hit are the owners of the 172-acre land who were neither paid any compensation nor allowed to cultivate.

The Statesman 5 July 2000 (P. 4).

Hungry tribals pay for unfinished dream plant

SHYAMSUNDAR ROY
STATESMAN NEWS SERVICE

KHARAGPUR, July 4. — This is the story of a dream sponge and pig-iron plant in Kharagpur's Kalaikunda region. And, the loss of 30,000 quintals of rice in chasing that dream that remained just that.

The Rs 400 crore dream project was approved by the West Bengal Industrial Development Corporation in early 1996. But till date, not a single brick has been laid on the 526-acre plot by the Mumbai-based company.

This huge piece of agricultural land in the process remains unutilised and barren and could have yielded at least 30,000 quintals of rice over the past four years that it lay wasted.

While the company informed the state government about its inability to set up the unit last year, the latter is yet to decide what to do with the plot. Much to the agony of local villagers, mostly tribals.

A study conducted by Vidyasagar University's anthropology department has revealed the adverse consequences of the acquisition of this fertile agricultural land by the state government.

The study, which was done in four villages — Shyamraipur, Baharapat, Kantapal and Mollachak — among 46 small and marginal farmers, shows that about 35 per cent of the affected families, all Lodhas, are languishing in their dilapidated mud houses and have given up all hope of getting back their farm land.

Prof Abhijit Guha, senior lecturer in the university's anthropology department, has said that in Kalaikunda's case, neither the panchayat nor any NGO has been doing anything to develop schemes for the landless tribals, bargadars and patta-holders, who are the worst victims of the unfinished project.

A government report of 21 June, 1996, stated: "It's a fact that since large quantum of land is being acquired for the company and people chiefly subsist on agriculture, many will be seriously affected in earning their livelihood."The report further stated: "The acquisition will affect at least 3,000 land owners, if not more". But still, all objections of the farmers were overruled.

A spokesman of the company said: "We had informed our decision to back out from the project last year itself because of the stiff competition in the market, particularly after the entry of Chinese and Austrian firms in the market."

It is evident from the attitude of the district land and land reforms department that it is undecided on the fate of the land. Officers confirm that no decision has been taken yet.

APPENDIX—C

Registered No.—W.B./SC-247 WB / 1876 / LA / MDP / 96

SL. NO.—I LA / G / 1

The Calcutta Gazette

EXTRAORDINARY

Published by Authority.

CHATRA—13 TUESDAY—2nd APRIL, 1996 SAKA – 1918

PART—I :—Orders and Notifications by the Governor of West Bengal, the High Court, Government Treasury, etc.

GOVERNMENT OF WEST BENGAL

LAND AND LAND REFORMS DEPARTMENT

LAND ACQUISITION BRANCH.

NOTIFICATION

MIDNAPORE No.1874—LA (11)

Dated 2. 4. 96

The following agreement is published under section 42 of the Land Acquisition Act, 1894 for general information.

AGREEMENT

Memorandum of Agreement made this second day of April, 1996 between the Century Textiles & Industries Limited Company, (a Company registered under the Indian Companies Act, 1882) and havings its registered office at Century Bhavan, Dr. Annie Beasant Road, Worli in Bombay – 400 025 and local office situated at Shivam Chambers, 53, Syed Amir Ali Avenue, Calcutta—700019 (hereinafter called "the company") of the one part and "the Governor" of the state of west Bengal (hereinafter called the Governor) of the other part.

Whereas for Purpose of the construction of Pig Iron and Steel plant the Company has applied to the Government of West Bengal for the acquisition under the provisions of the Land Acquisition Act, 1894 of the piece or parcel of land containing 526,71 acres (213,16 hectares) or thereabout situated in the village of Kalikapur JL No.—137 Rajpura JL No.—130. Chaksonadhar JL No. – 136. Knatageria JL No.—92, Sujatpur JL No. – 139. Dhekia JL No.—135, Panchrolya JL No.—91, Tarabamni JL No – 138 Niranjanbar JL No.—134, Malancha JL No. – 131 all of P. S. Kharagpur in the district of Midnapore and more particularly described in the schedule hereto and delineated in the plan hereunto annexed.

APPENDIX—D

Destination West Bengal

WBIDC, January 1999 (p 21)

KHARAGPUR

Location

112 Kms to the West of Calcutta, Kharagpur is connected to Calcutta by NH6 (connecting Calcutta to Mumbai and Chennai). But its main strength is as a railway junction on the South Eastern Railway line, connecting Calcutta, Mumbai, Chennai and the mining areas of the Eastern Region. Kharagpur is close to and well connected with the Integrated Steel Plants at Jamshedpur (TISCO), Rourkela (SAIL), Bokaro (SAIL) and Durgapur (SAIL). Home of the premier Indian Institute of Technology, it is served by the suburban train service from Calcutta.

The industrial giant of India, the Tatas, have located most of their manufacturing units in the state in Kharagpur because of its proximity to their steel city at Jamshedpur.

Existing Industrial Units

SE Railway Workshop	: Carriage, Wagon, Steam and Diesel Locomotive : Maintenance
Tata Bearings Ltd.	: Bearings and Castings
Tata Metaliks Ltd.	: Pig Iron Plant
Flender MacNeill	: Industrial Gears
Humboldt Wedag (I) Ltd.	: Slurry Pumps
Wellman Wacoma Ltd.	: Coke Oven
Aso Cement Ltd.	: Slag Cement
Tata Davy Ltd.	: Heavy Engineering

Upcoming Units

Century Textiles	: Pig & Sponge Iron
Aso Cement Ltd. (expansion)	: Cement

Industrial Area

Nimpura, located 7 Kms from Kharagpur on NH6 is a developed area with available railway siding and has a dozen working units, including two from the Tata group. Tisco is also building a Housing Complex within the Industrial Area.

Opportunities

Foundries, light engineering and steel downstream.

Glossary

Acre	A unit of land measure equal to 43,560 sq. ft.
Ail	Earthen dykes having a height of less than 12 inches prepared by the farmers on agricultural land to demarcate individual ownership.
Aman	The most important rice crop in Bengal which is sown in May and June and harvested in November and December.
Aus	A rice crop in Bengal sown around April and harvested in August and September.
Babu	A Bengali word meaning gentleman.
Bargadar	A sharecropper in West Bengal for whom a special legislation is made to secure his rights of cultivation and share of crop with the owner of the land.
Bastu	Homestead land.
Boro	A rice crop of Bengal sown in November and harvested in February and March.
Dhosa	Land in which aus paddy, pulses and oilseeds are grown.
Diara	Land near river formed by silt deposition.
Gram Panchayat	The third tier of elected panchayat in West Bengal consisting of a number of mouza villages.
Gram Samsad	The fourth tier of elected panchayat in West Bengal which operates at the mouza level.
Hectare	A metric unit of land measure equal to 10,000 square metres; equivalent to 2.471 acres.
Jal Awal	Land category within the *jal* variety used in Land and Land Records Department of the Government of West Bengal. In terms of qualitative ranking

developed by the Land Records Department. This category occupies the highest rank in terms of quality.

Jal Chaharam Official Land category occupying the fourth position.

Jal Soem Land category used by Land Records Department occupying the second position.

Jal Soem Official land category occupying the third position.

Jal A local term which refers to low clayey land which remains under water during the rains and rice is grown in it.

Kala A local term which refers to high sandy land found around the village sites above flood level and *rabi* crops are grown in it.

Mouza A revenue unit bearing a local name which may or may not overlap with the village defined by the local people.

Panchayat samity The second tier of the elected panchayat in West Bengal which operates at the block level.

Panchayat Local self-government in the rural areas of West Bengal having four tiers and the members are elected to office every five years.

Patta Land given to landless families by the government with the help of the Land and Land Reform Act, 1955. According to law patta land can be inherited but cannot be sold.

Pradhan Chairperson of the elected gram panchayat.

Rabi A variety of crops including wheat, pulses and winter vegetables sown after the rainy season.

Requiring body The government department or private company for which the Land Acquisition Department of the State Government in India acquires land for a public purpose by employing Land Acquisition Act.

Savapati Chairman of the elected panchayat samity.

Scheduled Caste A caste group in India enlisted in the government schedule for getting certain constitutional safeguards and privileges.

Scheduled Tribe A tribe in India enlisted in the government schedule for getting certain constitutional safeguards and privileges.

Solatium Thirty per cent of the land value given to the landloser as part of the compensation under the Land Acquisition Act of 1894. Before 1984 it was 15 per cent.

Til A summer oilseed.

Zamindary A system of exploitative land tenure arrangement based on a number of intermediaries introduced by the British colonial administration in India after the permanent settlement in 1795.

Zilla Parishad The highest tier of the elected local government in West Bengal which operates at the district level. The chairperson of the zilla parishad is termed Sabhadhipati.

References

Asthana, R. (1996): "Involuntary Resettlement: Survey of International Experience". *Economic and Political Weekly.* June 15, 1996, Vol. XXXI No. 24. pp. 1468-1475.

Bardhan, A.B. (1973): *The Tribal Problem in India,* New Delhi: Communist Party of India.

Barth, F. and T.R. Williams (1994): *Initial Resettlement Planning and Activity (1992-94) in a Large Scale Hydropower Project: The Ertan Dam in South-west China*. World Bank, Washington, D.C. Processed.

Block Development Office (1997): *Final Status Report of the Below Poverty Line Survey on Kharagpur I Block,* Medinipur District (Unpublished) Medinipur: Block Development Office, Kharagpur I.

Brokensha, D. and T. Scudder (1968): "Resettlement", in N. Rubin and W.W. Warren, eds. *Dams in Africa: An Interdisciplinary Study of Man-Made Lakes in Africa,* London: Frank Cass.

Butcher, D. (1971): *An Operational Manual for Resettlement: A Systematic Approach to the Resettlement Problem Created by Man-Made Lakes, with Special Relevance for West Africa, Rome:* FAO.

Cernea, M. (1991): "Involuntary Resettlement: Social Research, Policy and Planning" in M. Cernea, ed. *Putting People First: Sociological Variables in Development.* 2nd ed. New York: Oxford University Press.

—— (1995): "Understanding and Preventing Impoverishment from Displacement", *Journal of Refugee Studies* 8: 245-264.

——(1996a): "Public Policy Responses to Development-Induced Population Displacement", *Economic and Political Weekly,* June 15, 1996, Vol. XXXL. No. 24. pp. 1515-1523.

——(1996b): "Bridging the Research Divide: Studying Refugees and Development Oustees", in T. Allen ed., *In Search of Cool Ground: Displacement and Homecoming in North-east Africa,* London: James Currey.

——(1997): "The Risks and Reconstruction Model for Resettling Displaced Populations." *World Development* 25 (October): 1569-87.

——(1998): "Economics and the Private Sector: Open Issues in Resettlement Research". The 1998 Colson Lecture, University of Oxford, RSP, May 13. Processed.

——(1999a) "Mutual Reinforcement: Linking Economic and Social Knowledge about Resettlement, in *The Economics of Involuntary Resettlement:*

Questions and Challenges. Edited by M. Cernea, pp. 1-4. Washington D.C.: The World Bank.

——(1999b): Why Economic Analysis is Essential to Resettlement: A Sociologist's View, in M. Cernea (ed.), *The Economics of Involuntary Resettlement: Questions and Challenges*. Edited by M. Cernea, pp. 5-49 Washington D.C.: The World Bank.

——(2000): "Risks, Safeguards and Reconstruction: A Model for Population Displacement and Resettlement", *Economic and Political Weekly*. October 7, 2000 Vol. XXXV, No. 41, pp. 3659-3678.

——(2002): "For a New Economics of Resettlement: a Sociological Critique of the Compensation Principle", in *An Exchange on the Compensation Principle in Resettlement,* Working Paper, Department of Applied Economics and Management, Cornell University, Ithaca, New Youk.

Cernea, M. and S. Guggenheim (1993): (eds). *Anthropological Approaches to Resettlement: Policy, Practice, Theory*, Boulder Colorado: Westview Press.

Chakraborty, S. (1961): "Land Use Pattern of Western Midnapore" in *District Census Handbook, Midnapore,* Calcutta: Government of West Bengal.

Chambers, R. (ed.), (1970): *The Volta Resettlement Experience,* London: Pall Mall Press.

Chatterjee, P. (2000): *Recent Strategies of Resettlement and Rehabilitation in West Bengal.* Preliminary Draft presented in a Workshop on "Social Development Research in West Bengal" held during 6-7 July 2000 at the Centre for Studies in Social Sciences, Kolkata.

Coal India Limited (1994): *Resettlement and Rehabilitation Policy of CIL,* Coal India Ltd. Calcutta.

Colson, E. (1971): *The Social Consequences of Resettlement: The Impact of the Kariba Resettlement on the Gwembe Tonga*, Manchester, U.K. Manchester University Press.

Department of Agricullture (1967): *Report of the Group of Experts on Land Acquisition* Ministry of Food, Agriculture, Community Development and Cooperation, Government of India.

Department of Panchayat (1994) *Bidhi Nirdeshika* (Gram Panchayat) (Bengali) Government of West Bengal.

District Census Handbook (1951): *Midnapore* Calcutta: Government of West Bengal.

——(1961): *Midnapore* Calcutta: Government of West Bengal.

District Planning Committee (1985): *Village Based District Planning Process: An Outline of Methodology*. District Planning Committee, Midnapore, West Bengal.

District Statistical Handbook (1998): *Midnapore.* Bureau of Applied Economics and Statistics. Government of West Bengal.

Drèze, J. and A. Sen (1998): *Hunger and Public Action,* Delhi: Oxford University Press.

Eastern Anthopologist (2000): Vol. 53, Nos. 1-2, 2000 (January-June).

Economic and Political Weekly (1996) Vol. XXXI, No. 24, 1996 (June).

Fernandes, W. (1998): "The National Draft Policy for Rehabilitation: Principles of the NGO Alternative" in H.M. Mathur and D. Marsden (eds.) *Development Projects and Impoverishment Risks.* New Delhi: Oxford University Press.

——(2000): *Personal Communication,* June 2000. Guwahati: North Eastern Social Research Centre.

Fernandes, W., J.C. Das and S. Rao (1989): "Displacement and Rehabilitation: An Estimate of Extent and Prospects," in *Development Displacement and Rehabilitation* (eds.), W. Fernandes and E. Ganguly Thukral. New Delhi: Indian Social Institute.

Gans, H.J. (1968): *People and Plans: Essays on Urban Problems and Solutions.* New York: Basic Books.

Guha, A. L. Jana, T. Barman and R. Mondal (1996): "Plough, Policies, Pig-iron and Displacement in Medinipur in the Wake of Liberalisation". *Journal of the Indian Geographical Foundation.* Vol. 3, 1996.

Guha, A.L. Jana and T. Barman (1997): "Dispossession of the Tribal People from their Agricultural Land : a case study of Koras in Midnapore." *Man and Life*. Vol. 23, 1997.

Guha, A. (2004a): Dispossession of Peasants from Agricultural Land in West Medinipur: A Need for Radical changes in the Policy of the Government of West Bengal". *Society and Change* Vol. XII, No. 4, 2004.

Guha, A. (2004 b): " Land Acquisition in a West Bengal District". *Economic and Political Weekly*. October 16-22, 2004, Vol. XXXIX, No. 42.

——(2005): "Resettlement and Rehabilitation". *Economic and Political Weekly*, November 12-18, 2005, Vol. XL, No. 46.

——(2006a): "Eviction of Bargadars Under State Patronage in Leftist West Bengal: A Policy Perspective" in *Perspectives of Rural Development: Problems an Prospects* (eds.), R.K. Das, A. Basu and A. Guha. Kolkata: The India Anthropological Society and Department of Anthropology, Vidyasagar University.

——(2006b): "Dispossession of Peasants by Industrial Projects" in *The Economics and Politics of Resettlement in India* (eds.), S. Jain and M. Bala. New Delhi: Dorling Kindersley (India) Pvt. Ltd.

Hobsbawm, E. (1994): *Age of Extremes: The Short Twentieth Century,* New Delhi: Viking, Penguin India (P) Ltd.

International Rivers Network (1997): *Proceedings of the First International Meeting of People Affected by Dams*, March, 11-14, 1997, Curitiba, Brazil.

Johnson, A.W. (1978): *Research Methods in Social Anthropology,* London: Edward Arnold.

Kanbur, R. (2002): "Development Economics and the Compensation Principle", in An *Exchange on the Compensation Principle in Resettlement*, Working Paper, Department of Applied Economics and Management, Cornell University, Ithaca, New York.

Land Acquisition Department (1992): *Composite Revised Rate Report for Land Acquisition Cases of Pig-iron Project,* P.S. Kharagpur (Unpublished Report) Office of the Land Acquisition Department: Midnapore.

——(1993): *Land Acquisition Cases of Midnapore: Present Status, Problems, Future Strategy* (Unpublished Report) Office of the Collector: Midnapore.

——(1996): *Report on the Hearing of Objections for Land Acquisition for Century Textiles* (Unpublished). Office of the Land Acquisition Department: Midnapore.

Leiten, G.K. (1996) *Development, Devolution and Democracy, New Delhi:* Sage Publications.

Lokayan Bulletin (Special issue) (1995) Vol. 11, No. 5, 1995 (April).

Mahapatra, L.K. (1991) "Development for Whom? Depriving the Dispossessed Tribals". *Social Action* (July-September).

—— (1999). "Testing The Risks and Reconstruction Model on India's Resettlement Experiences", in M. Cernea (ed.), *The Economics of Involuntary Resettlement: Questions and Challenges.* The World Bank: Washington D.C.

Mathur, H.M. (1995): *Anthropology and Development in Traditional Societies.* 2nd ed. New Delhi: Vikas Publishing House.

Mathur, H.M. and D. Marsden. (eds.) (1998): *Development Projects and Improverishment Risks.* New Delhi: Oxford University Press.

McCully, P. (1996) *Silenced Rivers: The Ecology and Politics of Large Dams.* New Delhi: Orient Longman.

Ministry of Rural Development, Government of India (1994) *Draft National Policy for Rehabilitation of Persons Displaced as a Consequence of Acquisition of Land.* Reprinted in *The Ecologist Asia* 3 (6 Nov.-Dec. 1995).

Ministry of Water Resources, (1994): *Draft National Policy for Resettlement and Rehabilitation of Persons Affected by Reservior Projects.*

Mitra, A. (1951): *The Tribes and Castes of West Bengal, Census 1951,* Calcutta: Goverment of West Bengal.

Mukarji, N. and D. Bandopadhyay (1993): *New Horizon's for West Bengal's Panchayats,* Department of Panchayats, Goverment of West Bengal.

National Atlas and Thematic Mapping Organisation (1996): *Medinipur District.* New Delhi DST. Government of India.

National Thermal Power Corporation (1993): *Resetlement and Rehabilitation Policy.*

NCPR (1995): *National Policy for Development-induced Displacement and Rehabilitation of Persons Displaced as a Consequence of Acquisition of Land, 1995, Econet* and Indian Social Institute, New Delhi.

O'Malley, L.S.S. (1911): *Bengal District Gazetteers, Midnapore,* Reprinted in 1996. Calcutta: Governement of West Bengal.

Panchayat and Rural Development Department (1997): *Compendium on Socio-economic Survery of Rural Households.* Government of West Bengal.

Proceedings of the West Bengal Legislaltive Assembly (1956): *Vol. XV* Government of West Bengal.

Proceedings of the West Bengal Legislative Assembly (1957): *Vol. XVII* Government of West Bengal.

—— (1963): *Vol. XXXVI* Government of West Bengal.

—— (1967): *Vol. XLIV* Government of West Bengal.

—— (1970): *Vol. 50* Government of West Bengal.

—— (1972): *Vol. 52* Government of West Bengal.

—— (1973): *Vol. 54* Government of West Bengal.

—— (1978): *Vol. 69* Government of West Bengal.

—— (1983): *Vol. 80* Government of West Bengal.

—— (1989): *Vol. 92* Government of West Bengal.

—— (1991): *Vol. 98* Government of West Bengal.

—— (1992): *Vol. 99* Government of West Bengal.

—— (1994): *Vol. 103* Government of West Bengal.

Ramanathan, R. and S. Geetha (1999): "Land for Industrial Purposes". *Seminar* Vol. 474, February 1999.

Roy, S. (1996): *Bharater Krishak Bidroha O Ganatantrik Sangram* (Bengali). Kolkata: Book World.

Roy-Burman, B.K. (1961): *Social Processes in the Industrialization of Rourkela.* New Delhi: Census of India.

Scudder, T. (1985): "A Sociological Framework for the Analysis of New Land Settlements", in M. Cernea, ed. *Putting People First: Sociological Variables in Rural Development.* New York: Oxford University Press.

Scudder, T. (1962): *The Ecology of the Gwembe Tonga.* Manchester, U.K.: Manchester University Press.

——(1973): "The Human Ecology of Big Projects: River Basin Development and Resettlement", in B. Siegel, ed., *Annual Review of Anthropology.* Palo Alto: Annual Review.

Scudder, T. and E. Colson (1982): "From Welfare to Development: A Conceptual Framework for Analysis of Dislocated People", in A. Hansen and A. Oliversmith, eds. *Involuntary Migration and Resettlement.* Boulder, Colorado: West View Press.

Sen, A. (1999): *Poverty and Famines* New Delhi: Oxford University Press.

Singh, K. and R. Katyayan, (1989): *The Land Acquisition Act* (A Guide for Activists) New Delhi: Society for Participatory Research in Asia.

Smaranika (1994): Kalaikunda Gram Panchayat (Annual Report 1993-94). Kharagpur.

Smaranika (1995): Kalaikunda Gram Panchayat (Annual Report 1994-95). Kharagpur.

Social Action (1995): Edited Vol. 45, No. 3, 1995 (July-September).

Sudarsen, V. and M.A. Kalam Edited (1990): *The Uprooted: Development, Displacement and Resettlement,* New Delhi: Gian Publishing House.

The Land Acquisition Act, (1894)—Subordinate Legislation-being published separately, Ministry of Law and Justice, Government of India.

The Statesman (1996): *News item dated 10 January 1996,* Calcutta.

——(1996): *News item dated 2 May, 1996* Calcutta.

——(1998): *News item dated 12 March, 1998,* Calcutta.

——(1999): *News item dated 18 November, 1999,* Calcutta.

——(2000): *News item dated 5 July, 2000,* Calcutta.

Vaswani, K.,V. Dhagamwar and E. Ganguly Thukral (1990): *The Land Acquisition Act and You.* New Delhi: Multiple Action Research Group

Wenner-Gren Foundation for Anthropological Research (1991): *Report for 1990 and 1991* (Fiftieth Anniversary Issue). New York.

West Bengal Human Development Report (2004): Development and Planning Department. Government of West Bengal.

West Bengal Industrial Development Corporation (1999): *Destination West Bengal.* Calcutta: WBIDC.

——(2000): *West Bengal: Industry News Update.* Calcutta: WBIDC.

West Bengal Land Reforms Act, 1955 And the Rules Framed Thereunder. (1984): Directorate of Land Records and Survey, Government of West Bengal.

World Bank (1990): *Operational Directive* 4.30 "Involuntary Resettlement" Washington, D.C., Processed.

——(1994): *Resettlement and Development: The Bankwide Review of Projects Involving Involuntary Resettlement* 1986-1993 (2nd ed. 1996) Environment Department, Washington, D.C. Processed.

——(1998): *Recent Experience with Involuntary Resettlement Overview.* Operations Evaluation Department, Washington, D.C.

Index